D0077111

Behavioral
Business
Ethics

Shaping an Emerging Field

ORGANIZATION AND MANAGEMENT SERIES

Series Editors

Arthur P. Brief
University of Utah

Kimberly D. Elsbach
University of California, Davis

Michael Frese
University of Lueneburg and National University of Singapore

Ashforth (Au.): *Role Transitions in Organizational Life: An Identity-Based Perspective*

Bartel/Blader/Wrzesniewski (Eds.): *Identity and the Modern Organization*

Bartunek (Au.): *Organizational and Educational Change: The Life and Role of a Change Agent Group*

Beach (Ed.): *Image Theory: Theoretical and Empirical Foundations*

Brett/Drasgow (Eds.): *The Psychology of Work: Theoretically Based Empirical Research*

Brockner (Au.): *A Contemporary Look at Organizational Justice: Multiplying Insult Times Injury*

Chhokar/Brodbeck/House (Eds.): *Culture and Leadership Across the World: The GLOBE Book of In-Depth Studies of 25 Societies*

Darley/Messick/Tyler (Eds.): *Social Influences on Ethical Behavior in Organizations*

DeCremer/van Dick/Murnighan (Eds): *Social Psychology and Organizations*

DeCremer/Tenbrunsel (Eds.): *Behavioral Business Ethics: Shaping an Emerging Field*

Denison (Ed.): *Managing Organizational Change in Transition Economies*

Dutton/Ragins (Eds.): *Exploring Positive Relationships at Work: Building a Theoretical and Research Foundation*

Elsbach (Au.): *Organizational Perception Management*

Earley/Gibson (Aus.): *Multinational Work Teams: A New Perspective*

Garud/Karnoe (Eds.): *Path Dependence and Creation*

Harris (Ed.): *Handbook of Research in International Human Resource Management*

Jacoby (Au.): *Employing Bureaucracy: Managers, Unions, and the Transformation of Work in the 20th Century, Revised Edition*

Kossek/Lambert (Eds.): *Work and Life Integration: Organizational, Cultural and Individual Perspectives*

Kramer/Tenbrunsel/Bazerman (Eds.): *Social Decision Making: Social Dilemmas, Social Values and Ethical Judgments*

Lampel/Shamsie/Lant (Eds.): *The Business of Culture: Strategic Perspectives on Entertainment and Media*

Lant/Shapira (Eds.): *Organizational Cognition: Computation and Interpretation*

Lord/Brown (Aus.): *Leadership Processes and Follower Self-Identity*

Margolis/Walsh (Aus.): *People and Profits? The Search Between a Company's Social and Financial Performance*

Miceli/Dworkin/Near (Aus.): *Whistle-blowing in Organizations*

Behavioral Business Ethics

Shaping an Emerging Field

Edited by

David De Cremer
Rotterdam School of Management
Erasmus University
The Netherlands

Ann E. Tenbrunsel
Mendoza College of Business
University of Notre Dame
USA

Routledge
Taylor & Francis Group
New York   London

Routledge
Taylor & Francis Group
711 Third Avenue
New York, NY 10017

Routledge
Taylor & Francis Group
27 Church Road
Hove, East Sussex BN3 2FA

Printed in the United States of America on acid-free paper
Version Date: 20110610

International Standard Book Number: 978-0-415-87324-6 (Hardback)

Library of Congress Cataloging-in-Publication Data

Behavioral business ethics : shaping an emerging field / David De Cremer, Ann E. Tenbrunsel.
    p. cm. -- (Organization and management series)
    Summary: "This book presents a collection of chapters that contribute significantly to the field of business ethics by promoting much needed insights into the motives that drive people to act ethically or unethically. It acknowledges that business ethics plays a pivotal role in the way business is conducted and adds insights derived from a behavioral view that will make us more aware of morality and provide recommendations into how we can improve our actions"-- Provided by publisher.
    Includes bibliographical references and index.
    ISBN 978-0-415-87324-6 (hardback : acid-free paper)
    1. Business ethics. 2. Corporate culture--Moral and ethical aspects. I. De Cremer, David. II. Tenbrunsel, Ann E.

HF5387.B427 2011
174'.4--dc23
                                  2011020516

Visit the Taylor & Francis Web site at
http://www.taylorandfrancis.com

and the Psychology Press Web site at
http://www.psypress.com

Contents

SECTION 4   Fairness and Morality

SECTION 5   Bounded Ethicality

Series Foreword

[Un]ethical behavior has often been described like bad cinema: it's hard to define exactly what it is, but you know it when you see it. Impressively, the current volume goes a long way toward uncovering exactly what it is that you "see" when you witness ethical and unethical behavior. In particular, this volume reveals the situational, normative, and cognitive underpinnings of ethical behavior and illustrates how we are influenced and constrained in our ethicality by factors such as the behavior of followers, norms of obligation, and stereotypical beliefs and biases. [Un]ethical behavior, it turns out, is not just the product of deliberate actions by rational (and sometimes ruthless) individuals. It is also the product of routine and unconscious behaviors enacted in everyday situations by regular people trying to do their best. There is no better time for such an addition to our collective wisdom on organizational and business ethics, and we are proud to have this volume in the series.

Kimberly Elsbach, Michael Frese, and Arthur Brief
Series editors

Editors' Biographies

David De Cremer is professor of behavioral business ethics at Rotterdam School of Management, Erasmus University; scientific director of the Erasmus Centre of Behavioral Ethics; and professor of organizational behavior at London Business School, United Kingdom. He is the recipient of many scientific awards, including the British Psychology Society award for Outstanding Ph.D. Thesis in Social Psychology, the Jos Jaspars Early Career Award for Outstanding Contributions to Social Psychology, the Comenius European Young Psychologist Award, and the International Society for Justice Research Early Career Contribution Award. He has published extensively in the main journals in the fields of psychology, management, and organizational behavior; edited five books and nine special issues; and written a book, *When Good People Do Bad Things: Illustrating the Psychology Behind the Financial Crisis*. His work has been discussed in the *American Scientist*, *The Economist*, and *The Financial Times*. He writes regular columns and opinion pieces in the financial newspapers and magazines in the Netherlands, Belgium, and United Kingdom. In 2009, he was elected as the best publishing economist in the Netherlands. Previously, De Cremer held teaching and research positions at New York University (Department of Psychology and Center of Experimental Social Sciences); Harvard University (Kennedy School of Government); Maastricht University (Department of Organization Studies and Department of Psychology); and Tilburg University (Department of Psychology). De Cremer holds a PhD in social psychology from the University of Southampton, England, and an MA in social psychology from the University of Leuven, Belgium.

Ann E. Tenbrunsel (PhD, Northwestern University; MBA, Northwestern University; BSIOE, University of Michigan) is a professor in the Mendoza College of Business at the University of Notre Dame and the Arthur F. and Mary J. O'Neil codirector of the Institute for Ethical Business Worldwide. Her research interests focus on the psychology of ethical decision making, with her dissertation on this topic winning the State Farm Dissertation Award. Her work in this area has focused partially on the situational factors that lead to unethical decision making, including the role that temptation, uncertainty, power, and sanctions play in the ethical decision-making process. More recently, she has explored the process of ethical fading, arguing that individuals often make unethical decisions because the ethical aspects of the decision are hidden to the decision maker. She has also examined the role that organizations play in promoting unethical decisions, including the influence of formal and informal systems. In addition to recently coauthoring a review of the ethics field, she is the coeditor of four books on these topics and has published her research in a variety of journals, such as *Administrative Science Quarterly, Academy of Management Review, Academy of Management Journal, Organizational Behavior and Human Decision Processes, Journal of Applied Psychology,* and *Journal of Personality and Social Psychology.* She is currently serving on the editorial board of *Business Ethics Quarterly* and *Organizational Behavior and Human Decision Processes* and has served as a guest editor for the *Journal of Business Ethics.* Ann has received grants from the National Science Foundation to pursue her work and has published teaching materials on ethical and environmental issues that have been used both domestically and internationally.

Contributors

Max Bazerman
Harvard Business School
Harvard University

Arthur Brief
Management Department
University of Utah

Michael Brown
Sam and Irene Black School of
    Business
The Pennsylvania State University

Jason Dana
Department of Psychology
University of Pennsylvania

David De Cremer
Department of Business–Society
    Management
Rotterdam School of Management
Erasmus University Rotterdam
and
London Business School

Erik de Kwaadsteniet
Department of Social and
    Organizational Psychology
Leiden University

Rob Folger
College of Business
    Administration
Department of Management
University of Central Florida

Francesca Gino
Harvard Business School
Harvard University

Morela Hernandez
Michael G. Foster School of
    Business
University of Washington

Lukas Koning
Department of Social Psychology
University of Amsterdam

George Loewenstein
Department of Social and
    Decision Sciences
Carnegie Mellon University

Manuela Priesemuth
College of Business
    Administration
Department of Management
University of Central Florida

Marshall Schminke
College of Business Administration
Department of Management
University of Central Florida

Lisa L. Shu
Harvard Business School
Harvard University

Sim Sitkin
The Fuqua School of Business
Duke University

Ann Tenbrunsel
Mendoza College of Business
Management Department
University of Notre Dame

Tom R. Tyler
Department of Psychology
New York University

Eric van Dijk
Department of Social and
   Organizational Psychology
Leiden University

Gary Weaver
Department of Business
   Administration
Alfred Lerner College of
   Business and Economics
University of Delaware

Roberto Weber
Department of Social and
   Decision Sciences
Carnegie Mellon University

Section 1

Introduction

1

On Understanding the Need for a Behavioral Business Ethics Approach

David De Cremer
Erasmus University Rotterdam and London Business School

and

Ann E. Tenbrunsel
University of Notre Dame

INTRODUCTION

The numerous international scandals in business such as those at AIG, Tyco, WorldCom, Enron, and Ahold have made all of us concerned about the emergence of unethical and irresponsible behavior in organizations. Bad leadership behavior, as shown by the arrest of the former chief executive officer (CEO) of Converse in Namibia, the CEO at United Healthcare being forced to step down, and Patricia Dunn of Hewlett Packard being charged in an ethics scandal, are no exception anymore. More recently, our concerns over ethics have become even stronger due to the worldwide financial crisis, in which it became strikingly clear that the irresponsible (and unethical) behavior of managers and organizations inflicts pain on society and its members (De Cremer, 2011). In addition to the unethical behavior of those who contributed to the crisis, we see continued moral lapses in institutions like AIG, who have doled out millions in bonuses to the very people who drove the company and the country into a financial crisis. It seems that no matter where we look today, the erosion of ethics and basic moral principles of right and wrong have taken us to the point at which trust in our institutions and the very systems that make our society work is in imminent danger of oblivion.

The seemingly unending occurrence of instances of corruption and fraud has also activated consciousness about ethics in general and business ethics in particular (Bazerman & Tenbrunsel, 2011; De Cremer, Mayer, & Schminke, 2010). Although there may be no universal definition of business ethics, and one scholar likened defining it to "nailing Jello on a wall" (Lewis, 1985), most definitions focus on *evaluating* the moral acceptability of the actions of management, organizational leaders, and their employees. As the morals and actions of the representatives of the business world seem to go downhill at Rollerblade speed, it becomes increasingly necessary not only to evaluate these actions but also to understand how and why unethical behavior can emerge so easily, despite the presence of multiple control and monitoring systems (De Cremer, 2010; Tenbrunsel & Smith-Crowe, 2008).

A NORMATIVE AND BEHAVIORAL BUSINESS ETHICS APPROACH

Business ethics generally deals with evaluating whether practices of employees, leaders, and organizations as a whole can be considered morally acceptable (Ferrell, Fraedrich, & Ferrell, 2008). The standard approach to the study of ethics in business and management has been a normative or prescriptive approach, which focuses on what managers, employees, and people in general "should" do to act as morally responsible actors (Jones, 1991; Messick & Tenbrunsel, 1996; Rest, 1986; Trevino & Weaver, 1994). The prescriptive tones that are inherent in this literature are clearly reflected in the popularity of organizational codes of conduct and moral guidelines issued by management (Adams, Taschchian, & Shore, 2001; Weaver, 2001). An interesting and important underlying assumption of this approach is that it promotes the idea that individuals are rational, purposive actors who act in accordance with their intentions and understand the implications of their actions. That is, it assumes that all people are aware of the moral dilemmas they face and therefore in a conscious and controlled manner can decide what to do: do "good" or do "bad." This rational nature is clearly reflected in the important work of Kohlberg (1981) on moral development. Because the approach advocated in his work relied heavily on Piaget's theory of cognitive development (1932), reasoning was considered crucial in understanding people's moral experience.

This approach leads to the rather erroneous conclusion that most business scandals must be the responsibility of a few bad apples. Indeed, an important consequence of a rational approach is that people interpret moral dilemmas in a conscious manner in which cognitive corrections can be applied. If this rational process is valid, then it also implies that if people engage in bad behavior they do so consciously. In other words, bad behavior suggests actions by a bad apple. This logic is consistent with early explanations of business scandals. Charles Ponzi, the originator of the now-infamous Ponzi scheme and Bernie Madoff's forefather, clearly knew that he was doing wrong (Dunn, 1975). Larger corporate scandals also tend to focus on the actions and the responsibility of a few "bad apples" (De Cremer, 2009).

This assumption is intuitively compelling and attractive in its simplicity. On a practical level, it also facilitates both identification and actual punishment of those deemed responsible. More generally, a normative perspective suggests, or at least implies, that people interpret moral dilemmas in a conscious manner, and that cognitive guidelines can be used to avoid ethical lapses. This rational approach, however, may not be able to account for the emergence of a wide range of unethical behaviors. Ethicality and intentionality are two important but distinct dimensions: Individuals make both intentional and unintentional ethical and unethical choices (Tenbrunsel & Smith-Crowe, 2008). For instance, there is considerable evidence indicating that good people sometimes do bad things (Bersoff, 1999) and may not even realize that they are doing so. Research on ethical fading (Tenbrunsel & Messick, 2004, p. 204) asserts that, "Individuals do not 'see' the moral components of an ethical decision, not so much because they are morally uneducated, but because psychological processes *fade* the 'ethics' from an ethical dilemma." As a result, we fall prey to bounded ethicality, engaging in behavior that goes against our own morals and values without awareness that we are doing so (Chugh, Banaji, & Bazerman, 2005).

How can we explain this? To do this, a common understanding has emerged that, in addition to a prescriptive approach in which a moral principle is communicated and evaluated, we need a *descriptive* approach that examines how individuals make actual decisions and engage in real actions when they are faced with ethical dilemmas. For this reason, in the field of business ethics we also need a behavioral approach that zooms in on why people do the things they do.

The behavioral approach that we advocate explicitly argues that much unethical behavior occurs outside the awareness of individual actors (in contrast to the assumption of deliberate cheating in the principal agent models). This approach enhances our understanding of how ethical awareness and norms are interpreted and how they influence decision making and behavior. Improving our knowledge in this way will help to enhance an ethical climate that can lead to sustainable and effective management.

The idea that our decisions and judgments are not always colored by conscious reasoning processes is supported by recent research on morality, intuition, and affect. This intuitionist framework suggests that moral judgments and interpretations are the consequence of automatic and intuitive affective reactions. Haidt (2001, p. 818), for instance, defined moral intuition as "the sudden appearance in consciousness of a moral judgment, including an affective valence (good-bad, like-dislike), without any conscious awareness of having gone through steps of searching, weighing evidence, or inferring a conclusion." This approach suggests that moral judgments are (or at least can be) quick and affect laden rather than driven exclusively by elaborated and reflexive reasoning processes.

Evidence for this moral intuition view can be found in experiments using the trolley problem. Consider, for example, a variant of the familiar trolley car problem discussed by philosophers. You are standing on a footbridge when you see an out-of-control trolley car about to strike a group of five people standing on the tracks ahead. There is a large stranger standing next to you, and if you push him off the bridge onto the tracks below, his body will derail the trolley, in the process killing him but sparing the lives of the five strangers. Utilitarianism would predict that people should push the large stranger from the bridge since this would result in a net savings of four lives. Yet, when people are asked what they think should be done in this situation, most feel strongly that it would be wrong to push the stranger to his death. This finding illustrates that moral intuition plays a significant role in making moral decisions and judgments. Research examining this trolley problem by means of functional magnetic resonance imaging (fMRI) techniques has revealed that emotions, rather than reflexive cognitive processes, are indeed influencing people's decisions (Greene, Sommerville, Nystrom, Darley, & Cohen, 2001).

Based on this recent research, it becomes increasingly clear that it is not a select few who succumb to unethical action. Instead, almost everyone is susceptible to the forces that ultimately result in questionable decisions and unworthy actions, "There but for the grace of God go I." This research takes the perspective that most individuals involved, both within and outside the business world, know that a range of behaviors is not acceptable in the workplace, the marketplace, and society. Businesspeople, in particular, are aware of appropriate, ethical decision rules and moral behaviors and how they might be promoted (e.g., the rules in a code of conduct for a company or the ethical guidelines of a profession). Despite this awareness, however, irresponsible and unethical behaviors and decisions still emerge. In essence, some contexts may be sufficiently compelling for almost anyone to engage in unethical behavior. Arriving at a more complete understanding of these circumstances should enable leaders to create organizations that are more ethical. This is a fundamental, foundational idea in the emerging field of behavioral ethics.

A major assumption of the behavioral business ethics approach is that many of the ethical failures witnessed in society and organizations are not the result of so-called bad apples (some are, but the majority of such events are not) but come from a much wider set of individuals (Bazerman & Banaji, 2004). Research on this issue suggests that all of us may commit unethical behaviors, given the right circumstances. Treviño, Weaver, and Reynolds (2006, p. 952) defined behavioral ethics as a notion that "refers to individual behavior that is subject to or judged according to generally accepted moral norms of behavior." Tenbrunsel and Smith-Crowe (2008, p. 548) interpret this definition as saying that "behavioral ethics is primarily concerned with explaining individual behavior that occurs in the context of larger social prescriptions." Because of its focus on the actual behavior of the individual (i.e., advocating thus a descriptive approach rather than a prescriptive one), it becomes clear that research in behavioral ethics largely draws from work in psychology. The field of psychology is indeed referred to as the scientific study of human behavior and thought processes (Morris & Maisto, 2001). In 1996, Messick and Tenbrunsel called for the intersection of psychology and business ethics. In 2001, Dinehart, Moberg, and Duska compiled a series of papers entitled, entitled *The Next Phase of Business Ethics: Integrating Psychology and Ethics*, aimed at the synergy to be gained through the intersection of these two fields. Bazerman and Banaji (2004, p. 1150) noted "that efforts to improve ethical decision making are better aimed at understanding our psychological tendencies." We concur with these authors and propose that psychology can provide an ideal foundation for examining and promoting our understanding of why good people sometimes can do bad things.

It thus stands to reason that a behavioral ethics approach is well suited to enhance our understanding of how ethical behavior in organizations and management can be promoted (De Cremer, van Dick, Tenbrunsel, Pillutla, & Murnighan, 2011) and ethical failures can be dealt with effectively (De Cremer, Tenbrunsel, & van Dijke, 2011). We would like to note immediately, however, that looking at behavior is one thing, but we also need to understand the processes *underlying* the behavior (De Cremer, 2010). Therefore, a behavioral ethics approach should thus not only include a focus on what kind of behavior is actually engaged in but also attempt to identify the psychological processes underlying the different behaviors. This approach, in which we combine the search for a smoking gun with a focus on the psychology of the behavior, should be the primary scientific task of behavioral ethics.

OVERVIEW OF THE BOOK

The present book is divided into five sections. Section 1 is composed of this introductory chapter by David De Cremer and Ann Tenbrunsel presenting a short overview of how business ethics has been studied so far and how a behavioral approach can add to the value and approach of the business ethics field. Section 2 provides a chapter by Art Brief (Chapter 2) discussing the field of business ethics and how behavioral approaches can help develop the field. In so doing, Brief outlines what behavioral business ethics researchers should be studying. For example, he suggests that research attention should be paid to (a) the moral domains of in-group/loyalty, authority/respect, and purity/sanctity; (b) virtues and character; (c) the role of implicit affect and associations as drivers of moral behavior; and (d) perhaps most of all, the possibility that the mechanisms producing moral behaviors vary as a function of the moral nature of the issues encountered. All of the suggestions provided reflect a belief that the "business" in "behavioral business ethics," at least sometimes, matters.

In Section 3, we zoom in on how ethics is influenced by the situation. The social context can have a significant impact on people's decisions and behaviors, but people's decisions can also shape the context in which business emerges. Thus, context dictates ethical behavior to a certain extent, whereas some individuals (like leaders) can influence the setting in which ethics can become more or less salient. Marschall Schminke and Manuela Priesemuth (Chapter 3) argue that scholars from a variety of disciplines explore the causes and consequences of ethical behavior, with a special focus on business and organizational settings. However, they also note that, as with other research that explores behavior in organizations, the impact of the organization itself is often overlooked. The goal of their chapter is to establish the importance of organizational context as a central concern in behavioral ethics research. They provide a brief review of the role context has played in the development of behavioral ethics research. They then catalog the primary strengths and weaknesses of this context-related work and craft a set of directives for researchers interested in taking context seriously as a foundational concept in behavioral business ethics. They conclude that organizational context represents an important basis for understanding behavioral ethics in organizational settings and call on scholars to take its influence seriously in both conceptual and empirical work.

Morela Hernandez and Sim Sitkin (Chapter 4) focus on the topic of leadership in the context of ethics. They note that while a growing body of evidence has demonstrated how leaders play a particularly influential role in creating principled organizational contexts, relatively little theorizing has explained the effect of followers on the leader's ethicality. In their chapter, they begin to address this important gap by examining how the leader might be systematically influenced by four types of follower behaviors: modeling, eliciting, guiding, and sensemaking. In particular, they discuss how each follower behavior can influence a leader's ethicality and outline the cognitive, affective, and behavioral causal mechanisms through which this influence can be exercised.

In Section 4, we focus on the role that fairness and morality play in the development of ethical behavior in social groups and organizations and their influence on the judgments that people make in those settings. Van Dijk, de Kwaadsteniet, and Koning (Chapter 5) attempt to define behavioral business ethics by discussing the findings obtained in two distinct but related fields of research: social dilemmas and bargaining. Discussing two motives—self-interest and fairness—and their impact on choice behavior, the authors make a distinction between instrumental and true fairness. This distinction sheds light on decisions in social dilemmas and bargaining settings and identifies the motives and processes that underlie ethical and unethical conduct.

Rob Folger (Chapter 6) presents a theoretical analysis of the duties and obligations people experience and how they influence their behavior. This idea is elaborated upon in deonance theory (DT). DT cuts across philosophical traditions but remains neutral about their content, assuming that studying the psychological *processes* whereby moral norms influence behavior is independent of the *content* of such norms. As such, in this chapter, it is advocated that DT is a process theory that proposes a hypothetical construct, the psychological state of deonance, whose arousal occurs when a situation brings to bear beliefs about the relevance of moral directives.

Gary Weaver and Michael Brown (Chapter 7) argue that much research on ethically related phenomena in organizations focuses on two key types of ethical concerns: fairness and harm/benefit. Recent empirical research makes clear, however, that harm and fairness are but two of several core ethical concerns animating the thought and behavior of many people. According to moral foundations theory and research, strong moral intuitions concerning the avoidance of impurity, the value of authority and hierarchy, and in-group commitment function alongside concerns for avoiding harm and promoting fairness in the moral thoughts and behaviors of many, if not most, individuals in Western societies and around the world. In their chapter, these authors summarize the importance of considering those additional ethical concerns and then elaborate on the implications for future research on ethically relevant behavior specifically in organizations.

Tom Tyler (Chapter 8) argues that behavioral business ethics is concerned with the role that principled values and ethical judgments play in shaping the behavior of the people in work organizations (i.e., with moral motivation). In doing this, he argues for the value of a distinction among judgments about appropriateness of conduct linked to ends versus means. This distinction leads to concern about ends-based ethics (moral value congruence) and means-based ethics (appropriateness of conduct). Two types of means-based ethics are important: first, judgments about whether management makes decisions ethically; second, whether management generally follows the principles of procedural justice. His overall suggestion is that people in work organizations want to engage in appropriate conduct, and when they feel that the policies and practices of their work organizations are moral, ethical, and reflect principles of procedural justice, they are motivated to work voluntarily on behalf of those organizations.

Section 5 focuses on the topic of bounded ethicality. When making decisions, it is important that people are aware of the moral implications of their actions. Too often, however, we—in an objective way—know what the moral standards should be, but which nevertheless are not taken into account. The concept of *bounded ethicality* refers to the idea that we make use of many heuristics (rules of thumbs) and stereotypical beliefs that often have an intuitive character. As such, people easily develop or adhere to cognitions (biases, beliefs) that legitimize behaviors that they would deem inappropriate and wrong if they would reflect on or be aware of them. In other words, bounded ethicality leads people to be able to see themselves as ethical persons while making unethical decisions, thereby reducing or even eliminating their moral awareness (Chugh, Banaji, & Bazerman, 2005).

Jason Dana, George Loewenstein, and Roberto Weber (Chapter 9) make the argument that a study of behavioral ethics that takes its cue from the burgeoning field of behavioral economics can explain when and why ethically minded individuals behave unethically. They argue that just as people often fail to achieve their own goals or behave consistently, due to systematic errors and biases in judgment and decision making and to varying subtle features of the choice context, people can also systematically fail to live up to their own ethical standards. In their chapter, they discuss experimental research examining three different "tactics" people use—diffusing responsibility, exploiting uncertainty, and seeking justifications—to avoid holding themselves ethically accountable.

Lisa Shu, Francesca Gino, and Max Bazerman (Chapter 10) examine the psychological processes of two very different mechanisms by which unethical behavior occurs—that which occurs without as well as with our awareness—both of which are argued to lead to inflated views of one's ethicality. Their chapter identifies several mechanisms that contribute to such behavior, including the tendency to overweight the importance of the individual while underweighting the importance of the situation, the asymmetries in judgments of one's own behavior versus that of others, and the discrepancies in evaluating the same good and bad deeds depending on whether they have occurred in the past or will occur in the future. The processes that allow individuals to reconcile their immoral actions with their ethical goals through the process of moral disengagement and selective forgetting are then explored. The chapter closes with an identification of strategies that help to eliminate the ethical discrepancy between the unethical people we are and the ethical people that we strive to be.

To conclude, the book presents a collection of chapters that all contribute significantly to the field of business ethics. It does so by promoting much needed insights into the motives that drive people to act ethically or unethically and how it influences oneself, others, and the organization and business as a whole. The field of business ethics is increasingly being recognized as having a pivotal role in the way business is done, and as such adding the insights derived from a behavioral view will not only make us more aware of morality but also provide recommendations into how we can improve our actions. We sincerely believe that this development will only promote the interest of business in the long run. We hope that this book therefore will both motivate and intrigue readers because the advances that we hope for cannot be achieved by a small group of scholars; rather, we need to engage the collective in this endeavor to better ourselves, our organizations, and our society. Overall, the contributions in this volume lead us to conclude that the future of behavioral business ethics is not only in good hands (looking at the quality of scholars involved) but also appears very promising.

REFERENCES

Adams, J. S., Taschchian, A., & Shore, T. H. (2001). Codes of ethics as signals for ethical behavior. *Journal of Business Ethics, 29,* 199–211.

Bazerman, M. H., & Banaji, M. H. (2004). The social psychology of ordinary ethical failures. *Social Justice Research, 17,* 111–115.

Bazerman, M. H., & Tenbrunsel, A. E. (2011). *Blind spots: Why we fail to do what's right and what to do about it.* Princeton, NJ: Princeton University Press.

Bersoff, D. M. (1999). Why good people sometimes do bad things: Motivated reasoning and unethical behavior. *Personality and Social Psychology Bulletin, 25,* 28–39.

Chugh, D., Banaji, M. R., & Bazerman, M. H. (2005). Bounded ethicality as a psychological barrier to recognizing conflicts of interest. In D. A. Moore, M. Cain, G. Loewenstein, & M. H. Bazerman (Eds.), *Conflicts of interest: Problems and solutions from law, medicine, and organizational settings.* London: Cambridge University Press.

De Cremer, D. (2009). Being unethical or becoming unethical: An introduction. In D. De Cremer (Ed.), *Psychological perspectives on ethical behavior and decision making* (pp. 3–13). Greenwich, CT: Information Age.

De Cremer, D. (2010). On the psychology of preventing and dealing with ethical failures: A behavioral ethics approach. In M. Schminke (Ed.), *Managerial ethics* (pp. 111–125). New York: Routledge.

De Cremer, D. (2011). *When good people do bad things: Illustrations of the psychology behind the financial crisis.* Leuven/The Hague, Netherlands: Acco.

De Cremer, D., Mayer, D., & Schminke, M. (2010). On understanding ethical behaviour and decision making: A behavioral business ethics approach. *Business Ethics Quarterly, 20,* 1–6.

De Cremer, D., Tenbrunsel, A., & van Dijke, M. (2011). Regulating ethical failures: Insight from psychology. *Journal of Business Ethics, 95,* 1, 1–6.

De Cremer, D., van Dick, R., Tenbrunsel, A., Pillutla, M., & Murnighan, J. K. (2011). Understanding ethical behaviour and decision making in management: A behavioural ethics approach. *British Journal of Management, 22:* S1–S4.

Dinehart, J., Moberg, D., & Duska, R. (Eds.). (2001). *The next phase of business ethics: Integrating psychology and ethics.* Oxford, UK: Elsevier Science.

Dunn, D. (1975). *Ponzi: The incredible true story of the king of financial cons.* New York: Broadway.

Ferrell, C., Fraedrich, J., & Ferrell, L. (2008). *Business ethics: Ethical decision making and cases* (7th ed.). Boston: Houghton Mifflin.

Greene, J. D., Sommerville, R. B., Nystrom, L. E., Darley, J. M., & Cohen, J. D. (2001). An fMRI investigation of emotional engagement in moral judgment. *Science, 293,* 2105–2108.

Haidt, J. (2001). The emotional dog and its rational tail: A social intuitionist approach to moral judgment. *Psychological Review, 108,* 814–834.

Jones, T. M. (1991). Ethical decision making by individuals in organizations: An issue-contingent model. *Academy of Management Review, 16,* 366–395.

Kohlberg, L. (1981). *The philosophy of moral development: Moral states and the idea of justice.* San Francisco: Harper and Row.

Lewis, P. V. (1985). Defining "business ethics": Like nailing Jello to a wall. *Journal of Business Ethics, 4,* 377–383.

Messick, D. M., & Tenbrunsel, A. E. (Eds.). (1996). *Codes of conduct: Behavioral research into business ethics.* New York: Russell Sage.

Morris, C. G., & Maisto, A. A. (2001). *Psychology: An introduction* (11th ed.). Englewood Cliffs, NJ: Prentice Hall.

Piaget, J. (1932). *The moral judgment of the child.* London: Kegan Paul, Trench, Trubner.

Rest, J. R. (1986). *Moral development: Advances in research and theory.* New York: Praeger.

Tenbrunsel, A. E., & Messick, D. M. (2004). Ethical fading: The role of self-deception in unethical behavior. *Social Justice Research, 17,* 223–236.

Tenbrunsel, A. E., & Smith-Crowe, K. (2008). Ethical decision making: Where we've been and where we're going. *The Academy of Management Annals, 2,* 545–607.

Treviño, L. K., & Weaver, G. R. (1994). Business ethics: One field or two? *Business Ethics Quarterly, 4,* 113–128.

Treviño, L. K., Weaver, G. R., & Reynolds, S. J. (2006). Behavioral ethics in organizations: a review. *Journal of Management, 32,* 951–990.

Weaver, G. (2001). Ethics programs in global businesses: Culture's role in managing ethics. *Journal of Business Ethics, 30,* 3–15.

Section 2

A View of Behavioral Business Ethics

2

The Good, the Bad, and the Ugly: What Behavioral Business Ethics Researchers Ought to Be Studying

Arthur P. Brief
University of Utah

INTRODUCTION

Kristin Smith-Crowe and her colleagues have written some pretty potent words that those of us who identify as behavioral business ethics researchers should hear. Warren and Smith-Crowe (2008) wrote the following: "While behavioral ethics is descriptive rather than prescriptive, good social science requires a thorough understanding and definition of one's constructs—researchers only want to predict and describe ethical behavior, but in doing so, they must define what is ethical, and, therefore, they must be in some sense prescriptive" (p. 84). Tenbrunsel and Smith-Crowe (2008), in their terrific review of the literature, go further by stating, "The [behavioral] ethics field is in a quandary. If we don't believe it is important to define what an ethical decision is, or don't believe it is our place to do so, then we are a field without meaning" (p. 551).

The goal of this chapter is not to define what an "ethical decision" is but rather merely to nibble around the edges of such a definition. I begin by first placing the study of behavioral business ethics in context and, in doing so, explain why I am not directly attacking the definitional problem. After attempting to position our field, historically and in terms of its relationships to philosophy, psychology, and other disciplines, I become prescriptive, identifying what we ought to be seeking to predict and describe: the *good*–ethical versus unethical behaviors; the *bad*–conventional but overly narrow construals of unethical behaviors; and the *ugly*–moral norms, largely ignored, whose violations can produce strong reactions such as disgust. The chapter concludes with a discussion of the potential implications of my nibbling.

WHERE WE CAME FROM

Moral philosophy, the study of ethics' home, can be thought of as organized into three overlapping areas of inquiry: metaethics, normative ethics, and applied ethics (see Figure 2.1). Metaethics is a very broad area of study that often is difficult for laypersons (e.g., me) to put their arms around. It entails such questions as: Are there moral facts? And if so, where do they come from? How do people learn about them? How do they bind human behavior (Sayre-McCord, 2007)? From these example questions, it can be seen that metaethics can concern the otherworldly or supernatural origins of moral facts and the psychological bases of moral judgments and behaviors. The former recognizes the area of moral theology, which in part rests on the idea that God is the source of moral facts (e.g., the Ten Commandments;

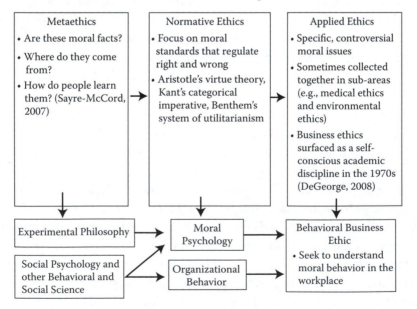

FIGURE 2.1
A crude depiction of where we came from.

Murphy, 2009). The latter recognizes the obvious: that philosophy and psychology are entwined intimately (e.g., James, 1890/1950). Moral philosophy, for instance, has long appreciated that moral assessments entail emotions (Hume, 1777/1960; also see Ayer, 1946). In psychology, this appreciation is most evident in moral psychology (Shweder & Haidt, 1993), an area of study also cohabited by some philosophers. "Moral psychology" is concerned with how people function in moral contexts and how that functioning may affect ethical theory (Doris & Stich, 2006).

Haidt (2007) provided a provocative synthesis of moral psychology that entails recognition of "the importance of moral intuitions, the social functional (rather than truth seeking) nature of moral thinking, and the coevolution of moral minds with cultural practices and institutions that create diverse world communities" and of morality being "about more than harm and fairness" (p. 998). Aligned with but distinct from moral psychology is experimental philosophy, which as the term suggests, involves philosophers employing experimental methods similar to psychologists (Knobe & Nichols, 2008). For more on this unusual (to me at least) mode of inquiry, see, for example, Appiah (2008) and Doris and Stich (2005).

I hope I have not given the impression that moral psychology and experimental philosophy speak only to questions of metaethics, for that is not true. They also address questions of normative ethics, the second branch of moral philosophy. Normative ethics focuses on the moral standards that regulate right and wrong behavior. Some of the principal theories intended to guide one to choose between right and wrong pertain to virtues (e.g., Aristotle's virtue theory), duties (e.g., Kant's categorical imperative), and the consequences of our actions (e.g., Bentham's system of utilitarianism). Following the lead of Williams (e.g., 1985), Doris and Stich (2006) forcefully tie moral psychology and empirical philosophy to normative ethics by asserting that "an ethical conception that commands relationships, commitments, or life projects that are at odds with the sort of attachments that can be reasonably expected to take root in and verify actual human lives is an ethical conception with—at best—a very tenuous claim to our assent" (para. 2).

The third branch of moral philosophy is applied ethics. It is concerned with the application of normative ethical theories to specific, controversial moral issues (e.g., abortion) that sometimes are collected together into identifiable subareas of inquiry (e.g., medical ethics and environmental ethics). The 1970s gave birth to business ethics as a self-conscious academic discipline (De George, 2008).

This portrayal of moral philosophy should be viewed with at least a bit of skepticism, for my one undergraduate course in philosophy does not qualify me as an expert. Indeed, my lack of formal training in philosophy is what leads me not to want to tackle the problem of defining the object of what we behavioral business ethics researchers study and, rather, to nibble around its edges. I think a lot of other social scientists interested in ethics are in the same boat.

Now, on to mapping territory more familiar to me—what has been called empirical (e.g., Doris & Stich, 2005) or behavioral ethics (e.g., Treviño, Weaver, & Reynolds, 2006). "Behavioral ethics" entails the social scientific study of ethical behavior. Like Haidt (2008), my list of relevant social science is rather lengthy—psychology (developmental, social, cultural, evolutionary, organizational, and moral), sociology, sociobiology, and behavioral economics. I do not know if I can get away with listing primatology and neuroscience as social sciences; nevertheless, they also are relevant. Finally, we come to the subarea of behavioral business ethics, which is concerned with understanding the nature and causes of ethical behavior *in business settings*. Does the "in business settings" part matter? I think so, at least sometimes. But, it is both a theoretical and an empirical question if and, if so, when the results obtained in behavioral ethics, more generally construed, hold in business settings. Of course, the economics of business settings may drive behaviors in ways not seen in other life domains. In my own work, I have argued that the accountability (Tetlock, 1985) inherent in organizational hierarchies is important for understanding ethical behavior in the workplace (e.g., Brief, Buttram, & Dukerich, 2001; Brief, Buttram, Elliott, Reizenstein, & McCline, 1995; Brief, Dietz, Cohen, Pugh, & Vaslow, 2000; Brief, Dukerich, & Doran, 1991). I am afraid that too many who stand up as behavioral business ethics researchers fail to ask the "if and, if so, when" questions. Further in the chapter, I hope the importance of such questions become even more apparent.

The relationship between normative and behavioral business ethics has been written about often, perhaps too often (e.g., Donaldson, 1994; Greenberg & Bies, 1992; Hartman, 2008; Rosenthal & Buchholz, 2000; Treviño & Weaver, 1994; Werhane, 1994). Here is the take on the relationship I enjoy most: "The division of normative and empirical, while methodologically clarifying … is not a chasm but rather a swamp with descriptive and normative islands and a great deal of wetland and quicksand" (Werhane, 1994, p. 177). Moral psychologists, in part, see themselves as bridging these empirical and normative islands by enlightening normative theories through their empiricism. Greene (2003), for instance, has observed gently that "we can respect the distinction between how things are and how things ought to be while acknowledging ... that scientific facts have the potential to influence our moral thinking in a deep way" (p. 849; also see Doris & Stich, 2005). The aims of behavioral business ethics researchers are different. I do not believe we seek to influence normative theories (although we might unintentionally one day); rather, most of us, I imagine, see our empiricism contributing to the development of social science theories of ethical behavior that speak to the practice of business.

Two books mark the birth of behavioral business ethics as an identifiable area of inquiry. Messick and Tenbrunsel's (1996) *Codes of Conduct: Behavioral Research Into Business Ethics* and Treviño and Weaver's (2003) *Managing Ethics in Business Organizations*. The publication date of the Treviño and Weaver book is a bit misleading, for it mostly summarizes research conducted by Treviño and her colleagues in the 1990s. The book is representative of social science research appearing in the management literature during that period, when behavioral business ethics research was becoming more visible and cohesive. I am leaving organizational justice research out of this story because with few exceptions,[1] it did not explicitly concern itself with ethics; rather, it principally has been focused on the linkage between perceived justice and outcomes deemed relevant to the economic performance of firms. For instance, virtually no attention has been paid to why or why not managers behave fairly toward their subordinates (see Brockner, Wiesenfeld, & Diekmann, 2009, for an exception). Returning to Treviño and Weaver, the research they examined included the influence of executive leadership (e.g., leader values and commitments) and external pressures (e.g., from government and the media) on formal ethics programs and informal ethics practices, as well as the influence of individual characteristics (e.g., age, locus of control, and cognitive moral development) and ethical issue characteristics (e.g., moral intensity)—including the aforementioned formal and informal aspects of the organization—on ethical judgments and behaviors in organizations. Work in this vein continues (e.g., Brown & Treviño, 2006; Brown, Treviño, & Harrison, 2005; Reynolds, 2006; Treviño, Brown, & Hartman, 2003; Treviño, Weaver, & Brown, 2008).

While Treviño and Weaver (2003) reflected on traditional management research, spiced up a bit by Kohlberg's (e.g., 1971) notions about moral development, Messick and Tenbrunsel (1996) broke the mold. They stated, "This book is based on the conviction that there are many domains of research in psychology and behavioral economics that are relevant to business ethics" (p. 2). Consistent with that conviction, Messick and Tenbrunsel assembled an amazing group of scholars (e.g., John Darley, Robert Cialdini, Robert Franks, Suzan Fiske, Marilyn Brewer, Johnathan Baron, George Loewenstein, Jousha Klayman, Baruch Fischoff, and Robyn Dawes) who, in large part, speculated how their particular takes on social psychology could influence understandings of ethical behavior in business. Many of the ideas advanced were fresh, invigorating, and most certainly, not then attended to by those aligned with traditional management research. More than a decade and a half after the publication of Messick and Tenbrunsel's work, we have a changing world populated by an increasing number of social-psychological-driven articles (e.g., Chugh, Bazerman, & Banaji, 2005; Gino, Gu, & Zhong, 2009; Gino & Pierce, 2009a, 2009b; Moore, Tetlock, Tanlu, & Bazerman 2006; Paharia, Kassam, Greene, & Bazerman, 2009; Tenbrunsel, 1998; Tenbrunsel, Diekmann, Wade-Benzoni, & Bazerman, in press; Tenbrunsel & Messick, 1999; Warren & Smith-Crowe, 2008).

We have traveled the road from the metaethics of moral philosophy to behavioral business ethics. The purpose of the trip was to place in context what is to come: an examination of the latter's focus of attention—ethical behavior in business settings. So, what is the nature of the ethical behaviors we study? Based on an analysis of four reviews of the literature (Kish-Gephart, Harrison, & Treviño, 2010; O'Fallon & Butterfield, 2005; Tenbrunsel & Smith-Crowe, 2008; Treviño et al., 2006), *it does not matter.* That is, the literature does not reflect a concern for the ethical behavior being studied, thus, implicitly considering all ethical behaviors equivalent. A somewhat distal exception to this conclusion is the research on Jones's (1991) "moral intensity" construct "that captures the extent of issue-related moral imperative in a situation" (p. 372) and is posited to influence ethical behavior. Scenario-based research does demonstrate that moral intensity is related to "ethical judgment" (Rest, 1986), another presumed precursor of ethical behavior.

I will argue that the nature of the ethical behavior being considered matters. For instance, it may be the case that the same theory does not predict a professor sexually exploiting a student, falsifying data, and taking home a pad of paper to his child. Next, I begin to examine different sorts of ethical behaviors and their status in the behavioral ethics research literature.

THE GOOD

"Bad is stronger than good" (Baumeister, Bratslavsky, Finkenauer, & Vohs, 2001) certainly is a truism in the behavioral business ethics literature. Good largely is ignored, with unethical behaviors of individuals, groups, and organizations capturing most of the attention. Of course, there is the corporate social responsibility literature; but regrettably, it has almost exclusively concerned itself with making a so-called business case for corporate social responsibility by seeking to demonstrate a positive relationship between corporate social performance and financial performance (Margolis & Walsh, 2003). Doing good because it is morally correct takes a backseat, at best. The same can be said about the study of so-called prosocial organizational behaviors (Brief & Motowidlo, 1986), for which the objectives have been to predict their occurrences and relationship to organizational effectiveness (e.g., Podsakoff & MacKenzie, 1997; Podsakoff, MacKenzie, Paine, & Bachrach, 2000).

My colleagues and I (Bradley, Brief, & Smith-Crowe, 2008) have addressed the import and difficulties of studying the "good corporation." To do so, we claimed one could construe of a corporation as an "artificial person" (but see Wolgast, 1992). Moreover, we argued that "behaviors defined as good … are not necessarily the polar opposite of those defined as bad. Theft, for instance, is a bad action that has no correspondent in the goodness category because abstaining from theft is not enough to be labeled as good" (Bradley et al., 2008, p. 179). Thus, "good," "decent," and "bad" were conceptualized as categorically distinct. We go on to (a) specify further the boundaries of a definition for the "good corporation," relying considerably on Kantian ethics; (b) consider how one might measure goodness; and (c) examine how a corporation may become good and stay good. The point is that behavioral business ethics researchers have neglected what is good, and good behavior is not the opposite of bad (or unethical) behavior.

An alternative to moral principles (e.g., Kant's) is virtue ethics, which shifts the focus of the behavioral researcher to character (for a business ethics take on virtues, see Solomon, 1992). Two positive psychologists defined character (or really "character strengths") as the distinguishable routes (psychological processes or mechanisms) to displaying one or another of the virtues (Peterson & Seligman, 2004). The only active and intriguing program of research in behavioral business ethics germane to character is that pursued by Aquino and his colleagues (e.g., Aquino & Freeman, 2009). Aquino and Reed (2002) defined *moral identity* as a self-schema organized around a set of trait associations that relate to a distinct mental image of what a moral person is likely to think, feel, and do (also see Blasi, 1983, 1984, 2005). But, Aquino and his colleagues saw their work resting more on a social-cognitive than a character perspective (Shao, Aquino, & Freeman, 2008).

So, behavioral ethics researchers have considerable room to maneuver in pursuing the virtues as an explanation for goodness in the workplace. But, what are these virtues? Peterson and Seligman (2004) claimed they identified six "core virtues" that converge historically and cross-culturally. They derived their lists from analysis of texts and their virtue catalogs evident in three "traditions"—China, South Asia, and the West—designated by Smart (1999) as the most influential traditions of thought in human history (wow). The six are as follows: courage (physical, moral, and psychological); justice (that which makes life fair); humanity (doing more than what is fair through generosity, kindness, and understanding); temperance (control over excess); transcendence (the connection to something higher); and wisdom (knowledge hard fought for and then used for good). Peterson and Seligman went on to identify positive traits (i.e., character strengths) associated with each virtue. For instance, integrity, authenticity, and honesty, along with bravery, persistence, and vitality, were identified as traits indicative of courage. In discussing measures of these traits, Peterson and Seligman identified tests often used in business to select honest employees (e.g., London House, 1999). Industrial psychologists have closely examined these sorts of tests, finding support for their predictive validity (e.g., Berry, Sackett, & Wiemann, 2007; Ones, Viswesvaran, & Schmidt, 1993; Sackett & Wanek, 1996). I am unaware of a behavioral ethics researcher taking advantage of this research.

Whether it is the good corporation, the virtuous worker, or some other alternative, it is time for behavioral business ethics researchers to take goodness much more seriously. Businesses can do much to ameliorate social ills (Margolis & Walsh, 2003). We have a responsibility to better understand ways that encourage them to do so.

THE BAD

Given that we are captivated by bad behaviors, yet do not conceptually differentiate among them, this section briefly examines the nature of unethical business behaviors. I begin with a somewhat self-serving observation. Much of my research in the moral domain is not recognized as such in the behavioral business ethics literature. I study the causes, nature, and consequences of unfair discrimination in work settings, for example, the treatment of employees or prospective employees based on their skin color or sex (e.g., Brief et al., 1995, 2000, 2005; Deitch, Barsky, Butz, Chan, & Bradley, 2003; James, Brief, Dietz, & Cohen, 2001). Clearly, unfair employment discrimination falls into the moral domain (e.g., Brief, 2008; Brief & Hayes, 1997); yet, in the four recent reviews of the behavioral business ethics literature previously cited (Kish-Gephart et al., 2010; O'Fallon & Butterfield, 2005; Tenbrunsel & Smith-Crowe, 2008; Treviño et al., 2006), *not one* such study was noted.

Why do behavioral business ethics researchers—with extremely few exceptions (e.g., Bazerman & Moore, 2009)—ignore race, sex, and other forms of unfair employment discrimination as unethical behaviors? I simply do not know.

I do know, however, that what currently is construed as the behavioral business ethics literature may be informed by the employment discrimination literature. I provide one quick example. The study of implicit biases is well recognized in the discrimination literature (e.g., Greenwald & Krieger, 2006; Jost et al., 2009; Ziegert & Hanges, 2005; but see Tetlock & Mitchell, 2009). Nevertheless, the idea that such implicit attitudes may drive unethical business behaviors other than employment discrimination has yet to be considered (for a rare exception, see Chugh, 2004). A common measure of these unconscious attitudes is the Implicit Association Test (IAT) (Greenwald, McGhee, & Schwartz, 1998). I would love to see, for instance, an IAT developed to measure implicit associations toward money (maybe construed as greed) and examine its relationship to, say, fraudulent sales practices. How, if at all, does one's unconscious attraction to money influence these unsavory behaviors, and how do contextual factors such as socialization, work group norms, pressures from bosses, and compensation systems interact with it?

What other unethical business behaviors besides unfair discrimination are not attended to adequately? To answer the question, I turned to several basic business ethics textbooks (e.g., Beauchamp & Bowie, 1997; Buchholz & Rosenthal, 1998; De George, 1999; Donaldson & Werhane, 2008; Velasquez, 2006). These books are heavily normative, typically opening with a review of ethical theories, then proceeding to application of those theories to business issues. The sorts of concerns addressed include, for example, false and deceptive advertising; unsafe products; workplace hazards; environmental pollution; employment at will; employee testing (drug, genetic, and psychological); employment discrimination (including pay inequality and sexual harassment); bluffing in negotiations; deceptive sales practices; competitor intelligence gathering; conflicts of interest; and bribery in foreign countries. On the behavioral side, most of these ethical issues have not been a focus of attention or simply have been ignored. Again, such inattention is *not* problematic *if* all forms of unethical business behavior are conceptually equivalent and, therefore, subject to the same casual forces. I, however, have never seen an argument, for example, that environmental pollution, sexual harassment, and bluffing in negotiations are somehow equivalent other than being of ethical concern. Maybe there are good reasons that such arguments are not evident, and that we need to attend to how unethical behaviors are alike and different and structure our theories accordingly.

Another way the nature of bad behaviors has not been adequately recognized in the behavioral business ethics literature is the failure to study carefully how moral dilemmas at work are resolved. The unethical behaviors we study almost always are obviously bad, entailing a choice, at least on the surface, between right and wrong. Thus, they include various forms of lying, cheating, stealing, or illegal acts. The morally correct course of action is apparent, but a different path is chosen to satisfy one's pleasures, interests, or desires, leaving behind duties, obligations, or principles. In such a situation, the choice between right and wrong does not constitute a moral dilemma; neither does the more obvious case of when we know the right thing to do and do it (Lemmon, 1962).

As a layperson, I concede the possibility of moral dilemmas, but it should be noted that among moral philosophers there is considerable debate about whether those dilemmas are possible (e.g., Gowans, 1987; McConnell, 2006; Sinnott-Armstrong, 1988; Williams, 1965). Proceeding as if they are, it also should be noted that the resolution of moral dilemmas assumes making conscious choices that rest on moral reasoning. This is an assumption I have already raised and attend to in the next section of the chapter.

Lemmon (1962) identified the simplest variety of a moral dilemma: a person both ought to do something and ought not to do the same thing. Such dilemmas seem to abound in business. The general case that intrigues me the most is when an employee believes that his organizational superior wants him to perform act X, and the employee has judged performing X as morally wrong (e.g., overbilling a client) but that *not* performing X also morally seems wrong. Not responding to one's organizational superior may fall into the moral domain for two reasons, both of which have to do with the likely virtue of loyalty. I say "likely" because of its ambiguous status as a virtue in moral philosophy (e.g., Ewin, 1992; Kleinig, 2007; Oldenquist, 1982); nevertheless, let us consider loyalty to one's employer and to one's family (regarding the latter I am assuming the focal employee is a breadwinner; Bernard, 1982). So, not performing X is judged by the employee as failing in his duties to the employer and family (again regarding the latter I am thinking of the loss of family income due to "poor" job performance). Clearly, I have gone on too long about my pet interest. The overarching concern is that we do not study the processes organizational members use to resolve such moral dilemmas and the factors that influence these processes. Alternatively, we simply study the choice between right and wrong, not the potential struggle between two rights or two wrongs. But, of course, this assumes people think—on to that assumption.

THE UGLY

Behavioral business ethics researchers have touched on the work of Jonathan Haidt, a moral psychologist (e.g., Sonenshein, 2007). In this section, his work takes center stage. I begin with (to me) his and his colleagues' unique efforts to map, both conceptually and empirically, the moral domain (e.g., Graham, Nosek, et al., 2009; Haidt & Graham, 2007; Haidt & Joseph, 2004). My discussion of this mapping will lead us to the ugliness missing in behavioral business research or, more precisely, to a consideration of disgust.

Starting with the belief that common principles of human morality are to be found in moral feelings, Haidt and Joseph (2004) analyzed five works rich in detail about moral systems (Brown, 1991; de Waal, 1996; Fiske, 1991; Schwartz & Bilsky, 1990; Shweder, Much, Mahapatra, & Park, 1997). Their analysis produced five moral modules: harm/care, fairness/reciprocity, in-group/loyalty, authority/respect, and purity/sanctity (Haidt & Bjorklund, 2007; Haidt & Joseph, 2007). Haidt and Kesebir (2010) told a compelling story that I do not repeat here, about how moral psychologists, following the lead of 18th-century European philosophers, came to almost exclusively study how individuals resolve quandaries pulled by self-interest on the one side and harm/care (including concerns about suffering, nurturance, and the welfare of others) or fairness/reciprocity (including justice and related notions of rights) on the other side as moral concerns. Behavioral business ethics researchers largely have gone down the same narrow path.

Given our familiarity with the ideas that people are vulnerable and often need protection (harm/care) and that people have rights to certain resources or kinds of treatment (fairness/reciprocity) (Haidt, 2007), I put a little more flesh on the three underresearched moral modules (in-group/loyalty, authority/respect, and purity/sanctity)—first in a general way, then with a focus on business. *In-group/loyalty* addresses concerns related to obligations of group membership, such as self-sacrifice and vigilance against betrayal (Haidt & Kesebir, 2010). The module is triggered when there is a threat or challenge to one's group, with *group* referring, for example, to country, family, or team (Graham, Nosek, et al., 2009; Haidt & Joseph, 2007). Characteristic emotions elicited by its engagement include group pride, belongingness, and rage at traitors (Haidt & Joseph, 2007).

While Haidt and his colleagues are not explicit about in-group/loyalty concerns pertaining to one's employing organization, it does not take much imagination to see its applicability. Indeed, organization scholars have long been studying loyalty (e.g., Hirschman, 1970; Salancik, 1977), and now students of positive organizational studies are advocating organizations as communities with commensurate loyalties (e.g., Dutton & Ragins, 2006). But again, organizational loyalty has not been pursued, to my knowledge, in a moral sense; I must admit, I am somewhat uncomfortable in doing so. Haidt and his colleagues supply an explanation for my discomfort (Graham, Haidt, & Nosek, 2009; Haidt & Graham, 2007; also see Haidt & Hersh, 2001). I consider myself politically liberal, and Haidt and his colleagues hypothesized and found across four studies that liberals show greater endorsement and use of harm/care and fairness/reciprocity compared to the other three modules, while conservatives endorse and use all five modules more equally. In part, their hypothesis rested on the following observations:

> Liberals historically have taken an optimistic view of human nature and of human predictability; they hold what Sowell (2002) calls an "unconstrained vision" in which people should be left as free as possible to pursue their own course of personal development. Conservatism in contrast, is best understood as a "positional ideology," a reaction to the challenges to authority and institutions that are so often mounted by liberals. (Muller, 1997)

Conservatives have traditionally taken a more pessimistic view of human nature, believing people are inherently selfish and imperfectible. They therefore hold what Sowell called a "constrained vision in which people need the constraints of authorizing, institutions, and traditions to live civilly with each other" (Graham, Haidt, et al., 2009, pp. 1029–1030).

I do not know how Haidt and his colleagues would explain why I am comfortable with pursing in-group/loyalty concerns in a moral sense as they pertain to the family. I think I have written previously about how people's moral obligations to their families influence their responses to their jobs without being aware I did so. That is, I studied how the financial obligations created by one's family condition reactions to work (e.g., Doran, Stone, Brief, & George, 1991; George & Brief, 1990) without explicitly interpreting those obligations as moral duties to one's family. As I suggested, such duties likely enter into moral reasoning in regard to workplace dilemmas.

Authority/respect addresses concerns related to social order and the obligations of hierarchical relationships such as obedience, respect, and proper role fulfillment (Haidt & Kesebir, 2010). It is triggered by signs of dominance and submission but also by adherence (or not) to the traditions of society (Graham et al., 2009; Haidt & Joseph, 2007). Characteristic emotions elicited by it are respect and fear. In addressing the authority/respect module, organizations clearly were in Haidt and Joseph's (2007) mindset, for, in doing so, they used the terms *bosses* and *respected professionals*. This is one of those modules liberals deemphasize; regardless of our political colors, however, authority/respect is too central to what we study as behavioral business ethics researchers for us to continue to ignore it. We do study what unfolds morally in organizations that are hierarchically structured (and sometimes, populated with respected professionals). While some of us have embraced notions evident in Tetlock's (e.g., 1985) treatment of accountability (e.g., Brief et al., 2000), in Sidanius and Pratto's (1999) social dominance theory (e.g., Umphress, Simmons, Boswell, & Triona, 2008), and in other ideas bound up in the notion of authority, what I am calling for is treatment of it as if obedience to it were a moral imperative.

At first blush, the applicability of the *purity/sanctity* module to behavior business ethics research may not necessarily be apparent. Relevant to it are cleanliness, charity, temperance, and piety (Haidt & Joseph, 2004, 2007), and when these are violated, a characteristic emotional reaction is disgust (e.g., Haidt, Koller, & Dias, 1993; Horberg, Overs, Keltner, & Cohen, 2009; Rozin, Lowery, Imada, & Haidt, 1999). Probing just a little yields several examples of ugliness at work potentially capable of producing disgust: a foul-smelling and dirty co-worker, a senior faculty member trading grades for sex with a freshman, and a boss who repeatedly shows up at work drunk. But, what about piety? How about the devout Catholic being disgusted with the ideas of distributing birth control or so-called morning-after pills in her work role as a pharmacist. Religion can enter the workplace in many ways (Chan-Serafin, Brief, & George, 2010), and clearly, the moral route is one such way.

In sum, Haidt and his colleagues' mapping of the moral domain provides considerable food for thought to the business ethics community. To us behavioralists, our research domain now appears much broader, limited only by our moral and scientific imaginations. Consideration of when and how the moral modules of in-group/loyalty, authority/respect, and purity/sanctity play themselves out in the workplace raises many interesting and potentially important questions. Here are a few examples: Under what conditions does organizational loyalty become a *moral* force in decision making? Is that moral force more powerful (as I suspect) in the U.S. Marine Corps than it is in some comparably sized business organization? If it is, then is that relative power a function of who chooses to join the Marines (e.g., political conservatives), the culture of the corps, or both? Haidt and Graham (2009) suggest that the more one endorses the moral import of authority/respect, the more one believes that hierarchy should be based on hard work and earned wealth; thus, it might be that the moral import of authority/respect influences how workers respond to the reward systems to which they are subjected (i.e., the more importance placed on authority/respect, the more morally correct pay-for-performance systems are judged). Might the import of purity/sanctity vary by organization type beyond the obvious expectation that its import would be greater in religious versus secular organizations? In organizations where cleanliness is central (e.g., hospitals and restaurants), would we find more workers endorsing purity/sanctity morals than in dirtier organizations (e.g., slaughterhouses and hog lots)? I trust you get the point and are enticed to let your imaginations run free.

Intuitive Responses

Thus far, I have not attended to perhaps Haidt's most influential and controversial idea: that moral reasoning is usually a post hoc construction generated after a judgment has been reached (Haidt, 2001). Obviously, this idea is inconsistent with the utility of most normative theories in moral philosophy and behavioral business ethics research that is characterized by a rationalist perspective. If moral reasoning does not produce moral judgment, then what does? The answer, according to Haidt (2001), is "moral intuition," which he defines as "the sudden appearance in consciousness of a moral judgment, including an affective valance (good-bad, like-dislike), without any conscious awareness of having gone through steps of searching, weighing evidence, or inferring a conclusion" (p. 818). His posed moral emotions–moral judgment–moral reasoning casual chain rests on a variety of evidence (e.g., Bargh & Chartrand, 1999; de Waal, 1996; Kahneman & Tversky, 1984; Nisbett & Wilson, 1977), including findings in neuroscientific moral psychology (e.g., Greene & Haidt, 2002; Haidt 2001, 2007; Haidt & Kesebir, 2010).

Haidt (e.g., 2007) recognized that affective reactions push but do not force moral judgments, and that those judgments sometimes are a product of reasoning. He discusses three instances in which immediate intuition is overridden: (a) conscious verbal reasoning (e.g., cost–benefit analysis); (b) reframing a situation to see a new angle or consequence, producing a second, competitive flash intuition; and (c) talking with others who raise new arguments, triggering new flashes of intuition followed by reasoning. Regrettably, Haidt did not adequately address when these instances might occur (for other criticisms of his ideas, see, for example, Huebner, Dwyer, & Hauser, 2009; Narvaez, 2010; but see Haidt, 2010; Pizarro & Bloom, 2003; also see Haidt, 2003, 2004; Saltzstein & Kasachkoff, 2004).

So, when do we decide before we react? Monin, Pizarro, and Beer (2007) attempted to provide an answer. They asserted that the moral judgment literature empirically is dominated by two types of moral encounters:

moral dilemmas entailing a tension between conflicting moral claims and witnessing shocking moral transgression (e.g., someone is reported to have sex with a chicken before cooking and eating it). Monin et al. essentially went on to claim that the more complex dilemmas principally produce reasoning before judgment, and that judgments regarding the shocking transactions principally are a product of affect. Most assuredly, the distinction they draw between investigators pursuing dilemma–reasoning–judgment or shock–affect–judgment situations is correct and important. But, Monin et al.'s reasoning seems somewhat insensitive to several facts: (a) Haidt's model rests on several seemingly well-accepted observations (e.g., individuals make rapid evaluative judgment of others; moral judgments involve brain areas related to emotions; and reasoning often is guided by desires; Haidt & Kesebir, 2010); (b) the data assessing Haidt's model beyond the purity/sanctity domain is very, very thin (i.e., we do not know if it applies to other domains like harm/care and fairness/reciprocity, from which most of the studied dilemmas were drawn); and (c) some data (albeit very few) indicate that, outside the purity/sanctity domain (in this case in regard to the footbridge dilemma), individual affective states can shape moral judgments (Valdesolo & DeSteno, 2006). This said, I am not disagreeing with Monin, Pizarro, and Beer's (in press) conclusion about the influence of prototypes of ethical encounters; rather, I am reserving judgment. Perhaps the answer will lie in a dual-process theory of moral judgment and the controversy surrounding it (e.g., Cushman & Young, 2009; Greene, 2007, 2009; Greene, Nystrom, Engell, Darley, & Cohen, 2004; Greene, Sommerville, Nystrom, Darley, & Cohen, 2001; Koenigs et al., 2007, 2008; McGuire, Langdon, Coltheart, & Mackenzie, 2009; Young & Koenigs, 2007).

The theory posits that characteristically deontological judgments (i.e., those entailing the recognition that no matter how morally good their consequences, some choices are morally forbidden; Alexander & Moore, 2007) are driven by automatic emotional responses, while characteristically utilitarian judgments (consequentialism) are driven by controlled cognitive processes. Most, but not all, of the data addressing the theory were obtained by collecting functional magnetic resonance images or reaction times (see Greene, Morelli, Lowenberg, Nystrom, & Cohen, 2008, for an exception). Given the controversy and the neuroscience link (which I am apprehensive about due to lack of training), I am hesitant to take a stand on the theory other than that I find it intriguing.

Monin et al. (in press) built on their earlier work and provided four different portraits of the virtuous person: (a) the philosopher, who thinks clearly about morality, interpreting and applying abstract principles to everyday life; (b) the sheriff, who views life as governed by quick flashes of affect-laden approval or disapproval, with virtue resulting from these flashes being appropriate; (c) the monk, who sees morality as a struggle between his principles and passions, with moral strength leading to long-term lofty benefits; and (d) the wrestler, who recognizes when an emotion is a valid moral input and when it is not, necessitating taming and juggling how he or she feels. Regrettably, Monin et al. stopped there, providing no indication when one might run into one of their metaphorical prototypes.

In the end, where are we left—moral psychologists and behavioral business ethics researchers alike? Concisely, we need broader tests of existing theory and more theorizing about how the roles of emotion and reasoning may vary in influencing moral judgments *and* ethical behaviors across an array of ethical encounters.

SUMMING UP AND MOVING ON

If my nibbling around the edges of a definition of moral behavior in the workplace has convinced you of nothing else, I hope it has persuaded you that Tenbrunsel and Smith-Crowe (2008) and Warren and Smith-Crowe (2008) were right that we need to get a much better handle on the object of our study. A principal reason for doing so is the ample evidence indicating that the nature of the moral encounter stimulating the behavior influences what sort of process drives the behavior (e.g., the process could be dominated by emotions or by reasoning). Stated somewhat differently, it clearly is not safe to assume that all ethical behaviors are conceptually equivalent and therefore the product of the same underlying process. The research we now do is bounded in ways we have yet to understand. Solving this mystery must be at the top of our research agenda. Its solution likely will entail a better understanding of what it means to do behavioral *business* ethics. That is, as I have implied previously, the moral issues encountered at work may be distinct in ways we do not yet adequately appreciate from those encountered in other settings.

Next in line on that agenda I would place explorations of the moral domains of in-group/loyalty, authority/respect, and purity/sanctity. We probably should begin by examining when they are encountered in the workplace and the nature of those encounters. There is evidence indicating that the importance of these domains varies across individuals (political conservatives versus liberals). This source of variance warrants attention, as does possible variation in the import of the domains across organizations.

By pursing in-group/loyalty, authority/respect, and purity/sanctity, the breadth of moral behaviors we consider will broaden, but not enough. Immoral workplace behaviors arbitrarily excluded from the behavioral business ethics literature (e.g., race and sex discrimination) need to be embraced, as does a long list of unsavory business practices that simply have yet to be attended to adequately (e.g., deceptive advertising and sales practices.) Given that ethical behavior may not be the opposite of unethical behavior, special attention should be focused on doing good. There is a difference between not being complicit in human rights abuses and actively supporting the protection of human rights. Why are some firms and individual businesspersons engaged in the latter and most are not? It would be helpful to know. The same holds true for firms that actively (a) uphold the right to collective bargaining, (b) support the abolition of slavery and child labor, and (c) promote environmental responsibility. The list of goods could go on and on, including corporate philanthropy not tied to potential economic gain.

The next item on my dream agenda is the study of virtues. I have friends in the behavioral business ethics community who have a general disdain for the inclusion of individual differences, and most certainly, some philosophers, in some cases based on social psychological evidence, question the case for virtue ethics (e.g., Doris, 1998, 2002; Harman, 1999). Nevertheless, I am intrigued by Haidt's arguments in support of the import of virtues (e.g., Haidt & Joseph, 2004), the idea that society benefits from a focus on virtues (e.g., Himmelfarb, 1995), and the promise of virtues in applied ethics (e.g., Solomon, 1992; Walker & Ivanhoe, 2007). However, I would urge behavioral researchers who contemplate pursuing the virtues construct to be sensitive to the Aristotelian notion of a virtue as a disposition to act and feel and to "practical wisdom" (i.e., mindfulness of the consequences of possible actions) as a necessary condition for virtues to be translated into virtuous actions (Hursthouse, 2007). That said, the study of virtues will not be an easy road to travel, but there may be a pot of gold at the end.

The final agenda item I would like to raise is the unconscious. I recognized the potential import, yet neglect, of unconscious (or implicit) associations and stereotypes in what to date has been construed as the behavioral business ethics literature. Now, I would like to address the import of "implicit affect," defined as "affective processes activated or processed outside of conscious awareness that influence ongoing thought, behavior, and conscious emotional experience" (Barsade, Ramarajan, & Westen, 2009, p. 136; also see, for example, Westen, 1998; Winkielman & Berridge, 2004). Barsade et al. (2009) identified three categories of implicit affect: (a) The emotion is consciously experienced but its source or its influence remain unconscious; (b) the emotion is unconscious and influences cognitions, motivations, and behaviors; and (c) emotions are implicitly regulated, and such regulation influences cognitions, motivations, or behaviors. Each of these categories could be evident in processes that drive moral behaviors in the workplace. Some data support my assertion. For instance, implicit affect regulation has been shown to increase honesty (Randolph-Seng & Nielsen, 2007) and volunteering to help a charity (Pichon, Boccato, & Saroglou, 2007). Interestingly, in both studies, implicit regulation was primed by religious content, which provides additional evidence for examining further religion=moral behavior connections (see Graham & Haidt, 2010, for a provocative take on the subject)—including negative ties (e.g., Hall, Matz, & Wood, 2010; Salvador, Smith-Crowe, Chan-Serafin, & Brief, 2007).

The idea of implicit affect brings us full circle back to my first agenda item, which concerned what sort of process drives moral behavior, given the nature of the moral issue encountered. Table 2.1 provides a crude summary of what the possible encounter-process options might look like. All the cells are empty because, while we have some clues, we really do not know which encounters prime which process. This state of affairs is challenging enough, but matters really are more complex than depicted: Table 2.1 does not recognize contextual factors in the workplace (e.g., policies, practices, procedures, hierarchical forces, informal social influences, etc.); individual differences (e.g., conservatism, religiosity, virtuousness, etc.); and interactions between factors that may also influence which process dominates (see Table 2.1).

You have arrived at the end, and I am exceedingly impressed with your patience. My reward for the read you have generously given me is the possibility that you might help lead behavioral business ethics along the sort of path I have partially mapped. Thank you for sticking with me.

TABLE 2.1

Some of What We Do Not Know: Drivers of Moral Behavior

Moral Domain	Conscious			Unconscious	
	Amoral Reasoning	Moral Reasoning	Affectively Driven	Cognitively Driven	Affectively Driven
Harm/care					
Fairness/reciprocity					
In-group/loyalty					
Authority/respect					
Purity/sanctity					

NOTE

1. For examples of exceptions, see Cropanzano, Goldman, & Folger (2004); Folger, Cropanzano, & Goldman (2005); Schminke, Ambrose, & Noel (1997); Turillo, Folger, Lavelle, Umphress, & Gee (2002).

REFERENCES

Alexander, L., & Moore, M. (2007). Deontological ethics. *Stanford Encyclopedia of Philosophy*. Retrieved from http://plato.stanford.edu/entries/ethics-deontological/

Appiah, K. A. (2008). *Experiments in ethics*. Cambridge, MA: Harvard University Press.

Aquino, K., & Freeman, D. (2009). Moral identity and business solutions. In. D. Narvaez & D. K. Lapsley (Eds.), *Personality, identity, and character* (pp. 375–395). New York: Cambridge University Press.

Aquino, K., & Reed, A., II. (2002). The self-importance of moral identity. *Journal of Personality and Social Psychology, 83*(6), 1423–1440.

Ayer, A. J. (1946). *Language, truth, and logic* (2nd ed.). New York: Dover.

Bargh, J. A., & Chartrand, T. L. (1999). The unbearable automaticity of being. *American Psychologist, 54*, 462–479.

Barsade, S. G., Ramarajan, L., & Westen, D. (2009). Implicit affect in organizations. *Research in Organizational Behavior, 29*, 135–162.

Baumeister, R. F., Bratslavsky, E., Finkenauer, C., & Vohs, K. D. (2001). Bad is stronger than good. *Review of General Psychology, 5*(4), 323–370.

Bazerman, M. H., & Moore, D. (2009). *Judgment in managerial decision making* (7th ed.). New York: Wiley.

Beauchamp, T. L., & Bowie, N. E. (1997). *Ethical theory and business* (5th ed.). Upper Saddle River, NJ: Prentice Hall.

Bernard, J. (1982). *The future of marriage.* New Haven, CT: Yale University Press.

Berry, C. M., Sackett, P. R., & Wiemann, S. (2007). A review of recent developments in integrity test research. *Personnel Psychology, 60,* 271–301.

Blasi, A. (1983). Moral cognition and moral action: A theoretical perspective. *Developmental Review, 3,* 178–210.

Blasi, A. (1984). Moral identity: Its role in moral functioning. In W. M. Kurtines & J. L. Gewirtz (Eds.), *Morality, moral behavior, and moral development* (pp. 128–139). New York: Wiley.

Blasi, A. (2005). Moral character: A psychological approach. In D. K. Lapsley & F. C. Power (Eds.), *Character psychology and character education* (pp. 67–100). Notre Dame, IN: University of Notre Dame Press.

Bradley, J. C., Brief, A. P., & Smith-Crowe, K. (2008). The good corporation. In D. B. Smith (Ed.), *The people make the place: Exploring dynamic linkages between individuals and organizations* (pp. 175–223). Mahwah, NJ: Erlbaum.

Brief, A. P. (2008). *Diversity at work.* Cambridge, MA: Cambridge University Press.

Brief, A. P., Buttram, R. T., & Dukerich, J. M. (2001). Collective corruption in the corporate world: Toward a process model. In M. E. Turner (Ed.), *Groups at work: Advances in theory and research* (pp. 471–499). Hillsdale, NJ: Erlbaum.

Brief, A. P., Buttram, R. T., Elliott, J. D., Reizenstein, R. M., & McCline, R. L. (1995). Releasing the beast: A study of compliance with orders to use race as a selection criterion. *Journal of Social Issues, 51,* 177–193.

Brief, A. P., Dietz, J., Cohen, R. R., Pugh, S. D., & Vaslow, J. B. (2000). Just doing business: Modern racism and obedience to authority as explanations for employment discrimination. *Organizational Behavior and Human Decision Processes, 81,* 72–97.

Brief, A. P., Dukerich, J. M., & Doran, L. I. (1991). Resolving ethical dilemmas in management: Experimental investigations of values, accountability, and choice. *Journal of Applied Social Psychology, 21,* 380–396.

Brief, A. P., & Hayes, E. L. (1997). The continuing "American dilemma": Studying racism in organizations. In C. L. Cooper & D. M. Rousseau (Eds.), *Trends in organizational behavior* (pp. 89–106). Chichester, UK: Wiley.

Brief, A. P., & Motowidlo, S. (1986). Prosocial organizational behaviors. *Academy of Management Review, 11,* 710–725.

Brief, A. P., Umphress, E. E., Dietz, J., Burrows, J. W., Butz, R. M., & Scholten, L. (2005). Community matters: Realistic group conflict theory and the impact of diversity. *Academy of Management Journal, 4*(48), 830–844.

Brockner, J., Wiesenfeld, J. B., & Diekmann, K. A., (2009). Towards a "fairer" conception of process fairness: Why, when and how more may not always be better than less. *The Academy of Management Annals, 3,* 183–216.

Brown, D. E. (1991). *Human universals.* Philadelphia: Temple University Press.

Brown, M., & Treviño, L. (2006). Socialized charismatic leadership, values congruence, and deviance in work groups. *Journal of Applied Psychology, 91,* 954–962.

Brown, M., Treviño, L., & Harrison, D. (2005). Ethical leadership: A social learning perspective for construct development and testing. *Organizational Behavior and Human Decision Processes, 97*, 117–134.

Buchholz, R. A., & Rosenthal, S. B. (1998). *Business ethics: The pragmatic path beyond principles to process.* Upper Saddle River, NJ: Prentice Hall.

Chan-Serafin, S., Brief, A. P., & George, J. M. (2010). *Does God matter? Religion and the organizational sciences.* Manuscript submitted for publication.

Chugh, D. (2004). Societal and managerial implications of implicit social cognition: Why milliseconds matter. *Social Justice Research, 17*(2), 203–222.

Chugh, D., Bazerman, M. H., & Banaji, M. R. (2005). Bounded ethicality as a psychological barrier to recognizing conflicts of interest. In D. A. Moore, D. M. Cain, G. Loewenstein, & M. X. Bazerman (Eds.), *Conflicts of interest: Challenges and solutions in business, law, medicine, and public policy* (pp. 74–95). New York: Cambridge University Press.

Cropanzano, R., Goldman, B., & Folger, R. (2004). Deontic justice: The role of moral principles in workplace fairness. *Journal of Organizational Behavior, 24*(8), 1019–1024.

Cushman, F., & Young, L. (2009). The psychology of dilemmas and the philosophy of morality. *Ethical Theory and Moral Practice, 12*(1), 9–24.

De George, R. T. (1999). *Business ethics* (5th ed.). Upper Saddle River, NJ: Prentice Hall.

De George, R. T. (2008). Business ethics. *Stanford Encyclopedia of Philosophy.* Retrieved from http://plato.stanford.edu/entries/ethics-business/

Deitch, E. A., Barsky, A., Butz, R. M., Chan, S., & Bradley, J. C. (2003). Subtle yet significant: The existence and impact of everyday racial discrimination in the workplace. *Human Relations, 56*, 1299–1324.

de Waal, F. (1996). *Good natured: The origins of right and wrong in humans and other animals.* Cambridge, MA: Harvard University Press.

Donaldson, T. (1994). When integration fails: The logic of prescription and description in business ethics. *Business Ethics Quarterly, 4*(2), 157–169.

Donaldson, T., & Werhane, P. (2008). *Ethical issues in business: A philosophical approach* (8th ed.). Upper Saddle River, NJ: Prentice Hall.

Doran, L. I., Stone, V. K., Brief, A. P., & George, J. M. (1991). Behavioral intentions as predictors of job attitudes: The role of economic choice. *Journal of Applied Psychology, 76*, 40–45.

Doris, J. M. (1998). Persons, situations, and virtue ethics. *Nous, 32*(4), 504–530.

Doris, J., (2002). *Lack of character: Personality and moral behavior.* New York: Cambridge University Press.

Doris, J., & Stich, S. (2005). As a matter of fact: Empirical perspectives on ethics. In F. Jackson & M. Smith (Eds.), *The Oxford handbook of contemporary analytic philosophy* (pp. 114–152). New York: Oxford University Press.

Doris, J., & Stich, S. (2006). Moral psychology: Empirical approaches. *Stanford Encyclopedia of Philosophy.* Retrieved from http://plato.stanford.edu/entries/moral-psych-emp/

Dutton, J. E., & Ragins, B. R. (2006). *Exploring positive relationships at work: Building a theoretical and research foundation.* Mahwah, NJ: Erlbaum.

Ewin, R. E. (1992). Loyalty and virtues. *Philosophical Quarterly, 42*(169), 403.

Fiske, A. P. (1991). *Structures of social life.* New York: Free Press.

Folger, R., Cropanzano, R., & Goldman, B. (2005). What is the relationship between justice and morality? In J. Greenberg & J. A. Colquitt (Eds.), *Handbook of organizational justice* (pp. 215–245). Mahwah, NJ: Erlbaum.

George, J. M., & Brief, A. P. (1990). The economic instrumentality of work: An examination of the moderating effects of financial requirements and sex on the pay-life satisfaction relationship. *Journal of Vocational Behavior, 37*, 357–368.

Gino, F., Gu, J., Zhong, C. (2009). Contagion or restitution? When bad apples can motivate ethical behavior. *Journal of Experimental Social Psychology, 45*(6), 1299–1302.

Gino, F., & Pierce, L. (2009a). The abundance effect: Unethical behavior in the presence of wealth. *Organizational Behavior and Human Decision Processes, 109*(2), 142–155.

Gino, F., & Pierce, L. (2009b). Dishonesty in the name of equity. *Psychological Science, 20*(9), 1153–1160.

Gowans, C. W. (1987). *Moral dilemmas.* New York: Oxford University Press.

Graham, J., & Haidt, J. (2010). Beyond beliefs: Religions bind individuals into moral communities. *Personality and Social Psychology Review, 14*(1), 140–150.

Graham, J., Haidt, J., & Nosek, B. A. (2009). Liberal and conservatives rely on different sets of moral foundations. *Journal of Personality and Social Psychology, 96*(5), 1029–1046.

Graham, J., Nosek, B. A., Haidt, J., Iyer, R., Koleva, S., & Ditto P. H. (2009). *Broadening and mapping the moral domain: Development and validation of the moral foundations questionnaire.* Manuscript in preparation.

Greenberg, J., & Bies, R. J. (1992). Establishing the role of empirical studies of organizational justice in philosophical inquiries into business ethics. *Journal of Business Ethics, 11*(5/6), 433–444.

Greene, J. (2003). From neural "is" to moral "ought": What are the moral implications of neuroscientific moral psychology? *Nature Reviews Neuroscience, 4*, 846–849.

Greene, J., & Haidt, J. (2002). How (and where) does moral judgment work? *Trends in Cognitive Sciences, 6*, 517–523.

Greene, J. D. (2007). Why are VMPFC patients more utilitarian? A dual-process theory of moral judgment explains. *Trends in Cognitive Sciences, 11*(8), 322–323.

Greene, J. D. (2009). Dual-process morality and the personal/impersonal distinction: A reply to McGuire, Langdon, Coltheart, and Mackenzie. *Journal of Experimental Social Psychology, 45*(3), 581–584.

Greene, J. D., Morelli, S. A., Lowenberg, K., Nystrom, L. E., & Cohen J. D. (2008). Cognitive load selectively interferes with utilitarian moral judgment. *Cognition, 107*(3), 1144–1154.

Greene, J. D., Nystrom, L. E., Engell, A. D., Darley, J. M., & Cohen, J. D. (2004). The neural bases of cognitive conflict and control in moral judgment. *Neuron, 44*, 389–400.

Greene, J. D., Sommerville, R. B., Nystrom, L. E., Darley, J. M., & Cohen, J. D. (2001). An fMRI investigation of emotional engagement in moral judgment. *Science, 293*(5537), 2105–2108.

Greenwald, A. G., & Krieger, L. H. (2006). Implicit bias: Scientific foundations. *California Law Review, 94*, 945–967.

Greenwald, A. G., McGhee, D. E., & Schwartz, J. L. K. (1998). Measuring individual differences in implicit cognition: The implicit association test. *Journal of Personality and Social Psychology, 74*, 1464–1480.

Haidt, J. (2001). The emotional dog and its rational tail: A social intuitionist approach to moral judgment. *Psychological Review, 108*(4), 814–834.

Haidt, J. (2003). The emotional dog does learn new tricks: A reply to Pizarro and Bloom (2003). *Psychological Review, 110*, 197–198.

Haidt, J. (2004). The emotional dog gets mistaken for a possum. *Review of General Psychology, 8*, 283–290.

Haidt, J. (2007). The new synthesis in moral psychology. *Science, 316*, 998–1002.

Haidt, J. (2008). Morality. *Perspectives on Psychological Science, 3*, 65–72.

Haidt, J. (2010). Moral psychology must not be based on faith and hope: Commentary on Narvaez (2010). *Perspectives on Psychological Science, 5*, 182–184.

Haidt, J., & Bjorklund, F. (2007). Social intuitionists answer six questions about moral psychology. In W. Sinnott-Armstrong (Eds.), *Moral psychology: The cognitive science of morality* (Vol. 2, pp. 181–217). Cambridge, MA: MIT Press.

Haidt, J., & Graham, J. (2007). When morality opposes justice: Conservatives have moral intuitions that Liberals may not recognize. *Social Justice Research, 20*(1), 98–116.

Haidt, J., & Graham, J. (2009). Planet of the Durkheimians, where community, authority, and sacredness are foundations of morality. In J. T. Jost, A. Kay, & H. Thorisdottir (Eds.), *Social and psychological bases of ideology and system justification* (pp. 371–401). New York: Oxford University Press.

Haidt, J., & Hersh, M. A. (2001). Sexual morality: The cultures and emotions of conservatives and liberals. *Journal of Applied Social Psychology, 31*(1), 191–221.

Haidt, J., & Joseph, C. (2004). Intuitive ethics: How innately prepared intuitions generate culturally variable virtues. *Daedalus, 133*(4), 55–66.

Haidt, J., & Joseph, C. (2007). The moral mind: How five sets of innate intuitions guide the development of many culture-specific virtues, and perhaps even modules. In P. Carruthers, S. Lawrence, & S. Stich (Eds.), *The innate mind* (Vol. 3, pp. 367–392). Oxford, UK: Oxford University Press.

Haidt, J., & Kesebir, S. (2010). Morality. In S. T. Fiske, D. Gilbert, & G. Lindzey (Eds.), *The handbook of social psychology* (5th ed., Vol. 2, pp. 791–832). Hoboken, NJ: Wiley.

Haidt, J., Koller, S. H., & Dias, M. G. (1993). Affect, culture, and morality, or is it wrong to eat your dog? *Journal of Personality & Social Psychology, 65*(4), 613–628.

Hall, D. L., Matz, D. C., & Wood, W. (2010). Why don't we practice what we preach? A meta-analytic review of religious racism. *Personality and Social Psychology Review, 14*, 126–139.

Harman, G. (1999). Moral philosophy meets social psychology: Virtue ethics and the fundamental attribution error. *Proceedings of the Aristotelian Society, 99*, 315–31.

Hartman, E. M. (2008). Reconciliation in business ethics: Some advice from Aristotle. *Business Ethics Quarterly, 18*(2), 253–265.

Himmelfarb, G. (1995). *The de-moralization of society*. New York: Knopf.

Hirschman, A. O. (1970). *Exit, voice, and loyalty: Responses to decline in firms, organizations, and states*. Cambridge, MA: Harvard University Press.

Horberg, E. J., Overs, C., Keltner, D., & Cohen, A. B. (2009). Disgust and the moralization of purity. *Journal of Personality and Social Psychology, 97*(6), 963–976.

Huebner, B., Dwyer, S., & Hauser, M. (2009). The role of emotion in moral psychology. *Trends in Cognitive Sciences, 13*(1), 1–6.

Hume, D. (1960). *An enquiry concerning the principles of morals*. La Salle, IL: Open Court. (Original work published 1777)

Hursthouse, R. (2007). Virtue ethics. *Stanford Encyclopedia of Philosophy*. Retrieved from http://plato.stanford.edu/entries/ethics-virtue/

James, W. (1950). *The principles of psychology*. New York: Dover. (Original work published 1890)

James, E. H., Brief, A. P., Dietz, J., & Cohen, R. R. (2001). Prejudice matters: Understanding the reactions of whites to affirmative action programs targeted to benefit blacks. *Journal of Applied Psychology, 86*, 1120–1128.

Jones, T. M. (1991). Ethical decision making by individuals in organizations: An issue contingent model. *Academy of Management Review, 16*, 366–395.

Jost, J. T., Rudman, L. A., Blair, I. V., Carney, D. R., Dasgupta, N., Glaser, J., et al. (2009). The existence of implicit bias is beyond reasonable doubt: A refutation of ideological and methodological objections and executive summary of ten studies that no manager should ignore. *Research in Organizational Behavior, 29*, 39–69.

Kahneman, D., & Tversky, A. (1984). Choices, values, and frames. *American Psychologist, 39*, 341–350.

Kish-Gephart, J. J., Harrison, D. A., & Treviño, L. K. (2010). Bad apples, bad cases, and bad barrels: Meta-analytic evidence about sources of unethical decisions at work. *Journal of Applied Psychology, 95*(1), 1–31.

Kleinig, J. (2007). Loyalty. *Stanford Encyclopedia of Philosophy*. Retrieved from http://plato.stanford.edu/entries/loyalty/

Knobe, J., & Nichols, S. (2008). An experimental philosophy manifesto. In J. Knobe & S. Nichols (Eds.), *Experimental philosophy* (pp. 3–14). Oxford, UK: Oxford University Press.

Koenigs, M., Young, L., Adolphs, R., Tranel, D., Cushman, F., Hauser, M., et al. (2007). Damage to the prefrontal cortex increases utilitarian moral judgments. *Nature, 446*, 908–911.

Koenigs, M., Young, L., Adolphs, R., Tranel, D., Cushman, F., Hauser, M., et al. (2008). Koenigs et al. reply. *Nature, 452*(7185), E5–E6.

Kohlberg, L. (1971). From is to ought: How to commit the naturalistic fallacy and get away with it in the study of moral development. In T. Mischel (Ed.), *Cognitive development and epistemology* (pp. 151–235). New York: Academic Press.

Lemmon, E. J. (1962). Moral dilemmas. *The Philosophical Review, 71*(2), 139–158.

London House, Incorporated. (1999). *Personnel selection inventory*. Park Ridge, IL: Author.

Margolis, J. D., & Walsh, J. P. (2003). Misery loves companies: Whither social initiatives by business. *Administrative Science Quarterly, 48*, 268–305.

McConnell, T. (2006). Moral dilemmas. *The Stanford Encyclopedia of Philosophy*. Retrieved from http://plato.stanford.edu/entries/moral-dilemmas/

McGuire, J., Langdon, R., Coltheart, M., & Mackenzie, C. (2009). A reanalysis of the personal/impersonal distinction in moral psychology research. *Journal of Experimental Social Psychology, 45*(3), 577–580.

Messick, D. M., & Tenbrunsel, A. E. (1996). Behavioral research into business ethics. In D. M. Messick & A. E. Tenbrunsel (Eds.), *Codes of conduct: Behavioral research into business ethics* (pp. 1–10). New York: Russell Sage.

Monin, B., Pizarro, D. A., & Beer, J. S. (2007). Deciding versus reacting: Conceptions of moral judgment and the reason-affect debate. *Review of General Psychology, 11*(2), 99–111.

Monin, B., Pizarro, D. A., & Beer, J. S. (in press). Reason and emotion in moral judgment: Different prototypes lead to different theories. In K. D. Vohs, R. F. Baumeister, & G. Loewenstein (Eds.), *Do emotions help or hurt decision making? A hedgefoxian perspective*. New York: Russell Sage Foundation.

Moore, D. A., Tetlock, P. E., Tanlu, L., & Bazerman, M. H. (2006). Conflicts of interest and the case of auditor independence: Moral seduction and strategic issue cycling. *Academy of Management Review, 31*(1), 10–29.

Muller, J. Z. (1997). What is conservative social and political thought? In J. Z. Muller (Ed.), *Conservatism: An anthology of social and political thought from David Hume to the present* (pp. 3–31), Princeton, NJ: Princeton University Press.

Murphy, M. C. (2009). Morality and divine authority. In T. Flint & M. Rea (Eds.), *Oxford handbook of philosophical theology* (pp. 306–331). New York: Oxford University Press.

Narvaez, D. (2010). Moral complexity. *Perspectives on Psychological Science, 5,* 163–181.

Nisbett, R. E., & Wilson, T. D. (1977). Telling more than we can know: Verbal reports on mental processes. *Psychological Review, 84,* 231–259.

O'Fallon, M. J., & Butterfield, K. D. (2005). A review of the empirical ethical decision making literature: 1996–2003. *Journal of Business Ethics, 59,* 375–413.

Oldenquist, A. (1982). Loyalties. *The Journal of Philosophy, 79*(4), 173–193.

Ones, D. S., Viswesvaran, C., & Schmidt, F. L. (1993). Comprehensive meta-analysis of integrity test validities: Findings and implications for personnel selection and theories of job performance. *Journal of Applied Psychology, 78,* 679–703.

Paharia, N., Kassam, K. S., Greene, J. D., & Bazerman, M. H. (2009). Dirty work, clean hands: The moral psychology of indirect agency. *Organizational Behavior and Human Decision Processes, 109*(2), 134–141.

Peterson, C., & Seligman, M. E. P. (2004). *Character, strengths, and virtues: A handbook and classification.* Oxford, UK: Oxford University Press.

Pichon, I., Boccato, G., & Saroglou, V. (2007). Nonconscious influences of religion on prosociality: A priming study. *European Journal of Social Psychology, 37,* 1032–1045.

Pizarro, D. A., & Bloom, P. (2003). The intelligence of the moral intuitions: A comment on Haidt (2001). *Psychological Review, 110,* 193–196.

Podsakoff, P. M., & MacKenzie, S. B. (1997). Impact of organizational citizenship behavior on organizational performance: A review and suggestions for future research. *Human Performance, 10,* 133–151.

Podsakoff, P. M., MacKenzie, S. B., Paine, J. B., & Bachrach, D. G. (2000). Organizational citizenship behaviors: A critical review of the theoretical and empirical literature and suggestions for future research. *Journal of Management, 26*(3), 513–563.

Randolph-Seng, B., & Nielsen, M. E. (2007). Honesty: One effect of primed religious representations. *International Journal for the Psychology of Religion, 17,* 303–315.

Rest, J. R. (1986). *Moral development: Advances in research and theory.* New York: Praeger.

Reynolds, S. J. (2006). Moral awareness and ethical predispositions: Investigating the role of individual differences in the recognition of moral issues. *Journal of Applied Psychology, 91,* 233–243.

Rosenthal, S. B., & Buchholz, R. A. (2000). The empirical-normative split in business ethics: A pragmatic alternative. *Business Ethics Quarterly, 10*(2), 399–408.

Rozin, P., Lowery, L., Imada, S., & Haidt, J. (1999). The CAD triad hypothesis: A mapping between three moral emotions (contempt, anger, disgust) and three moral codes (community, autonomy, divinity). *Journal of Personality and Social Psychology, 76*(4), 574–586.

Sackett, P. R., & Wanek, J. E. (1996). New developments in the use of measures of honesty, integrity, conscientiousness, dependability, trustworthiness, and reliability for personnel selection. *Personnel Psychology, 49,* 787–829.

Salancik, G. R. (1977). Commitment and control of organizational behavior and belief. In B. M. Staw & G. R. Salancik (Eds.), *New directions in organizational behavior* (pp. 1–54). Chicago: St. Clair.

Saltzstein, H. D., & Kasachkoff, T. (2004). Haidt's moral intuitionist theory: A psychological and philosophical critique. *Review of General Psychology, 8,* 273–290.

Salvador, R., Smith-Crowe, K., Chan-Serafin, S., & Brief, A. P. (2007, August). Religious identity and destructive conformity. In D. E. Warren & A. K. Vadera (Co-Chairs), *Doing good or doing evil? Identity and deviance in organizations.* Symposium conducted at the annual meeting of the Academy of Management, Philadelphia.

Sayre-McCord, G., (2007). Metaethics. *The Stanford Encyclopedia of Philosophy.* Retrieved from http://plato.stanford.edu/entries/metaethics/

Schminke, M., Ambrose, M. L., & Noel, T. W. (1997). The effect of ethical frameworks on perceptions of organizational justice. *Academy of Management Journal, 40,* 1190–1207.

Schwartz, S. H., & Bilsky, W. (1990). Toward a theory of the universal content and structure of values: Extensions and cross-cultural replications. *Journal of Personality and Social Psychology, 58,* 878–891.

Shao, R., Aquino, K., & Freeman, D. (2008). Beyond moral reasoning: A review of moral identity research and its implications for business ethics. *Business Ethics Quarterly, 18*(4), 513–540.

Shweder, R. A., & Haidt, J. (1993). The future of moral psychology: Truth, intuition, and the pluralist way. *Psychological Science, 4*(6), 360–365.

Shweder, R. A., Much, N. C., Mahapatra, M., & Park, L. (1997). The "big three" of morality (autonomy, community, and divinity) and the "big three" explanations of suffering. In A. M. Brandt & P. Rozin (Eds.), *Morality and health* (pp. 119–169). New York: Routledge.

Sidanius, J., & Pratto, F. (1999). *Social dominance: An intergroup theory of social hierarchy and oppression.* New York: Cambridge University Press.

Sinnott-Armstrong, W. (1988). *Moral dilemmas.* Oxford, UK: Blackwell.

Smart, N. (1999). *World philosophies.* New York: Routledge.

Solomon, R. C. (1992). Corporate roles, personal virtues: An Aristotelian approach to business ethics. *Business Ethics Quarterly, 2*(3), 317–339.

Sonenshein, S. (2007). The role of construction, intuition, and justification in responding to ethical issues at work: The sensemaking-intuition model. *Academy of Management Review, 32,* 1022–1040.

Sowell, T. (2002). *A conflict of visions: The ideological origins of political struggles.* New York: Basic Books.

Tenbrunsel, A. E. (1998). Misrepresentation and expectations of misrepresentation in an ethical dilemma: The role of incentives and temptation. *Academy of Management Journal, 41,* 330–339.

Tenbrunsel, A. E., Diekmann, K. A., Wade-Benzoni, K. A., & Bazerman, M. H. (in press). The ethical mirage: A temporal explanation as to why we aren't as ethical as we think we are. *Research in Organizational Behavior.*

Tenbrunsel, A. E., & Messick, D. M. (1999). Sanctioning systems, decision frames, and cooperation. *Administrative Science Quarterly, 44,* 684–707.

Tenbrunsel, A. E., & Smith-Crowe, K. (2008). Ethical decision making: Where we've been and where we're going. *The Academy of Management Annals, 2,* 545–607.

Tetlock, P. E. (1985). Accountability: A social check on the fundamental attribution error. *Social Psychology Quarterly, 48,* 227–236.

Tetlock, P. E., & Mitchell, G. (2009). Implicit bias and accountability systems: What must organizations do to prevent discrimination? *Research in Organizational Behavior, 29,* 3–38.

Treviño, L. K., Brown, M. E., & Hartman, L. P. (2003). A qualitative investigation of perceived executive ethical leadership: Perceptions from inside and outside the executive suite. *Human Relations, 56,* 5–38.

Treviño, L. K., & Weaver, G. R. (1994). Business ethics/business ethics: One field or two? *Business Ethics Quarterly, 4,* 113–128.

Treviño, L. K., & Weaver, G. R. (2003). *Managing ethics in business organizations: Social scientific perspectives.* Stanford, CA: Stanford University Press.

Treviño, L. K., Weaver, G. R., & Brown, M. E. (2008). It's lovely at the top: Hierarchical levels, identities, and perceptions of organizational ethics. *Business Ethics Quarterly, 18,* 233–252.

Treviño, L. K., Weaver, G. R., & Reynolds, S. J. (2006). Behavioral ethics in organizations: A review. *Journal of Management, 32*(6), 951–991.

Turillo, C. J., Folger, R., Lavelle, J. J., Umphress, E. E., & Gee, J. O. (2002). Is virtue its own reward? Self-sacrificial decisions for the sake of fairness. *Organizational Behavior and Human Decision Processes, 89,* 839–865.

Umphress, E. F., Simmons, A. C., Boswell, W., & Triona, M. C. (2008). Managing discrimination in selection. The impact of accountability and social dominance orientation. *Journal of Applied Psychology, 93,* 982–988.

Valdesolo, P., & DeSteno, D. (2006). Manipulations of emotional context shape moral judgment. *Psychological Science, 17*(6), 476–477.

Velasquez, M. G. (1996). Business ethics, the social sciences, and moral philosophy. *Social Justice Research, 9*(1), 97–107.

Velasquez, M. G. (2006). *Business ethics: Concepts and cases* (4th ed.). Upper Saddle River, NJ: Prentice Hall.

Warren, D. E., & Smith-Crowe, K. (2008). Deciding what's right: The role of external sanctions and embarrassment in shaping moral judgments in the workplace. *Research in Organizational Behavior, 28,* 81–105.

Walker, R. L, & Ivanhoe, P. J. (2007). *Working virtue: Virtue ethics and contemporary moral problems.* New York: Oxford University Press.

Werhane, P. H. (1994). The normative/descriptive distinction in methodologies of business ethics. *Business Ethics Quarterly, 4,* 175–180.

Westen, D. (1998). Implicit cognition, affect, and motivation: The end of a century-long debate. In R. Bornstein & J. Masling (Eds.), *Empirical studies of unconscious processes.* Washington, DC: American Psychological Association.

Williams, B. A. O. (1965). Ethical consistency. *Proceedings of the Aristotelian Society, 39,* 103–124.

Williams, B. A. O. (1985). *Ethics and the limits of philosophy.* Cambridge MA: Harvard University Press.

Winkielman, P., & Berridge, K. C. (2004). Unconscious emotion. *Current Directions in Psychological Science, 13,* 120–123.

Wolgast, E. (1992). *Ethics of an artificial person: Lost responsibility in professions and organizations.* Stanford, CA: Stanford University Press.

Young, L., & Koenigs, M. (2007). Investigating emotion in moral cognition: A review of evidence from functional neuroimaging and neuropsychology. *British Medical Bulletin, 84,* 69–79.

Ziegert, J. C., & Hanges, P. J. (2005). Employment discrimination: The role of implicit attitudes, motivation, and a climate for bias. *Journal of Applied Psychology, 90*(3), 553–562.

Section 3

Ethics and Social Context

3

Behavioral Business Ethics: Taking Context Seriously

Marshall Schminke and Manuela Priesemuth
University of Central Florida

INTRODUCTION

To understand ethical behavior, one must consider the context in which it evolves. In business settings, this requires that we recognize the influence of the organizations in which it occurs. Our goal in this chapter is to facilitate that conversation, and we proceed in four steps. First, we highlight the important role context has played in improving our understanding of behavioral ethics. Second, we outline a critique of the extant literature by identifying four recurring challenges that emerge in this research. Third, we build on this critique by advancing a set of directives aimed at improving the quality and quantity of research devoted to understanding the role of context in behavioral business ethics. Finally, we position these thoughts into the larger stream of emergent research by providing a brief background and history of the emergence of behavioral ethics as an area of study. In all, our aim is to highlight the critical role context plays in understanding behavioral ethics in organizations and to call on scholars to take seriously the challenge it represents for crafting quality research on both theoretical and empirical fronts.

THE ROLE OF CONTEXT IN BEHAVIORAL ETHICS RESEARCH

Behavioral ethics research has long graced the pages of top scholarly journals. However, it has only recently been organized under that moniker.

Two efforts stand out as providing a solid inventory of what is known about behavioral ethics. Treviño, Weaver, and Reynolds (2006) and Tenbrunsel and Smith-Crowe (2008) have cataloged, organized, and interpreted the broad array of empirical work in the area. We build on the results of these two reviews and other related work to provide the foundation for our discussion of the role of context in behavioral ethics. However, we refer the interested reader to these helpful and insightful works for an even broader assessment of the literature.

Both Treviño et al. (2006) and Tenbrunsel and Smith-Crowe (2008) reviewed multiple themes that have emerged in behavioral ethics research. These include influences on ethical decision making and behavior that include both individual and contextual factors, as well as the nature of the specific ethical event itself. In this chapter, we focus in particular on the impact of context on ethical decision making and behavior.

Scholars like Lewin (1947) have long recognized the importance of context in understanding behavior in organizations. Subsequent work by Mischel (1977), Schneider (1983), Cappelli and Sherer (1991), Mowday and Sutton (1993), Rousseau and Fried (2001), and Johns (2001, 2006) has reiterated the critical role played by organizational context in shaping a broad array of individual attitudes and behavior.

The focus of this chapter is on the extent to which context matters in behavioral ethics. We adopt Johns's definition of *context* as "situational opportunities and constraints that affect the occurrence and meaning of organizational behavior as well as functional relationships between variables" (2006, p. 386). Further, we agree with Johns that the impact of context may play out in multiple ways. Context may exert main or direct effects on ethical behavior, or it may occupy more complex moderating or mediating roles. In all, our interest lies in summarizing and cataloging the several aspects of context that have demonstrated a relationship with behavioral ethics.

Although the Treviño et al. (2006) and Tenbrunsel and Smith-Crowe (2008) reviews take different paths in organizing and interpreting behavioral ethics research, each points to organizational context as a critical component for understanding behavioral ethics. We briefly catalog the work presented in these two reviews and revisit themes that have emerged elsewhere in summaries of contextual influences (e.g., Arnaud & Schminke, 2007; O'Fallon & Butterfield, 2005). We also consider relevant research completed since these reviews appeared. Finally, we draw on related research that considers variables like abusive supervision and employee deviance, domains that, as noted in Treviño et al., overlap significantly with behavioral ethics.

Three notes are in order before we proceed. First, we do not offer this overview as an exhaustive review of all studies that have explored the impact of context on ethics in organizations. Rather, it seeks to illustrate the type of contextual influences that have interested scholars, both conceptually and empirically, and how those contextual factors influence organizational events and outcomes. Second, we limit our observations to organizational characteristics. Although some studies have explored additional situational influences such as industry type (see O'Fallon & Butterfield, 2005, for a review) or the intensity of the ethical issue itself (Jones, 1991), these do not represent organizational characteristics and are not addressed here.

Finally, we have not limited our review to studies of ethical or unethical behavior per se. Rather, we follow Treviño et al. (2006) in considering ethics-related behaviors such as deviance, organizational misconduct, counterproductive work behavior, and whistle-blowing. Treviño et al. argue behavioral constructs like these share conceptual space with behavioral ethics on several fronts. First, they share a common set of antecedents, such as whether employees are treated fairly, whether effective codes of conduct are in place, and whether ethical leadership is displayed in the work unit. Second, they comprise a constellation of behaviors that represent violations of generally accepted moral norms or rules. Finally, they focus on behaviors that are intentional. We add to this collection of ethics-related behaviors constructs like abusive supervision, bullying, and incivility. Because of the characteristics they share with ethical and unethical behavior, we suggest each has the potential to provide useful insights regarding patterns of evidence relevant to behavioral ethics research.

Ethical Infrastructure

Ethical infrastructures include both the formal and the informal aspects of organizational structures and systems related to ethics (Tenbrunsel, Smith-Crowe, & Umphress, 2003). Formal aspects include ethical codes, surveillance systems, and sanctioning systems. Informal aspects include ethical climate, culture, and informal communication systems and norms (Treviño, Butterfield, & McCabe, 1998).

Formal Dimensions

The formal components of ethical infrastructure like ethical codes have been shown to influence ethical decision making and behavior in a number of ways. For example, ethical codes have been shown to influence moral awareness (Weaver & Treviño, 1999) and are positively related to both ethical decision making (Ford & Richardson, 1994; Loe, Ferrell, & Mansfield, 2000; O'Fallon & Butterfield, 2005) and ethical behavior (Greenberg, 2002; McCabe, Treviño, & Butterfield, 1996; Peterson, 2002b; Weaver & Treviño, 1999).

Similarly, Somers (2001) showed that accountants who worked at organizations with ethical codes in place reported less misconduct than did those in organizations without codes of ethics. Likewise, Andreoli and Lefkowitz (2009) examined the impact of formal mechanisms such as codes of ethics, ethical practices, and pressure to comply. Results show that formal ethical practices are negatively related to both one's own misconduct and observed misconduct by others. In all, findings show formal dimensions of ethics within organizations impact individuals' ethical reasoning and behavior.

Informal Dimensions

The informal components of ethical infrastructure like ethical culture and climate have also been shown to influence ethical decision making and behavior. For example, ethical work climate (Victor & Cullen, 1988; Arnaud & Schminke, in press) relates to a variety of ethical outcomes like moral awareness (VanSandt, 2003), deviant behavior (Peterson, 2002a), and ethical behavior (Peterson, 2002b; Vardi, 2001; Wimbush, Shepard, & Markham, 1997). Ethical climate has been associated with more general outcomes as well, including job attitudes (e.g., Koh & Boo, 2001). Other research suggests ethical climate may also play a moderating role in organizational ethics. For example, Barnett and Vaicys (2000) found that ethical climate may moderate the relationship between an individual's moral judgments and behavioral intent. That is, ethical climate may influence whether an individual will engage in a morally questionable activity when the person does not personally find the activity to be objectionable. (For a more complete review of the antecedents and consequences of ethical work climate, see Arnaud and Schminke, 2007.)

Ethical culture (Treviño, 1990), a close cousin to ethical climate, has also been shown to influence ethical outcomes. Treviño et al. (1998), for example, found that when ethics codes were in place, ethical culture exerted a strong influence on ethical behavior. They also found ethical culture influenced more general outcomes like organizational commitment.

Informal ethical infrastructures extend beyond climate and culture. They also include informal sanctioning processes such as those involved in informal reward and punishment systems (Tenbrunsel et al., 2003). These have also been shown to influence organizational ethics. For example, both Hegarty and Sims (1978) and Tenbrunsel (1998) found informal incentives to behave unethically exerted a significant influence on unethical behavior, a finding generally supported in other reviews (e.g., Ford & Richardson, 1994; O'Fallon & Butterfield, 2005). Likewise, informal ethical infrastructures also include communication patterns with respect to ethics. Research shows more open discussion of ethics in an organization is predictive of ethical conduct (Treviño, Weaver, Gibson, & Toffler, 1999), whereas a lack of open communication about ethics appears to support increased misconduct (Bird, 1996).

Here, we have addressed the formal and informal dimensions of ethical infrastructure separately. However, both conceptual (Tenbrunsel et al., 2003) and empirical (Weaver, Treviño, & Cochran, 1999) research suggests formal and informal systems typically operate as a system. In particular, informal components like climate and culture are generally viewed as influencing the effectiveness of more formal components like ethical codes.

Other Contextual Influences

Nonethical Infrastructure

Research also suggests other aspects of the organizational context have the capacity to influence ethics. For example, characteristics of the organizational environment not explicitly oriented toward ethics may play an important role. Tenbrunsel and Smith-Crowe (2008), for example, concluded that environments characterized by competitive business practices may increase moral awareness. Likewise, research suggests that settings in which a strong emphasis is placed on obedience toward authority figures are associated with higher levels of unethical behavior (Treviño et al. 1998, 1999).

Organizational structure is also not generally considered part of the ethical infrastructure of organizations but has nonetheless been explored as a possible influence on organizational ethics. Weber (1995) demonstrated that work units devoted to technical core activities, buffering activities, and boundary-spanning activities (Thompson, 1967) differed in predictable ways with respect to their ethical climates (Victor & Cullen, 1988). Similarly, Schminke (1991) showed that organizational size and the rigidity or flexibility of organizational structure were related to the ethical decision-making styles of organizational members. Additional evidence with respect to a link between organizational size and ethics has been mixed. Earlier reviews (e.g., Ford & Richardson, 1994) suggested organizational size exerts a negative effect on ethics. More recent reviews (e.g., O'Fallon & Butterfield, 2005) suggest a more mixed picture, but some evidence continues to suggest size does influence organizational ethics. However, the processes by which it does so do not yet appear to be fully understood.

Leadership

In organizational settings, most individuals work for—or with—other individuals. Therefore, in addition to the impact of infrastructure, the ethical context of work often reflects the impact of other individuals such as leaders and peers.

Various aspects of leadership have been shown to influence organizational ethics. Brown, Treviño, and Harrison (2005) demonstrated that ethical leadership was associated with greater willingness to report ethical problems, as well as increased satisfaction with their supervisor and commitment to their job. Studies by Dukerich, Nichols, Elm, and Vollrath (1990) and Schminke, Wells, Peyrefitte, and Sebora (2002) demonstrated that leader ethics may shape the ethical tendencies of the group itself by establishing stronger agreement about appropriate ethical norms. Research also showed leaders may influence development of the ethical climate of their organizations, especially in younger organizations (Schminke, Ambrose, & Neubaum, 2005).

Peers

Research demonstrates that peers also provide a source of contextual influence on organizational ethics. Zey-Ferrell and Ferrell (1982), for example, showed peers exert an important influence on individual ethics, and those influences are stronger when peer interactions are more frequent and more intense. Similarly, employee antisocial behavior has been shown to be related to antisocial behavior of co-workers (Robinson & O'Leary-Kelly, 1998). In other work, Schmidtke (2007) explored co-worker effects on theft propensities. He found when consensus about the type of theft decreased, witnessing theft by a similar co-worker increased the likelihood an employee would imitate the behavior and decreased the likelihood of reporting the behavior. In all, peer influences on ethical behavior have been robust in the literature, appearing in experimental settings (e.g., Beams, Brown, & Killough, 2003; Jones & Kavanagh, 1996), field settings (e.g., Zey-Ferrell, Weaver, & Ferrell, 1979), and cross-cultural settings (Izraeli, 1988).

CHALLENGES FACING RESEARCHERS INTERESTED IN CONTEXTUAL INFLUENCES

In all, considerable evidence suggests a variety of contextual factors influence ethical awareness, decision making, and behavior in organizational settings. Further, this evidence suggests those influences manifest themselves in a variety of ways. However, as with most nascent research areas, several challenges have emerged for scholars exploring the impact of context on behavioral ethics. Addressing these issues will allow us to probe more carefully the relationship between context and ethics. In addition, it may strengthen the quality of our research in ways that will increase its impact on scholars beyond our own immediate circle.

In the next section, we identify four such challenges: definitions, theory development, model development, and research methods and analyses. We do so with the aim of providing a developmental critique of work in the area. Although we cite specific articles as representative of these challenges, the issues addressed here are not specific to any one author, article, or topic area. To demonstrate the broader applicability of these critiques, we expand our discussion of these challenges by including research topics beyond core areas like moral awareness and ethical decision making, to include related topics like deviance, bullying, violence, misconduct, and incivility. Finally, to ensure the reader understands that we provide this critique with the most positive intentions, and in the spirit of creating a supportive, developmental dialogue about how to improve our research efforts in this area, we include examples of our own work as illustrative of the specific challenges.

Challenge 1: Definitions

Definitions are difficult. Definitions of constructs related to ethics are especially difficult. This is not simply because ethics researchers are often forced to wrestle with the dual challenges of both normative and descriptive components of our definitions. It is also because we wrestle with constructs that are, in and of themselves, challenging to understand and therefore challenging to define.

One recent example of a difficult definition in the area of contextual influences is perceived violence climate (Spector, Coulter, Stockwell, & Matz, 2007). Building on the safety climate literature, Spector et al. examined how perceived violence climate influences outcomes like physical violence and verbal aggression. However, close examination of the article reveals a precise definition of perceived violence climate is elusive.

It is not that the authors did not provide considerable background on the construct. They described when a violence climate is likely to be perceived by employees, how it might be achieved, and how it would be expected to act on employees to influence important outcomes. In all, the authors provided a rich picture of the role perceived violence climate might play as a component of organizational context. However, they did not provide a specific definition of violence climate or a specific definition of violence itself from which the reader could work to create a definition of violence climate. For example, what makes violence distinct from bullying, aggression, harassment, or assault (all terms that also appear in the article) is never made fully clear. An understanding of the distinction between constructs like these might be assumed among scholars familiar with this family of work. But a new reader, interested in drawing this work back to his or her own area, would face substantial hurdles in knowing exactly how to do so.

An article on the topic of moral courage demonstrates this is not a challenge limited to contextual factors influencing ethics but is, rather, problematic throughout the behavioral ethics literature. Sekerka and Bagozzi (2007) define *moral courage* as "the ability to use inner principles to do what is good for others, regardless of threat to self, as a matter of practice" (p. 135). This definition provides a succinct, focused, and thoughtful definition of a difficult construct, clearly framing moral courage as an ability, a specific characteristic of the individual. However, two sentences prior to this definition, they state, "Moral courage is a consistent practice of having the virtue of willpower" (p. 135). At this point, the reader faces a challenge. A single construct cannot simultaneously be both an individual ability and a practice or process. As such, a researcher interested in exploring moral courage, or the impact of context on it, would face a quandary with respect to operationalizing the construct.

One additional issue tends to plague scholars attempting to define factors related to behavioral ethics. It involves constructs that are so broadly framed as to be of limited value. Employee misconduct is one such construct. For example, in exploring organizational antecedents of employee misconduct Andreoli and Lefkowitz (2009) (drawing on Kidder, 2005) describe employee misconduct as encompassing behaviors that range from spending five extra minutes on break to workplace homicide. We wonder whether any given set of antecedents or consequences is likely to bear a consistent relationship with such a broad array of actions. That is, would we expect similar antecedents to drive both workplace lateness and workplace homicide? Would we expect similar consequences to flow from lateness and from homicide? We must therefore wonder about the utility of researching a construct with such an expansive domain. It is noteworthy that Andreoli and Lefkowitz never explicitly define employee misconduct, in spite of a section in the article titled, "Defining Organizational Misconduct." Rather, they define three categories of behavior—organizational misbehavior, unethical behavior, and incivility, hostility, or rude behavior—that comprise what they call the domain of moral action. However, it is unclear whether their intent is to equate this domain of moral action with employee misconduct or whether it also represents a distinct construct.

Construct definitions represent the basic building blocks of everything we do: our theories, our models, and the means by which we operationalize and measure constructs in our empirical analyses. As our work on the impact of context on ethics begins to speak to larger and more diverse audiences, it is especially important that we apply the utmost in care and precision with regard to our definitions.

Challenge 2: Theory Development

Theory development is a second challenge facing scholars engaged in research integrating context and ethics. Our track record of building strong theoretical foundations for our work has not always been on par with leading edge research in other areas.

It is not that scholars do not recognize the benefits of theory-based research. They do (Lewin, 1945; Van de Ven, 1989). However, even with this recognition made explicit, research often falls short. For example, consider Deshpande and Joseph's (2009) work exploring the impact of two contextual influences (ethical climate and peer behavior) and emotional intelligence on ethical behavior of nurses. Deshpande and Joseph explicitly recognize the importance of theory-based research. They cite several recent reviews calling for more theory-based research in business ethics. However, neither their overall model nor any of their three hypotheses is grounded in formal theory.

The authors do make mention of theories. For example, they note the belief that co-workers serve as role models for other employees is based on social learning theory. However, beyond a single-sentence remark, social learning theory is neither described nor its basic tenets explained; those components are not mapped onto the issues at hand to develop new perspectives on the relationship between focal concepts. Similarly, several theoretical perspectives (e.g., ethical theory, ethical climate theory) are presented briefly when describing previous research showing a link between ethical climate and behavior. However, they are presented as being related to previous empirical findings, rather than as the foundation for a process-based story line aimed at understanding how ethical climate might influence ethical behavior.

In other cases, behavioral ethics research has built on explicitly atheoretical foundations. Consider, for example, Somers's (2001) examination of the impact of ethical codes and organizational values on employee behavior. Somers's interest lies squarely on understanding the impact of organizational context on ethical behavior. However, the study does not identify a particular theoretical perspective on which its research questions and hypotheses are based. This is not to say it does not provide a conceptual foundation for the work. It is grounded explicitly in what Somers terms the contextual-behavioral perspective, in which the individual represents the unit of analysis, but the purpose of the research is to understand contextual influences on the individual's behavior. However, Somers is explicit in noting the lack of theoretical foundation for making strong predictions about the relationships between his constructs of interest. As a result, this study is primarily—and explicitly—an exploration of several atheoretical research questions, rather than of formal, theory-generated, hypotheses.

This transparency is refreshing in that many authors are less willing to embrace an atheoretical approach openly. In such instances, readers are forced to discover for themselves whether the work is theory based.

A third type of theory development challenge involves a more explicit embrace of one or more specific theoretical perspectives, but one in which the theories represent more of a simple backdrop for hypotheses than a true foundation for the study and model. In such instances, a particular theoretical perspective may provide a general narrative or guide to the underlying processes at work. But, the research may not delve deeply into the nuances of the theory as a source of interesting, counterintuitive, or challenging hypotheses.

For example, Leung (2008) presents some interesting thoughts about the relationship between ethical context (climate) and organizational citizenship behavior (OCB). In establishing the link between ethical climate and ethical behavior, she invokes the notions of relational (Barnett & Schubert, 2002) and psychological (Lester, Turnley, Bloodgood, & Bolino, 2002) contracts. In extending this link to include OCB, she cites social exchange theory (Blau, 1964). Both of these theoretical perspectives appear as well, during hypothesis development, but no particular theory is explicated either deeply or precisely as a foundation for new, interesting, or novel linkages between the constructs. Rather, previous research is presented as being "consistent with the relational contract" (p. 46) or "linked to the social exchange theory" (p. 47). These are not accurate statements, so far as they go. The findings are indeed consistent with and linked to the theoretical perspectives cited. But although such links to theoretical foundations provide a sound starting point for theory-based research, they do not provide the basis for developing and extending our theoretical understanding of the issues.

Demonstrating that findings are consistent with a well-known theoretical phenomenon may be the basis for new empirical insights. However, the strongest research allows us to offer significant contributions on both empirical and theoretical fronts. For behavioral ethics scholars interested in contextual effects, this means truly grounding our work in theory, not just applying it at a superficial level. Doing so will improve not only the quality of our scholarship but also the depth of our reach into other related areas of research that share our theoretical language.

Several theoretical perspectives appear to hold promise for advancing research in behavioral ethics, especially relating to contextual impacts on behavioral and attitudinal outcomes. Examples of these include social learning theory (Bandura, 1977), social information-processing theory (Salancik & Pfeffer, 1978), and Schneider's (1987) attraction-selection-attrition (ASA) perspective. These theories argue that perceptions about social context in the workplace emerge through social interaction, exchange, or amplification (Mayer, Kuenzi, Greenbaum, Bardes, & Salvador, 2009). In turn, these context-based perceptions influence behavior and attitudes.

For example, social learning theory states individuals look to role models in the work context, and model or imitate their behavior. Through social learning, people may adopt ethical behaviors, as evidenced by the impact of ethical leadership (Brown et al., 2005), or antisocial behaviors (Robinson & O'Leary-Kelly, 1998). It is notable that these role models may be either leaders or peers and thus may provide a sound theoretical foundation for studies like those of Deshpande and Joseph (2009).

Social information-processing theory also has potential for helping to understand the role of context on behavioral ethics. Social information processing of events in the workplace may influence both positive and negative behaviors and attitudes. It occurs when individuals interpret cues and information from the context of their immediate social work environments to understand and develop appropriate attitudes and behaviors (Salancik & Pfeffer, 1978). Extended to organizational ethics, it suggests employees read and interpret ethical codes and organizational values that will guide their behavior at work. As such, it has the capacity to inform relationships like those indicated by Somers (2001), which explored the relationship between ethical codes and values on employee behavior.

Finally, Schneider's (1987) ASA perspective argues the reason individuals and organizations come to exhibit congruent traits is that people analyze their work environments and may adjust their behavior accordingly. People select workplaces and environments to which they are more attracted and to which they feel greater levels of similarity. Heightened levels of attraction and similarity lead individuals to be more prone to adapt common behaviors, cognitions, and attitudes. These outcomes may extend to ethical factors; thus, Schneider's ASA perspective offers potential theoretical explanations for how contextual factors may influence individuals' behavior and attitudes. In all, each of these perspectives offers scholars a sound theoretical platform on which behavioral ethics research may be built.

Challenge 3: Model Development

The world is not a main-effects-only place. The same is true for behavioral ethics. It is true that some of the most basic, introductory-level questions one might ask about the impact of contextual factors on ethical outcomes reflect main or direct effects. Do ethical codes influence ethical behavior? Does organizational size influence employee ethics? Does an ethical climate affect ethical outcomes? All of these are sensible, foundational, main-effects-only questions. However, as researchers we recognize that knowing whether X is related to Y may be an important starting point, but it is just a starting point. As soon as main effects questions are probed, our thoughts immediately turn to questions of a more sophisticated theoretical nature.

At their most basic level, these more advanced models come down to two basic types. The first explores *the process by which* X influences Y. These are mediation models. The second explores *the conditions under which* X influences Y. These are moderation models. Models of these two types, and combinations of them, hold the key for understanding the impact of context in a more fine-grained way than is possible with main-effects-only models.

We did not need to go far to identify models reflecting this challenge. Schminke (2001), for example, provided an example. This study explored the relationship between four contextual factors and individuals' ethical predispositions (whether they tended toward formalist or utilitarian moral reasoning). The four contextual factors were organizational size, structural formalization, and two dimensions of structural centralization. The study hypothesized main effects of each contextual factor on both types of ethical predispositions. Results demonstrated a strong effect for size. Members of larger organizations displayed higher levels of both ethical formalism and utilitarianism. In addition, one dimension of structural centralization (participation) was related to ethical utilitarianism, and structural formalization was marginally related to ethical formalism.

This study was one of the first to examine explicitly the link between organizational structure and individuals' ethical decision-making tendencies. However, its focus on simple, main-effects-only relationships severely limited its ability to help us understand how and why context matters. Yes, the impact of size on ethical predisposition was robust, but the effect was in the opposite direction from that hypothesized. (Schminke, 2001, had predicted ethical predispositions would be stronger in smaller organizations.) In addition, other hypotheses regarding structural formalization and centralization were only weakly supported, suggesting any underlying effects might be conditional ones, requiring that potential moderators be identified and tested. Further, the effects that did emerge provide limited insights about the process by which structure and size influence individuals' ethical predispositions because no mediation processes were included in the model. Although the study's narrative describes a process by which size and structure might influence individual ethics, it cannot support or refute those speculations because it neither measured nor modeled variables capable of reflecting those mediating processes.

Schminke (2001) is not alone in relying on main-effects-only modeling for exploring the impact of context on ethics. More recent models do so as well, although often not as explicitly. For example, Kidwell and Valentine (2009) proposed and tested a model of the impact of group context on organizational misbehavior. The pictorial representation of Kidwell and Valentine's framework links group context to misbehavior via multiple mediating processes involving job satisfaction and effort-performance expectancies. Thus, it represents a clear conceptual improvement over Schminke's (2001) main-effects-only model. However, although the illustration of the framework reflects mediation effects, the study's hypotheses do not address mediation effects explicitly. Each link in the pictorial depiction of the framework was hypothesized individually and was presented and tested in a main-effects-only format. No formal mediation hypotheses (e.g., "The impact of instrumental leadership on job effort will be mediated by ethical climate") are presented. Further, formal tests for mediation were not performed as part of the analysis of the structural relationships between variables. Standard tests for whether those mediation effects were most accurately modeled as full or partial mediation also were not performed.

Similar modeling limitations faced a study of the impact of the contextual factors of leadership and ethical climate on job effort and performance (Mulki, Jaramillo, & Locander, 2009). As in the previous study, leadership effects on job effort and performance were described pictorially in mediation terms, with leadership affecting behavior via its impact on ethical climate and job attitudes. However, as with the Kidwell and Valentine (2009) study, all hypotheses are presented as simple main effects. No explicit mediation hypotheses are offered or formal tests for mediation performed. So, although the studies by both Kidwell and Valentine and Mulki et al. are conceptually superior to studies such as that of Schminke

(2001), their modeling—at least as reflected in their formal hypothesis structure and testing—remains at the main-effects-only level.

Other limitations in modeling have afflicted research on the impact of context on ethics. We briefly raise three additional concerns here, each of which is also present in Schminke's (2001) work. The first involves model underspecification. By embracing only three contextual factors (size, structural formalization, and structural centralization), the Schminke model implicitly assumed no other factors—individual or contextual—affect individual ethical predispositions. But clearly, the potential exists for other contextual and individual factors to play a significant role in driving individual ethical predispositions. In regression settings, variance wants to be explained. But absent a more fully specified model, the variables included in an underspecified model will attempt to "take credit" for explaining variance that might be more accurately attributed to other factors. Of course, no single study can accommodate all factors thought to influence a particular outcome. But when making a specific case—such as establishing the importance of considering contextual as well as individual influences on an outcome—demonstrating that contextual factors matter is only half of the story. To argue strongly for their inclusion as a critical component in our thinking, we must be able to demonstrate they contribute above and beyond individual-level effects.

The second additional concern involves the functional form of the relationships we hypothesize between variables. In nearly all cases, researchers model and hypothesize simple linear relationships. But if the world is not a main-effects-only place, it is certainly also not a linear-effects-only place. Schminke (2001) recognized this with respect to the impact of organizational size and adjusted for potential nonlinearity by converting the number of employees via a log transformation that lessened the disproportionate impact of a few exceptionally large organizations in the sample. However, the study remained content with modeling simple linear relationships between the other structural characteristics and ethical predispositions. For example, it is reasonable to ask whether employees are likely to perceive that each additional unit of structural formalization (the presence of formalized work rules and regulation) represents an equally valuable (or harmful) thing. Most would agree that moving from organizational anarchy (no rules whatsoever) toward order (some formal rules) is a good thing. But do additional layers of rules and regulations necessarily make the workplace even more attractive? Beyond some point, most would view additional rules and regulations as offering a diminishing ability to improve workflow, innovation, productivity, and performance. At extremely high levels, most would anticipate additional structural formalization would become even more stifling and dysfunctional. Yet, for all of the intuitive appeal of such observations, nonlinear modeling of the relationships between contextual factors and ethical outcomes is rarely evident in our work.

A final concern involves the temporal dimension of our models. The conceptual story lines of many studies exploring the impact of context on ethics are implicitly longitudinal, but few scholars make this explicit in modeling and hypothesis development. Although this challenge reflects a legitimate modeling concern, it spills into methods and analysis concerns, which we address further in the chapter.

The solution to challenges in model development is not complicated. It requires simply that behavioral ethics scholars interested in contextual influences think more carefully about the broader constellation of relationships that might be at work in their models. We may do so at both the theory and construct levels.

Theory-Level Improvements to Modeling

The organization behavior and organization theory literatures provide examples of theoretical foundations oriented toward more complex nonlinear modeling of the relationship between individuals and the context in which they work. The person-organization (P-O) fit literature provides one example.

P-O fit research examines the impact of fit or misfit between individual and contextual (organizational) characteristics on a variety of outcomes, such as employee attitudes and behavior. Traditionally, P-O fit scholars conceptualized fit in terms of difference scores, the difference between the individual and organizational score on some metric. However, one implication of this conceptualization of fit is that all types of fit are deemed equal. In terms of ethics, for example, a saintly individual in a saintly organization represents a very strong fit, as does a devilish person in a devilish organization. Yet, few would predict that ethical fit at the saintly level would lead to the same type of ethical outcomes as ethical fit at the devilish level. Thus, P-O fit scholars have developed theoretical frameworks capable of coping with relationships beyond simple difference score main effects.

Scholars like Edwards (Edwards, 2001; Edwards & Parry, 1993) have addressed this issue, proposing conceptual and empirical solutions for complex, nonlinear examinations of P-O relationships. Adopting polynomial regression and response surface methodologies has allowed fit scholars to model more complex (and accurate) relationships between individual, organizational, and outcome variables. Researchers are now able to theorize about and model the impact of fit in nonlinear ways, predicting how different types of fit and misfit might differentially influence outcomes. Such approaches may provide a foundation for similar advances in understanding the relationship between the individual and the organizational context as applied to behavioral ethics.

Research on learning and problem solving suggests another venue in which nonlinear modeling might be extended to behavioral ethics research. For example, March (1991) proposed two distinct learning processes, exploration and exploitation. Exploration refers to searching for and exploring new knowledge. Exploitation describes the use of current and previous acquired knowledge when solving problems. Ample research has shown that these types of learning and problem-solving behaviors are curvilinear in nature (e.g., Katila & Ahuja, 2002). Using previous knowledge may improve decision making as errors are reduced, and processes are refined. However, relying too much on previous knowledge may create a so-called competency trap (Levinthal & March, 1993), as old knowledge may not apply to new problems. This in turn may limit one's ability to learn new things and solve new problems effectively.

We noted the role that learning—in the form of social learning—plays in behavioral ethics. Therefore, ethics scholars might benefit from adapting March's (1991) perspective to the social learning processes involved in organizational ethics. Learning from one's superiors or peers may not be a simple, linear, main effect process. Rather, it may involve a balance between drawing on one's historical understanding of organizational ethics and drawing on new, unique experiences involving leaders and peers.

Construct-Level Improvements to Modeling

In addition to embracing general theoretical perspectives that are better equipped to model more complex relationships, researchers interested in ethical context may benefit from considering a broader range of constructs that have added richness to main-effects-only models in other areas. Constructs that are able to explain the conditions under which one variable influences another (moderating effects) or the process by which one variable influences another (mediating effects) have the potential to expand our understanding of the role of context in organizational ethics.

For example, work climate research has explored the impact of a variety of work climate types (e.g., innovation, goals orientation, justice, and service) on outcomes. This research revealed that climate strength, the degree of agreement among unit members with respect to their climate perceptions (Lindell & Brandt, 2000), represents one of the most impactful moderators of the relationship between work climates and outcomes (Kuenzi & Schminke, 2009). For instance, González-Romá, Peiró, and Tordera (2002) demonstrated that strength of innovation climate moderated the relationship between level of innovation climate and job attitudes, and strength of goals orientation climate moderated the relationship between level of goals orientation climate and attitudes. Colquitt, Noe, and Jackson (2002) argued that strength of procedural justice climate moderates the relationship between level of procedural justice climate and team performance and team absenteeism. Similarly, Schneider, Salvaggio, and Subirats (2002) found that strength of service climate moderated the relationship between service climate level and customer satisfaction.

In all, organizational scholars have established the important role of climate strength—and by extension, the strength of agreement among organizational members with respect to any collective-level construct—as a potentially important moderator of main effect relationships. Scholars interested in ethical context should be cognizant of similar moderating influences at work in the relationships they explore.

Similarly, organizational scholars from other areas have found consistent patterns of mediation in seeking to explain the process by which certain variables influence other variables. Efficacy research provides an illustrative example.

Social cognitive theory (Bandura, 2001) suggests—and substantial research has confirmed—that efficacy provides the mechanisms by which an individual's desires or objectives are converted into successful outcomes. This work has been extended to the collective level, showing collective efficacy to be the conduit through which collective-level constructs influence behavior as well. For example, Bandura (1993) explored the relationship between school characteristics and academic achievement and found the collective efficacy of school staff mediated the impact of school characteristics on academic achievement. Prussia and Kinicki (1996) found the collective efficacy of brainstorming groups mediated the relationship between group characteristics and performance. Likewise, van Zomeren, Spears, Fischer, and Leach (2004) found that collective efficacy mediated the relationship between instrumental social support in groups and collective action of those groups. Similarly, Gibson (1999) found collective efficacy mediated the relationship between organizational training practices and performance of nursing teams. In all, efficacy—including collective efficacy—has been shown to be an important construct in explaining the process by which organizational actors convert their objectives into behavior.

These examples from the climate strength and efficacy literatures demonstrate organizational scholars have expanded their understanding of both the process by which interesting main effects unfold, as well as important boundary conditions of those main effects, by incorporating mediation and moderation considerations into their models. Researchers interested in understanding the impact of context on organizational ethics would benefit from doing the same.

Challenge 4: Research Methods and Analyses

There are no perfect studies. Research involves trade-offs among different methods, such as the realism provided by field settings versus the control offered by lab settings. However, when ethics scholars who edit and review for leading journals gather, the conversation often turns to stories of research that asks fascinating questions but is limited by flawed methods.

Some methodological limitations represent either minor issues or more major concerns that are relatively simple to repair. For example, the theoretical narrative for a model may describe conditional or moderating effects, but analyses may probe mediation effects. Such a slipup is easily remedied. A model may test effects of control variables, main effect variables, and interaction effects in isolation (e.g., via stepwise regression) rather than simultaneously, in a fully specified regression model. Again, such an error is easily remedied. Analysis concerns like these are relatively easy to sort out through the review and revision process.

Other methodological limitations involve issues that, individually, do not represent especially serious flaws, but collectively may snowball into a larger concern. For example, single-source data do not represent a fatal flaw or necessarily even represent a weakness in every case. The same is true for self-report-only data, cross-sectional designs, single-method data collection techniques, or the exclusive use of perceptual measures. But, the cumulative effect of multiple limitations of these types in any single study eventually exceeds a tipping point. When that happens, reviewers and editors are no longer able to place sufficient confidence in the data and, in turn, in the results of the study. As a result, it is difficult for a study that utilizes single-source, self-report, single-method, cross-sectional, and perceptual data to clear the empirical hurdles of top empirical journals.

Finally, some papers contain methodological shortcomings that are difficult or impossible to overcome. For example, an author may propose a model of top management team ethics but test the model on undergraduate subjects, whose reactions cannot be expected to reflect the theorizing by upper echelons that motivated the study. Similarly, a hypothesis may rest on a core construct like moral character, but the empirical test may substitute a measure of moral behavior. Likewise, a construct may be conceptualized at the work team or organizational level but operationalized and tested at the individual level. Methodological concerns like these are often deemed fatal.

Because all studies have limitations, it is impossible—and probably unfair—to attempt to catalog recent examples of all methodological and analytical shortcomings in behavioral ethics research related to context. So, rather than identifying specific examples of studies with particular methodological limitations, we defer the remainder of this discussion to the following section, in which we highlight positive approaches to methods that scholars in the area might benefit from emulating.

IMPROVING RESEARCH ON CONTEXTUAL INFLUENCES

Clearly, research on the contextual influences on ethics faces significant challenges on many fronts. In this final section, we offer a set of directives aimed at improving the quality and quantity of research devoted to understanding these issues.

Addressing the First Three Challenges

In the previous sections, we provided concrete examples of potential pitfalls in context-oriented behavioral ethics research and outlined some solutions to the first three challenges that are straightforward and emerge directly from the discussion of the challenges themselves: (a) Provide clear and consistent definitions of key constructs, (b) craft research questions around solid theoretical foundations, and (c) craft models that acknowledge the complexity of the relationship between context and ethics that explore either processes or boundary conditions (or both). In most cases, these challenges can all be removed as sources of concern with simple, but ample, doses of care and forethought.

Addressing the Fourth Challenge and Beyond

Methodological challenges are, in many ways, both easier and more difficult to handle. Careful attention to the first three challenges will take an author a long way toward avoiding a verdict of a "fatal flaw" because sound definitions, theory, and modeling make it much less likely, for example, that a key variable will be operationalized in a fatal way or that an inappropriate sample, incapable of providing an answer to the research question, will be pursued.

For the more common and less-serious errors noted, solutions are also relatively straightforward. Refresh one's basic research design and methods awareness and skills. Update one's understanding of current standards for applying analytical tools. Minimize the number of methodologically limiting (but not necessarily fatal) points in a single paper. Counteract those limitations with strengths on other fronts. Again, the key is to take these basic and easy-to-address concerns that threaten the success of so many papers off the table from the outset.

However, quality research methods are not simply an insurance policy against having a paper rebuffed. Rather, they represent an opportunity to extract the greatest possible insight and contribution from a good idea. Through thoughtful, creative, and appropriate use of research methods and analytic tools, a good study with interesting insights may become a great study providing truly striking insights. Quality research methods are not just about playing defense against reviewers and editors. Methods are an effective offensive tool as well, able to enhance the prospects of a paper getting noticed and its potential for making the greatest possible impact.

Because of this, we believe it is possible to gain as much from examining work by scholars who have used solid and creative research methods to enhance the value of their studies, as from those who have bobbled. In recent years, a number of bright lights have appeared on our research horizon, in both behavioral ethics and a variety of closely related research areas. We highlight several here. Our intent is not to identify every well-executed methodological attribute of research in our area. Rather, it is to present an array of well-executed features of several studies from which context-oriented behavioral ethics scholars might learn and benefit. We do so by considering issues related to sampling, design, analyses, and theory.

Use of Student Samples

We agree with Greenberg (1987) that students are real people. Thus, we do not dismiss out of hand behavioral ethics research that focuses on student samples. Two recent efforts demonstrate highly appropriate applications of student samples. The first involves applying them only to research questions for which they represent appropriate participants. Duffy, Shaw, Scott, and Tepper (2006) demonstrated this in a study of how self-esteem and neuroticism moderate the relationship between group undermining and individual-level undermining behavior. In two studies, Duffy, Shaw, et al. examined the moderating impact of these individual difference variables on the undermining behavior of student work teams. These teams remained intact for several months, collaborated on several work projects, and were evaluated and rewarded based on team performance (20–25% of their total semester evaluation). Thus, by most reasonable definitions, they represented "real" work teams, and none of the key variables in the studies appeared to be inappropriate for samples comprised of undergraduate and graduate students.

The second example of appropriate application of student samples demonstrates how they might successfully be supplemented with other samples. In another study of undermining, Duffy, Ganster, Shaw, Johnson, and Pagon (2006) explored the social context of undermining in four distinct samples: the national police force of Slovenia, U.S. National Guard soldiers, student teams, and restaurant employees. Results from the student work team sample supported those from the Slovenian national police and U.S. National Guard samples and allowed the authors to explore further the consequences of undermining in addition to their antecedents model.

Matching the Sample to the Research Question

In some cases, matching a study's sample to the research question at hand is not a critical concern; the focal constructs may be generally applicable to a variety of individuals and organizations. But in other cases, an appropriate match between research question and sample is critical and can add enormous value to a study. For example, Tangirala and Ramanujam (2008) explored the antecedents of employee silence (intentionally withholding information). More specifically, they examined the moderating effect of procedural justice climate on the relationship between antecedents such as work group identification and professional commitment on employee silence. Their sample consisted of 850 experienced hospital-based nurses. The authors provided convincing evidence of the critical role nurses play in detecting and reporting avoidable medical errors that may result in as many as 98,000 deaths per year in the United States alone. In this setting, silence may truly represent a difference between life and death. Thus, the study represents a very attractive match between question and sample, one that adds to both the theoretical and practical value of the work.

Lab Studies

Scholars have begun to embrace lab settings for conducting research on behavioral ethics, including research related to the impact of context. Garcia, Bazerman, Kopelman, Tor, and Miller (2010), for example, conducted a series of four lab experiments to explore how social categories influence ethical decision making with respect to allocation decisions. The four distinct settings created in the lab allowed the researchers to examine how allocation decisions were made within and between social categories, as well as how social categories influenced the decisions of third-party observers.

Longitudinal Designs

Johns (2006) declared that context may assert its influence on organizational outcomes in multiple ways. At least some of these (e.g., mediation effects) may be expected to play out over time. Therefore, longitudinal research designs represent an appropriate path for exploring the temporal impact of context on outcomes.

The literature has begun to see more longitudinal studies, such as Tepper, Henle, Lambert, Giacalone, and Duffy's (2008) examination of the relationship between supervisory abuse and subsequent deviance behavior. Tepper et al. hypothesized the impact of abuse on organizational deviance is mediated by affective commitment. Supportive results from a cross-sectional sample were supplemented by results from a two-wave longitudinal sample, providing considerable additional support for their conceptualization of commitment as the process by which abuse affects deviance. Duffy, Shaw, et al. (2006) also utilized a longitudinal design that allowed them to separate by time the measurement of their hypothesized antecedent (group undermining) and outcome (individual undermining) variables.

More Complex Designs

We noted the benefit of considering the mediation and moderation processes at work in our models. Methodological developments have allowed us to become even more precise in our thinking about these relationships. For example, work by Edwards and Lambert (2007) and Preacher, Rucker, and Hayes (2007) allows scholars to model, hypothesize, and test specific configurations of variables that involve simultaneous mediation and moderation effects (also known as conditional indirect effects). These tools have begun to find their way into our literature, such as in Tepper et al.'s (2008) tests of the mediated moderation effects present in the relationship between abusive supervision and employee deviance.

Multilevel Analyses

Ethical attitudes, decision making, and behavior are most commonly construed as individual-level constructs. Context, by contrast, typically reflects higher-level constructs that often manifest themselves at the level of the work group or the organization. Multilevel theorizing and modeling like this require multilevel analytic tools. Scholars are becoming increasingly aware of, and facile with, tools capable of performing multilevel analyses such as hierarchical linear modeling (HLM). HLM analyses are becoming almost commonplace in context-focused ethics research, as evidenced by work by Tangirala and Ramanujam (2008), Duffy and colleagues (Duffy, Ganster, et al., 2006; Duffy, Shaw, et al., 2006), and Dineen, Lewicki, and Tomlinson (2006).

Strong Tests of Theory

We noted insufficient theory development represents a challenge to our literature on several fronts. Strong theory not only helps scholars craft stronger models for testing but also creates an opportunity to perform stronger tests of the theory itself. Few studies in behavioral ethics do so. More should. An excellent example of a successful effort is provided by Rupp and Bell (2010). In this article, the authors draw on the deontic model of justice (Folger, 1998, 2001) to explore third-party reactions to injustice. However, the article was framed from the outset not only as a test of third-party reactions to injustice but also as a test and extension of the deontic model itself. It represents an impressive effort and a solid model for what more research should aim to do. Supporting or refuting particular links in a model may generate insights. But supporting, refuting, or extending entire theoretical perspectives represents a "force multiplier" in our efforts, from which we may benefit in more substantial ways.

Each of these aspects of research methods holds potential for improving the quality of behavioral ethics research. Notably, the studies cited in this section as exemplars of sound practices all appeared in journals widely recognized as top scholarly outlets, including *Business Ethics Quarterly, Journal of Applied Psychology, Organizational Behavior and Human Decision Processes,* and *Personnel Psychology.* That is no accident. Strong studies, with strong methods, have greater potential to be viewed positively by editors and reviewers at the best journals. In turn, the work has a better chance of impacting behavioral ethics scholarship more broadly.

In all, our goal in this section has been to provide a critique of research that explores the relationship between context and behavioral ethics. Of course, this list of challenges is not exhaustive. Other scholars reviewing the literature will detect challenges beyond those identified here. Further, our intent was not to identify particular studies as good or bad overall. To the contrary, several studies identified during our description and illustration of the first three challenges were quite strong overall, and many contained positive features that may partially or fully offset any weaknesses we identified. Rather, our goal was to identify common themes in the empirical literature (some positive and some negative) to provide concrete examples of these themes and to offer direction for how we might overcome them in the future. By doing so, we hope to identify a core set of foundational challenges that context researchers will need to take seriously, and to improve on, if we are to learn all we can about the impact of context on behavioral ethics.

PUTTING IT INTO PERSPECTIVE: A BRIEF HISTORY OF THE BEHAVIORAL ETHICS MOVEMENT

Behavioral ethics is not a new concept. Early philosophers grounded ethics solidly in behavior. Aristotle, for example, argued that the acquisition of moral character or virtue occurred through practiced behavior. He noted that people become builders by actually building, they become musicians by practicing musical skills, and they become ethical by participating in ethical actions (White, 1993). Aristotle's writings thus laid the foundation for a permanent relationship between behavior and ethics.

More recently, organizational scholars began to focus on the behavioral aspects of business ethics. For example, during the 1990s David Messick and Ann Tenbrunsel opened researchers' eyes to the potential for a behavioral perspective on ethics research (Messick & Tenbrunsel, 1996; Tenbrunsel & Messick, 1996). However, as a distinct area of research, the term *behavioral ethics* is a fairly new designation, and our best assessment points to Rob Folger as its father.

At the Presidential Luncheon of the Academy of Management meetings in Seattle in 2003, Rob shared some thoughts with Roy Lewicki about the emergence of a new area of inquiry that was becoming known as behavioral economics. Why, Rob wondered, couldn't a similar case be made for attempting to unify the diverse base of scholars who approached the study of ethics from a behavioral perspective? Interesting behavioral work on ethics was appearing among scholars in social psychology, neuroscience, industrial psychology, economics, organizational behavior, sociology, political science, and a host of other disciplines. Might it be possible to create an umbrella under which such diverse scholars could unite their efforts at understanding these ethical issues? Or, if not uniting them, at least provide a portal through which ideas and progress might be shared?

This bit of inspiration triggered a snowball-like series of events. The 2004 Academy of Management meetings found Rob leading a small handful of interested scholars in a short brainstorming event in an out-of-the-way corner of a conference hotel. In 2005, Rob successfully proposed a behavioral ethics caucus at the Academy of Management meetings in Honolulu. A difficult time slot in a cramped, hard-to-find hotel space did not prevent a beyond-capacity crowd from arriving to talk enthusiastically about the potential of behavioral ethics. Maybe a conference? Maybe a formal organization? Maybe a journal? Ideas filled the air, and a spark had landed on dry tinder.

In 2006, Rob hosted a research incubator at the Academy of Management meetings in Atlanta, aimed at fostering and developing nascent research in behavioral ethics. By 2008, Rob was hosting a formal research roundtable on behavioral ethics. For this event, top behavioral ethics scholars from around the world converged at the University of Central Florida for 3 days of thinking about, talking about, and developing behavioral ethics research. The event was repeated successfully on an even larger scale in 2010. Notably, at this meeting the conversation shifted from "How do we attract a critical mass of scholars?" to "How do we deal with growth and interest that makes it impractical to gather all interested scholars together in one place at a given time?" What a difference 5 years make.

Of course, research movements require more than a single leader or scholar. But, if there is a single person more responsible for the emergence of a set of researchers who now identify themselves as behavioral ethics scholars than Rob Folger, we do not know who that person is. His work, and the work of that small group of enthusiastic fellow travelers in the mid-2000s (they know who they are!), has concretized the concept of behavioral ethics research. Further, it has spawned a host of additional initiatives focused squarely on behavioral ethics as an area of study. Such efforts include the excellent review of behavioral ethics authored by Treviño et al. (2006) and the subsequent ambitious piece by Tenbrunsel and Smith-Crowe (2008). More recently, an entire special issue devoted to behavioral ethics has appeared in *Business Ethics Quarterly* (January 2010), with others on the horizon for *Organizational Behavior and Human Decision Processes*, *Human Relations*, and *Management and Organization Review*. The present volume, and the outstanding Notre Dame conference based on its contents, is the most recent example but certainly will not be the last.

We believe researchers now exist who identify themselves as behavioral ethics scholars, but whom Rob Folger does not know personally. In our view, that stands as evidence the area of behavioral ethics is now formally founded and well positioned to "burn on its own."

GETTING SERIOUS ABOUT CONTEXT: QUO VADIS?

The early success of behavioral ethics and behavioral ethics researchers naturally raises the question of where we go from here. Marketing experts identify four stages in a product life cycle: (a) market introduction, (b) growth, (c) maturity, and (d) saturation/decline. It is clear that behavioral ethics research has successfully cleared the market introduction hurdle and rests solidly in the growth stage. However, as with new products, this growth stage presents its own set of challenges and opportunities. In this chapter, we have sought to highlight some of the most critical of these challenges, the issues scholars must confront and manage successfully if we are to take context seriously as we seek to improve our understanding of behavioral ethics.

So, where do we go from here? The answer is nearly anywhere, as evidenced on at least four fronts. First, multiple disciplinary paths lead to behavioral ethics research; industrial psychology, organizational behavior, experimental economics, and experimental philosophy represent just a few. Thus, scholars may come to the conversation via any one of these conduits. Second, each of these disciplines encompasses multiple subareas of study. Within organizational behavior alone, research on ethical leadership, organizational justice, ethical decision making, moral identity, abusive supervision, employee deviance, ethical efficacy, social undermining, and ethical climate represents examination of just some of the topics that occupy important conceptual ground related to behavioral ethics. Third, each of these areas and subareas is growing. New questions spawn new research paths, and, successful answers to those questions spawn new research areas that may be of interest to an entirely new set of scholars. Finally, if there should exist a scholar interested in behavioral ethics who cannot quite find a home in one of these areas, we offer a single piece of advice: integrate. Some of the most promising new work in behavioral ethics seeks to combine the most appealing constructs, the most promising theoretical foundations, and the most effective tools that exist across these areas. Build bridges, and scholars will cross them.

REFERENCES

Andreoli, N., & Lefkowitz, J. (2009). Individual and organizational antecedents of misconduct in organizations. *Journal of Business Ethics, 85*, 309–332.

Arnaud, A., & Schminke, M. (2007). Ethical work climate: A weather report and forecast. In S. W. Gilliland, D. D. Steiner, & D. P. Skarlicki (Eds.), *Research in social issues in management, volume 5: Managing social and ethical issues in organizations* (pp. 181–227). Greenwich, CT: IAP.

Arnaud, A., & Schminke, M. (in press). The ethical climate and context of organizations: A comprehensive model. *Organization Science.*

Bandura, A. (1977). *Social learning theory.* New York: General Learning Press.

Bandura, A. (1993). Perceived self-efficacy in cognitive development and functioning. *Educational Psychology, 28,* 117–148.

Bandura, A. (2001). Social cognitive theory: An agentic perspective. *Annual Review of Psychology, 52,* 1–26.

Barnett, T., & Schubert, E. (2002). Perception of the ethical work climate and convenantal relationships. *Journal of Business Ethics, 36,* 279–290.

Barnett, T., & Vaicys, C. (2000). The moderating effect of individuals' perceptions of ethical work climate on ethical judgments and behavioral intention. *Journal of Business Ethics, 27,* 351–362.

Beams, J. D., Brown, R. M., & Killough, L. N. (2003). An experiment testing the determinants of non-compliance with insider trading laws. *Journal of Business Ethics, 45,* 309–323.

Bird, F. (1996). *The muted conscience: Moral silence and the practice of ethics in business.* Westport, CT: Quorum Books.

Blau, P. (1964). *Exchange and power in social life.* New York: Wiley.

Brown, M., Treviño, L. K., & Harrison, D. (2005). Ethical leadership: A social learning perspective for construct development and testing. *Organizational Behavior and Human Decision Processes, 97,* 117–134.

Cappelli, P., & Sherer, P. D. (1991). The missing role of context in OB: The need for a meso-level approach. *Research in Organizational Behavior, 13,* 55–110.

Colquitt, J., Noe, R., & Jackson, C. (2002). Justice in teams: Antecedents and consequences of procedural justice climate. *Personnel Psychology, 55,* 83–109.

Deshpande, S. P., & Joseph, J. (2009). Impact of emotional intelligence, ethical climate, and behavior or peers on ethical behavior of nurses. *Journal of Business Ethics, 85,* 403–410.

Dineen, B. R., Lewicki, R. J., & Tomlinson, E. C. (2006). Supervisory guidance and behavioral integrity: Relationships with employee citizenship and deviant behavior. *Journal of Applied Psychology, 91,* 622–635.

Dukerich, J. M., Nichols, M. L., Elm, D. R., & Vollrath, D. A. (1990). Moral reasoning in groups: Leaders make a difference. *Human Relations, 43,* 473–493.

Duffy, M. K., Ganster, D. C., Shaw, J. D., Johnson, J. L., & Pagon, M. (2006). The social context of undermining at work. *Organizational Behavior and Human Decision Processes, 101,* 104–126.

Duffy, M. K., Shaw, J. D., Scott, K. L., & Tepper, B. J. (2006). The moderating roles of self-esteem and neuroticism in the relationship between group and individual undermining behavior. *Journal of Applied Psychology, 91,* 1066–1077.

Edwards, J. (2001). Alternatives to difference scores: Polynomial regression analysis and response surface methodology. In F. Drasgow & N. W. Schmitt (Eds.), *Advances in measurement and data analysis* (pp. 350–400). San Francisco: Jossey-Bass.

Edwards, J., & Parry, M. (1993). On the use of polynomial regression equations as an alternative to difference scores in organizational research. *Academy of Management Journal, 36,* 1577–1613.

Edwards, J., & Lambert, L. S. (2007). Methods for integrating moderation and mediation: A general analytical framework using moderated path analysis. *Psychological Methods, 12,* 1–22.

Folger, R. (1998). Fairness as a moral virtue. In M. Schminke (Ed.), *Managerial ethics: Morally managing people and processes* (pp. 13–34). Mahwah, NJ: Erlbaum.

Folger, R. (2001). Fairness as deonance. In S. W. Gilliland, D. D. Steiner, & D. P. Skarlicki (Eds.), *Research in social issues in management* (pp. 3–31). Greenwich, CT: Information Age.

Ford, R. C., & Richardson, W. D. (1994). Ethical decision making: A review of the empirical literature. *Journal of Business Ethics, 13,* 205–221.

Garcia, S. M., Bazerman, M. H., Kopelman, S., Tor, A., & Miller, D. T. (2010). The price of equality: Suboptimal resource allocations across social categories. *Business Ethics Quarterly, 20,* 75–88.

Gibson, C. B. (1999). Do they do what they believe they can? Group efficacy and group effectiveness across tasks and cultures. *Academy of Management Journal, 42,* 138–152.

González-Romá, V., Peiró, J., & Tordera, N. (2002). An examination of the antecedents and moderator influences of climate strength. *Journal of Applied Psychology, 85,* 956–970.

Greenberg, J. (1987). The college sophomore as guinea pig: Setting the record straight. *Academy of Management Review, 12,* 157–159.

Greenberg, J. (2002). Who stole the money and when? Individual and situational determinants of employee theft. *Organizational Behavior and Human Decision Processes, 89,* 985–1003.

Hegarty, W. H., & Sims, H. P. (1978). Some determinants of unethical decision behavior: An experiment. *Journal of Applied Psychology, 64,* 451–457.

Izraeli, D. (1988). Ethical beliefs and behavior among managers: A cross-cultural perspective. *Journal of Business Ethics, 7,* 263–271.

Johns, G. (2001). In praise of context. *Journal of Organizational Behavior, 22,* 31–42.

Johns, G. (2006). The essential impact of context on organizational behavior. *Academy of Management Review, 31,* 386–408.

Jones, G. E., & Kavanagh, M. J. (1996). An experimental examination of the effects of individual and situational factors on unethical behavioral intentions in the workplace. *Journal of Business Ethics, 15,* 511–523.

Jones, T. M. (1991). Ethical decision making by individuals in organizations: An issue-contingent model. *Academy of Management Review, 16,* 366–395.

Katila, R., & Ahuja, G. (2002). Something old, something new: A longitudinal study of search behavior and new product introductions. *Academy of Management Journal, 45,* 1183–1194.

Kidder, D. L. (2005). Is it "who I am," "what I can get away with," or "what you've done to me"? A multi-theory examination of employee misconduct. *Journal of Business Ethics, 57,* 389–398.

Kidwell, R. E., & Valentine, S. R. (2009). Positive group context, work attitudes, and organizational misbehavior: The case of withholding job effort. *Journal of Business Ethics, 86,* 15–28.

Koh, H. C., & Boo, E. H. Y. (2001). The link between organizational ethics and job satisfaction: A study of managers in Singapore. *Journal of Business Ethics, 29,* 309–24.

Kuenzi, M., & Schminke, M. (2009). A fragmented literature? A review, critique, and proposed research agenda for the work climate literature. *Journal of Management, 35,* 634–717.

Lester, S. W., Turnley, W. H., Bloodgood, J. M., & Bolino, M. C. (2002). Not seeing eye to eye: Differences in supervisor and subordinate perceptions of and attributions for psychological contract breach. *Journal of Organizational Behavior, 23*, 39–56.

Leung, A. S. M. (2008). Matching ethical work climate to in-role and extra-role behaviors in a collectivist work setting. *Journal of Business Ethics, 79*, 43–55.

Levinthal, D. A., & March, J. G. (1993). The myopia of learning. *Strategic Management Journal, 14*, 95–112.

Lewin, K. (1945). The research center for group dynamics at Massachusetts Institute of Technology. *Sociometry, 8*, 126–135.

Lewin, K. (1947). Frontiers in group dynamics. *Human Relations, 1*, 5–41.

Lindell, M. K., & Brandt, C. J. (2000). Climate quality and climate consensus as mediators of the relationship between organizational antecedents and outcomes. *Journal of Applied Psychology, 85*, 331–348.

Loe, T. W., Ferrell, L., & Mansfield, P. (2000). A review of empirical studies assessing ethical decision making in business. *Journal of Business Ethics, 25*, 185–204.

March, J. G. (1991). Exploration and exploitation in organizational learning. *Organization Science, 2*, 71–87.

Mayer, D. M., Kuenzi, M., Greenbaum, R., Bardes, M., & Salvador, R. (2009). How does ethical leadership flow? Test of a trickle-down model. *Organizational Behavior and Human Decision Processes, 108*, 1–13.

McCabe, D., Treviño, L. K., & Butterfield, K. (1996). The influence of collegiate and corporate codes of conduct on ethics-related behavior in the workplace. *Business Ethics Quarterly, 6*, 441–460.

Messick, D. A., & Tenbrunsel, A. E. (Eds.) (1996). *Codes of conduct: Behavioral research into business ethics.* New York: Russell Sage Foundation.

Mischel, W. (1977). On the future of personality measurement. *American Psychologist, 32*, 246–254.

Mowday, R. T., & Sutton, R. I. (1993). Organizational behavior: Linking individuals and groups to organizational contexts. *Annual Review of Psychology, 44*, 195–229.

Mulki, J. P., Jaramillo, J. F., & Locander, W. B. (2009). Critical role of leadership on ethical climate and salesperson behaviors. *Journal of Business Ethics, 86*, 125–141.

O'Fallon, M. J., & Butterfield, K. D. (2005). A review of the empirical ethical decision-making literature: 1996–2003. *Journal of Business Ethics, 59*, 375–413.

Peterson, D. K. (2002a). Deviant workplace behavior and the organization's ethical climate. *Journal of Business and Psychology, 17*, 47–61.

Peterson, D. K. (2002b). The relationship between unethical behavior and the dimensions of the ethical climate questionnaire. *Journal of Business Ethics, 41*, 313–326.

Preacher, K. J., Rucker, D. D., & Hayes, A. F. (2007). Addressing moderated mediation hypotheses: Theory, methods, and prescriptions. *Multivariate Behavioral Research, 42*, 185–227.

Prussia, G. E., & Kinicki, A. J. (1996). A motivational investigation of group effectiveness using social-cognitive theory. *Journal of Applied Psychology, 81*, 187–198.

Robinson, S. L., & O'Leary-Kelly, A. M. (1998). Monkey see, monkey do: The influence of work groups on the antisocial behavior of employees. *Academy of Management Journal, 41*, 658–672.

Rousseau, D. M., & Fried, Y. (2001). Location, location, location: Contextualizing organizational research. *Journal of Organizational Behavior, 22*, 1–13.

Rupp, D. E., & Bell, C. M. (2010). Extending the deontic model of justice: Moral self-regulation in third-party responses to injustice. *Business Ethics Quarterly, 20,* 89–106.

Salancik, G. R., & Pfeffer, J. (1978). A social information processing approach to job attitudes and task design. *Administrative Science Quarterly, 23,* 224–253.

Schmidtke, J. M. (2007). The relationship between social norm consensus, perceived similarity, and observer reactions to coworker theft. *Human Resource Management, 46,* 561–582.

Schminke, M. (1991). Power in organizations. In *Proceedings of the annual meeting of the NE Decision Sciences Institute.* Decision Sciences Institute, Pittsburgh.

Schminke, M. (2001). Considering the business in business ethics: An exploratory study of the influence of organizational size and structure on individual ethical predispositions. *Journal of Business Ethics. 30,* 375–390.

Schminke, M., Ambrose, M. L., & Neubaum, D. O. (2005). The effect of leader moral development on ethical climate and employee attitudes. *Organizational Behavior and Human Decision Processes, 97,* 135–151.

Schminke, M., Wells, D., Peyrefitte, J., & Sebora, T. C. (2002). Leadership and ethics in work groups: A longitudinal assessment. *Group and Organization Management, 27,* 272–293.

Schneider, B. (1983). Work climates: An interactionist perspective. In N. W. Feimerand & E. S. Geller (Eds.), *Environmental psychology: Directions and perspectives.* New York: Praeger.

Schneider, B. (1987). The people make the place. *Personnel Psychology, 40,* 437–451.

Schneider, B., Salvaggio, A., & Subirats, E. (2002). Climate strength: A new direction for climate research. *Journal of Applied Psychology, 87,* 220–230.

Sekerka, L. E., & Bagozzi, R. P. (2007). Moral courage in the workplace: Moving to and from the desire and decision to act. *Business Ethics: A European Review, 16,* 132–142.

Somers, M. J. (2001). Ethical codes of conduct and organizational context: A study of the relationship between codes of conduct, employee behavior and organizational values. *Journal of Business Ethics, 30,* 185–195.

Spector, P. E., Coulter, M. L., Stockwell, H. G., & Matz, M. W. (2007). Perceived violence climate: A new construct and its relationship to workplace physical violence and verbal aggression, and their potential consequences. *Work & Stress, 21,* 117–130.

Tangirala, S., & Ramanujam, R. (2008). Employee silence on critical work issues: The cross-level effects of procedural justice climate. *Personnel Psychology, 61,* 37–68.

Tenbrunsel, A. E. (1998). Misrepresentation and expectations of misrepresentation in an ethical dilemma: The role of incentives and temptation. *Academy of Management Journal, 41,* 330–339.

Tenbrunsel, A. E., & Messick, D. A. (1996). Behavioral research, business ethics, and social justice. *Social Justice Research, 9,* 1–6.

Tenbrunsel, A. E., & Smith-Crowe, K. (2008). Ethical decision making: Where we've been and where we're going. *Academy of Management Annals, 2,* 545–607.

Tenbrunsel, A. E., Smith-Crowe, K., & Umphress, E. E. (2003). Building houses on rocks: The role of the ethical infrastructure in organizations. *Social Justice Research, 16,* 285–307.

Tepper, B. J., Henle, C. A., Lambert, L. S., Giacalone, R. A., & Duffy, M. K. (2008). Abusive supervision and subordinates' organization deviance. *Journal of Applied Psychology, 93,* 721–732.

Thompson, J. (1967). *Organizations in action.* New York: McGraw-Hill.

Treviño, L. K. (1990). A cultural perspective on changing and developing organizational ethics. In R. Woodman & W. Passmore (Eds.), *Research in organizational change and development* (Vol. 4, pp. 195–230). Stamford, CT: JAI Press.

Treviño, L. K., Butterfield, K., & McCabe, D. (1998). The ethical context in organizations: Influences on employee attitudes and behaviors. *Business Ethics Quarterly, 8,* 447–476.

Treviño, L. K., Weaver, G. R., Gibson, D., & Toffler, B. (1999). Managing ethics and legal compliance: What works and what hurts. *California Management Review, 41,* 131–151.

Treviño, L. K., Weaver, G. R., & Reynolds, S. J. (2006). Behavioral ethics in organizations: A review. *Journal of Management, 32,* 951–990.

Van de Ven, A. H. (1989). Nothing is quite so practical as a good theory. *Academy of Management Review,* 14, 486–489.

VanSandt, C. V. (2003). The relationship between ethical work climate and moral awareness. *Business & Society, 42,* 144–152.

Van Zomeren, M., Spears, R., Fischer, A. H., & Leach, C. W. (2004). Put your money where your mouth is! Explaining collective action tendencies through group-based anger and group efficacy. *Journal of Personality and Social Psychology, 87,* 649–664.

Vardi, Y. (2001). The effects of organizational and ethical climates on misconduct at work. *Journal of Business Ethics, 29,* 325–337.

Victor, B., & Cullen, J. B. (1988). The organizational bases of ethical work climates. *Administrative Science Quarterly, 33,* 101–125.

Weaver, G. R., & Treviño, L. K. (1999). Compliance and values oriented ethics programs: Influences on employees' attitudes and behavior. *Business Ethics Quarterly, 9,* 315–337.

Weaver, G. R., Treviño, L. K., & Cochran, P. L. (1999). Corporate ethics programs as control systems: Influences of executive commitment and environmental factors. *Academy of Management Journal, 42,* 539–552.

Weber, J. (1995). Influences upon organizational ethical subclimates: A multidepartmental analysis of a single firm. *Organization Science, 6,* 509–523.

White, T. I. (1993). *Business ethics: A philosophical reader.* New York: Macmillan.

Wimbush, J. C., Shepard, J. M., & Markham, S. E . (1997). An empirical examination of the relationship between ethical climate and ethical behavior from multiple levels of analysis. *Journal of Business Ethics, 16,* 1705–1716.

Zey-Ferrell, M., & Ferrell, O. C. (1982). Role-set configuration and opportunity as predictors of unethical behavior in organizations. *Human Relations, 35,* 587–604.

Zey-Ferrell, M. K., Weaver, M., & Ferrell, O. C. (1979). Predicting unethical behavior among marketing practitioners. *Human Relations, 32,* 557–569.

4

Who Is Leading the Leader?
Follower Influence on Leader Ethicality

Morela Hernandez
University of Washington

and

Sim B Sitkin
Duke University

INTRODUCTION

The issue of how to formulate an ethical organizational environment has become a mainstay in business. Given the breaches of ethical conduct in recent history, ethical behavior has come to represent a cornerstone of effective organizational functioning and performance. Accordingly, to maintain long-term performance and avoid the hazards of ethical misconduct, organizations routinely invest an extraordinary amount of resources into understanding and implementing ethics initiatives, focusing on such elements as structure, code of ethics, and core values within organizations (e.g., Johnson, 2007; Treviño, Weaver, Gibson, & Toffler, 1999).

Scholarly research has sought to examine various factors that can promote an *ethical climate*, defined as "organizational members' shared perceptions of the events, practices, and procedures and the kinds of behaviors that get rewarded, supported, and expected in a setting regarding ethics" (Tenbrunsel, Smith-Crowe, & Umphress, 2003, p. 294; cf. Schneider, 1990; Victor & Cullen, 1988). Past studies have focused on how ethical principles can be instilled within the organizational context through, for example, codes of conduct (e.g., McCabe, Treviño, & Butterfield, 1996) and sanctioning systems (e.g., Tenbrunsel & Messick, 1999) to explicate how these factors influence individual behavior in ethical situations (Treviño et al., 1999).

Underscoring the importance of understanding how individuals perceive ethical situations and how they act in those situations, the field of behavioral ethics has adopted a descriptive approach to explore the factors that can promote or constrain ethical conduct within organizational environments. Thus, with a focus not on normative moral standards (i.e., what individuals *should* do) but rather on how individuals are influenced by organizational systems to interpret morality, in this chapter we investigate how individual ethical behavior emerges within organizational settings. In particular, we take a key building block of social situations—leadership—to examine the dynamics that can unfold within interpersonal influence processes across all levels of the organization. Leadership is theorized to represent one avenue through which morality is interpreted within the organizational environment (Treviño, 1990). In line with the descriptive approach to behavioral ethics, we seek to examine why and how individuals are likely to behave when it comes to moral problems and, in particular, what role the leader–follower relationship plays in this process.

UTILIZING A BEHAVIORAL ETHICS LENS TO COUNTER BASIC ASSUMPTIONS WITHIN THE LEADERSHIP LITERATURE

The leadership field is based on the assumption that leaders can influence organizational outcomes via their ability to influence followers, as well as affect organizational routines and norms. This assumption has played a particularly important part in determining how ethical behavior can be promoted within the organization. Notably, past work has demonstrated that leaders can influence followers' ethical behavior by demonstrating normatively appropriate conduct (Brown, Treviño, & Harrison, 2005). They can influence follower cognition by shaping the ways in which followers think about moral justifiability (Beu & Buckley, 2004) and affect the moral reasoning level of a group through their own levels of principled reasoning (Dukerich, Nichols, Elm, & Vollrath, 1990). Research has also linked the moral development of the leader to the ethical climate and attitudes of the group (Schein, 1985). At the organizational level, leadership-based efforts to foster ethical behavior, such as ensuring organizationally fair procedures and structures, have been shown to reduce unethical behavior and increase employees' willingness to report problems to management (Treviño & Weaver, 2001).

Although a growing body of evidence has demonstrated the leader's influence on follower ethical behavior, relatively little theorizing has been done regarding the effect of followers on the leader's ethicality. Although peer influence in the workplace has been found to affect individual ethical behavior (Zey-Ferrell & Ferrell, 1982) through the need for moral approval from one's peers (Jones & Ryan, 1998), it is unclear how this need manifests itself in leader–follower relationships. Although one may typically conceptualize approval (moral or otherwise) as given to followers by leaders, leader behavior is most effective when leadership decisions are accepted by followers (Dornbusch & Scott, 1975). Thus, follower approval of leadership behavior may serve as a precursor to followership.

First introduced by Hollander and Webb (1955), the term *followership* is characterized as an interdependent relationship in which the leader's perceived legitimacy can affect the degree to which followers allow themselves to be influenced (Hollander & Julian, 1969). This early work highlights leadership as a reciprocal relationship in which followers play an active role not only by receiving but also by exerting influence (Homans, 1961), a point that has been echoed in more recent research (Avolio, 2007). Moreover, this past work emphasizes the role of social perceptions in defining the legitimacy of a leader. Defined as "a generalized perception or assumption that the actions of an entity are desirable, proper, or appropriate within some socially constructed system of norms, values, beliefs, and definitions" (Suchman, 1995, p. 574), we argue that the concept of legitimacy encompasses the socially construed morally normative boundaries of leadership behavior. Thus, followers' perceived legitimacy of their leader influences how they interpret the leader's ethically relevant behaviors within the context of larger social prescriptions and determines the degree to which followers may both receive and exert influence on those behaviors.

In this chapter, we focus on how followers go beyond mere legitimization to exercise influence on their leader's ethicality (see Kelley, 1988; Useem, 2001). While acknowledging that leaders play a potentially influential agentic role, we propose that a leader's ethical behavior not only

influences followers' ethical behavior but also is influenced by it. In proposing this, we debunk the familiar notion that leaders are impervious, or
at least more resistant than followers, to a social influence process. Indeed,
they may be especially susceptible to this influence when their legitimacy
is in question (Long, 2010; Long & Sitkin, 2006).

Because so little work has directly examined the influence of followers
on the leader's ethicality, ours is necessarily speculative. But, our goal is
hardly to settle such a nascent issue; we aim to be provocative and thus
stimulate more attention to theorizing about and empirically examining
this potentially important and fruitful line of inquiry. In the following
sections, we further discuss leader ethicality, examine the role of legitimacy in influencing a leader's predisposition to being influenced by
followers, and outline the follower behaviors through which this influence
is exercised, mainly through modeling, eliciting, guiding, and sensemaking
via cognitive, affective, and behavioral causal mechanisms.

LEADER ETHICALITY

Although the topic of leadership has a long and complex history in a variety of scholarly disciplines, a focus on ethics has only recently (re)gained
theoretical momentum. Nevertheless, most of the theoretical perspectives
that have emerged have espoused arguments pertaining to how leaders
should act, thereby adopting a prescriptive approach to ethical conduct.
For example, ethical leadership theory defines ethical leadership as "the
demonstration of normatively appropriate conduct through personal
actions and interpersonal relationships, and the promotion of such conduct to followers through two-way communication, reinforcement, and
decision-making" (Brown et al., 2005, p. 120). For ethical leaders to behave
morally in their roles, they should be seen as honest, caring, and principled individuals who make fair decisions and promote ethical conduct
in followers by helping them understand the implications for their own
decision making (Treviño, Hartman, & Brown, 2000). Servant leadership
adopts a similarly moral position by advocating a perspective that leaders
have a responsibility to serve their followers by helping them achieve and
improve, as well as by serving the interests of society and those who are
disadvantaged (Greenleaf, 1977). Spiritual leadership theory (Fry, 2003),

in which a leader's values, attitudes, and behaviors influence organizational outcomes through the fulfillment of followers' needs, is similarly prescriptive. Within the mainstream leadership literature, theories such as authentic leadership (Avolio, Gardner, Walumba, Luthans, & May, 2004) share a focus on the normatively moral aspect of leadership. Authentic leaders are individuals "who are deeply aware of how they think and behave and are perceived by others as being aware of their own and others' values/moral perspectives, knowledge, and strengths; aware of the context in which they operate; and who are confident, hopeful, optimistic, resilient, and of high moral character" (Avolio et al., 2004, pp. 802–803).

Although these approaches have advanced our understanding of how ethics and morality can define whether leaders are perceived as more or less ethical, they remain limited in their predictive and explanatory abilities. Their focus rests on delineating the characteristics that individuals ought to possess or the behaviors they should display as a leader, rather than on the causal factors that can drive leaders to exhibit ethical or unethical conduct. In particular, it remains unclear how a leader's attention and information processing, decision making, and behavior as they relate to ethics can be affected by followers. An integration of a follower perspective remains underdeveloped within the leadership field in general but, perhaps even more acutely, within this ethical space. Hence, we aim to provide a stronger theoretical basis for developing descriptive, empirically grounded insight into how and why leaders can act more or less ethically.

We begin our descriptive analysis by examining the dynamic interplay between leaders and followers and identifying how followers are able to influence leader ethicality. We define *leader ethicality* as the intention to demonstrate normatively appropriate conduct and to create an environment within which others will be encouraged to act ethically and discouraged from acting unethically. This definition implies that (a) demonstrating normatively appropriate conduct is in part determined by follower perceptions, thus leader intent is important; and (b) the leader exerts as well as receives influence from followers in promoting ethical behavior, thus creating an ethical milieu is important. Moreover, this definition takes into consideration the importance of moral perspectives; however, it also underscores the notion that ethical behavior is to some extent defined by how it is construed within the context of social prescriptions. In the following sections, we adopt this follower-based view of ethical conduct, turning our focus to explicating the causal mechanisms through which followers affect leader ethicality.

The Role of Legitimacy in Leader Vulnerability to Influence

Even though leaders exert influence on followers and have the power to shape the context, we propose that, because of their position, leaders are highly susceptible to scrutiny, to perhaps an even greater degree than are individuals without such power and status. We posit that the social perception of a leader's legitimacy may play an important role in determining how the leader's morally relevant actions are interpreted and, subsequently, the influence exerted by followers on the leader. We conceptualize legitimacy as a socially construed phenomenon, based on the normatively positive expectations of followers. The social context created by followers' normative expectations is thus a significant determinant of leader legitimacy, and violations of such expectations can cast doubt on the leader's position, authority, status, and influence.

The process through which legitimacy is conferred from followers to leaders has been studied in depth within the justice domain (e.g., Tyler, Boeckmann, Smith, & Huo, 1997). In reviewing why individuals choose to cooperate with the police, Tyler (2004) concluded that people obey police officers because they view the police as a legitimate legal authority. Such legitimacy conferral is brought about only when individuals' assessment of police behavior is construed as abiding by their positive expectations of law enforcement (e.g., actions associated with due process). Thus, when policing behaviors conform to their expectations of process-based justice, individuals are likely to voluntarily cooperate and support the police (Tyler, 2006). This line of inquiry highlights the reciprocal dynamic that takes place between leaders and followers. In particular, Tyler (1990; Tyler & Huo, 2002) demonstrated not only how normative expectations (i.e., the ethical milieu) are important, but also how motives underlying actions are construed (i.e., ethical intent) can determine whether individuals confer legitimacy to those in a position of authority.

The social context created by followers can therefore create the lens through which leadership is interpreted (Lord, Brown, & Freiberg, 1999; van Knippenberg, van Knippenberg, De Cremer, & Hogg, 2004). Drawing on categorization and person perception research, Lord and colleagues posited that followers have preconceived notions (implicit theories) about what a prototypical leader looks like and, when placed within an informationally ambiguous situation, seek confirming evidence of these notions (Lord, 1977; Lord, Foti, & De Vader, 1984; Lord, Foti, & Phillips, 1982). When leaders are viewed as prototypical of the organization or subgroup, or as an exemplar with whom the follower can individually identify, that follower is more likely to perceive and value leader actions. Thus, if cues are found that support the prototype, the person will be perceived as a leader; if the leader provides cues that conflict with the follower prototype, the perception of leadership is not likely to occur.

Similarly, in their study of how leaders can motivate followers to display prosocial behavior, De Cremer, Mayer, van Dijke, Schouten, and Bardes (2009) found that the effectiveness of a leader may depend on specific follower characteristics. In particular, for those followers who value being dutiful and responsible, characteristics associated with a prevention focus, a leader's self-sacrificial behavior can significantly influence the emergence of similarly prosocial behavior. The congruence between the values and goals that the leader activates and followers pursue is thus a determining factor in the effectiveness of leader behavior.

The activation of specific characteristics has also been shown to flow from followers to leaders. Followers can influence a leader's ethical decisions and behavior by affecting the leader's level of self-construal (van Gils, van Quaquebeke, & van Knippenberg, 2010). Van Gils and colleagues (2010) proposed that to the extent followers activate a leader's collective level of self-construal, the leader will display more collectively oriented behaviors, which followers equate with ethical behavior. In contrast, to the extent followers activate a leader's individual level of self-construal, the leader will display more self-serving behaviors, which followers equate with unethical behavior. Taken together, the dynamic interplay between leader and follower influence suggests that the very emergence of leadership may in part depend on follower perceptions (e.g., Hollander & Julian, 1969; Lord, 1977; Pfeffer, 1977).

Building on these insights, we posit that due to the socially construed nature of leader legitimacy, leaders are vulnerable to follower judgments. Leaders may gain legitimacy from followers when they allow themselves to receive follower influence and behave in accordance with followers' normative expectations. This influence process may be either conscious or subconscious and occur through multiple types of influence strategies over different time periods. As such, we propose that the leader–follower relationship is fundamentally affected by upward influence strategies on the part of followers, which tend to either promote or prohibit certain types of morally relevant leadership behavior.

FOLLOWER INFLUENCE ON LEADER ETHICALITY

Proposing a Typology of Follower Actions to Influence Leader Ethicality

Followers' attempts to affect leader ethicality can be directed toward increasing leader behaviors that enhance the level of ethicality or influencing leaders to forgo actions that would reduce the level of ethicality.[1] That is, followers can try to get leaders to behave more ethically or avoid doing the unethical. For followers, such attempts can involve personal and political risk, such as when whistleblowers "go public" to influence their organizations to curtail unethical actions (Grant, 2002). Follower actions taken to influence leader ethicality, however, can also be perceived by leaders as a demonstration of concern and support, being what has been referred to as a "trusted advisor" (Maister, Green, & Galford, 2000).

To systematize our theorizing about how followers can act to influence leader ethicality, we draw on Van Dyne, Cummings, and Mclean Parks's (1995) distinction between *affiliative/challenging* and *promotive/prohibitive* behaviors. The first dimension contrasts whether the behavior would likely strengthen or preserve the relationship (affiliative) or whether it creates a risk of damaging the relationship (challenging). The second dimension contrasts whether the behavior encourages something to occur (promotive) or to cease (prohibitive). Affiliative/promotive behaviors include helping, cooperative behaviors; challenging/promotive behaviors are those that may challenge the status quo but do so to improve a situation rather than criticize it. Affiliative/prohibitive behaviors aim to protect others from harm by preventing wrongdoings, and challenging/prohibitive behaviors confront wrongdoings. Accordingly, we utilize this framework to organize the underlying structure of follower influence actions and propose that followers can influence leader ethicality in four distinct ways (see Table 4.1).

TABLE 4.1

A Typology of Follower Influence on Leader Ethicality

	Promotive	Prohibitive
Affiliative	Modeling	Guiding
Challenging	Eliciting	Sensemaking

Source: Adapted from Van Dyne, L., Cummings, L. L., & Mclean Parks, J. P., Extra-role behaviors: In pursuit of construct and definitional clarity. *Research in Organizational Behavior,* 17: 215–287, 1995.

Followers can encourage leader ethicality, which Van Dyne et al. (1995) referred to as "promotive behaviors," in one of two ways: (a) by having the follower become a role model for how such behavior might look or be practically effective so that a leader who might not see how to be more ethical can be shown through the follower's *modeling* actions; or (b) by *eliciting* behavior by encouraging the leader to recognize and act on his or her own values, beliefs, and capabilities. Similarly, followers can discourage poor ethicality on the part of leaders, classified under what Van Dyne et al. (1995) referred to as "prohibitive behaviors," in two distinct ways: (a) by *guiding* the leader away from poor ethical choices, which can be accomplished by structuring a situation in a way that narrows the available options, such that poorer ethical choices are harder to see and pursue; or (2) by serving in a *sensemaking* role by providing information and interpretations that alter how a leader views the situation and its implications, thus helping the leader attend to problematic ethical implications that might have been overlooked or misunderstood.

Van Dyne et al. (1995) also distinguished between affiliative and challenging behaviors; followers' actions can be viewed through such a conceptual lens in terms of whether they explicitly confront (i.e., challenge) a leader to stimulate more ethicality, or if followers take a more tacit (i.e., affiliative) approach to preserve their relationship with the leader (or at least expose it to less risk). For followers, *modeling* and *guiding* behaviors are affiliative in that they are indirect, implicit, and aimed at avoiding threats to the relationship while still serving as "nudges" (Thaler & Sunstein, 2008) toward ethicality. By modeling the desired ethical response, a follower can show the leader how to behave more ethically without unduly pushing the issue onto the leader. Similarly, follower guiding behaviors shape the situation, often without the leader's awareness, in ways that gently channel the leader toward his or her "better angels" without doing so in an explicit, confrontational, or directive way. In contrast, eliciting and sensemaking follower behaviors are more direct and confrontational and thus challenge the leader to alter his or her behavior or beliefs through, for example, new data. Eliciting can be seen as a follower provoking the leader to engage in new or different behavior. Similarly, sensemaking can be viewed as arguing for the leader to change his or her interpretation of a morally relevant issue requiring action. This is not always problematic but could easily be viewed as challenging a leader's authority.

Taken together, these four types of follower influence on leader ethicality can be understood to systematically affect leader ethicality in predictable ways via explicable causal pathways. In the next section, we explore those causal mechanisms.

TOWARD A RUDIMENTARY THEORY OF FOLLOWER INFLUENCE ON LEADER ETHICALITY

We hypothesize that each type of follower behavior described affects leader ethicality through a combination of cognitive, affective, and behavioral mechanisms. Table 4.2 summarizes each causal mechanism; we explain the function of each mechanism in the sections that follow. Our underlying assumption throughout is that follower influence is a complex and often-challenging process, given the power disparities between leaders and followers.[2]

Modeling

Modeling has often been conceptualized as the primary mechanism through which a leader influences followers in that followers are aided by

TABLE 4.2

Causal Mechanisms by Which Follower Behavior Influences Leader Ethicality

FOLLOWER BEHAVIOR	CAUSAL MECHANISM		
	Cognition	Affect	Behavior
Modeling	Clarify understanding	Foster optimism	Demonstrate
Eliciting	Engage mindfulness	Rouse fervor	Stimulate
Guiding	Focus attention	Prompt dissatisfaction	Channel
Sensemaking	Persuade	Induce insecurity	Routinize

seeing what ethical behaviors might look like, how they may be accomplished successfully (in both the logistical and political sense), and that the leader is personally committed to such actions. Also, because followers can come to admire their leaders and wish to emulate them, leader modeling can be a powerful influence on follower ethicality. Ethical leadership theory (Brown et al., 2005), for example, adopts a social learning perspective (Bandura, 1977; 1986) to ethical influence, arguing that leaders influence followers through norms of reciprocity and social exchange. When the leader has developed a caring and just relationship with the followers, followers may wish to reciprocate this beneficent relationship with their own exhibition of ethical behavior (Hernandez, 2008; Treviño & Brown, 2004). In this case, followers are more likely to emulate their leaders, positively influencing their ethical decision making and prosocial behaviors and attitudes while subsequently decreasing counterproductive work behaviors (Brown & Treviño, 2006; Brown et al., 2005).

Cognitive Causal Path

When a leader engages in reciprocal exchanges with the follower, the leader may want to reciprocate the follower's ethical behavior with similarly principled action. In this way, the follower can become an ethical role model for the leader. Recent findings support this notion. In their study of ethical role modeling, Weaver, Treviño, and Agle (2005) found that ethical role modeling takes place through various interpersonal behaviors that promote other-oriented concern in the context of close working relationships. Followers who exhibit self-sacrifice, responsibility for their actions, and high standards may be "looked up to" by not only other followers, but also the leader. Accordingly, followers can clarify their leader's understanding of normatively appropriate conduct by personifying moral principles.

Affective Causal Path

When followers model ethicality for their leader, their actions not only help to explain social prescriptions, but also can reduce the fear of negative responses to ethically relevant behaviors. Consequently, leaders can become optimistic about the feasibility of ethicality. Past research has found that leaders can influence followers' emotions through their behavior (Ashkanasy & Tse, 2000; Gardner & Avolio, 1998), and in turn, the emotions leaders evoke in followers can influence the followers' own morally relevant behavior (Brown & Mitchell, 2010). We posit that follower behavior can have a similar effect on leader emotions. For example, by modeling ethicality, followers can demonstrate that they are truly committed, in deed as well as word, to the principles their ethical actions imply. Such a demonstration can encourage a similar commitment in the leader.

Behavioral Causal Path

In line with Brown et al.'s (2005) view of how ethical leaders "teach" ethical behavior to followers through their own behavior, we propose followers can influence leader ethicality through this same mechanism. In particular, followers' ethical behaviors demonstrate to the leader that an ethical course of action is possible by revealing unexplored ethical alternatives. In addition, through modeling the feasibility of ethical actions, followers can show how leader ethicality can be practically effective. It can be difficult to enact ethical actions when one has never seen them in practice; providing a model can facilitate mimicry or extension. In this way, modeling can encompass follower attempts to enact or adhere to the leader's instructions as a way of showing the leader how such behavior could look and work in practice, as well as its potential ramifications.

Eliciting

We propose that followers elicit ethical behavior from their leaders by engaging mindfulness with regard to morally relevant decisions, processes, and behavior. Followers can highlight a particular ethical issue to trigger a leader's moral schema, ultimately connecting the ethical issue to a leader's personal guilt, passion, or other powerful emotions. Similarly, we posit followers can stimulate leaders to undertake ethical actions through either provocation or seduction. Building on the work on social influence (e.g., Kipnis, Schmidt, & Wilkinson, 1980), Dutton and Ashford (1993) proposed that managers engage in "issue selling" as a way to direct superiors' attention to certain issues by framing them in particular ways (e.g., Sonenshein, 2006; 2009) and by mobilizing resources and routines. Issue selling is directed at changing the organizational agenda; while it can take the form of abstract ideas, it often arises out of a sense that a particular position represents an important organizational or personal opportunity (Ashford, Rothbard, Piderit, & Dutton, 1998). Analogous to issue selling, eliciting is an upward influencing behavior that engages consideration of particular perspectives.

Cognitive Causal Path

"Mindlessness," the lack of mindfulness, often entails analyzing information context free and treating it as true regardless of the circumstances (Langer, 1989, 1997). We posit that followers can curtail this sort of automatic processing by creating awareness of multiple morally relevant facets of a situation and by challenging their leader's habitual reaction with new information on ethically relevant factors or implications. Butterfield, Treviño, and Weaver (2000) found that moral awareness could be enhanced through such factors as the use of moral language in organizational routines and practices. Thus, by increasing a leader's sensitivity to ethical issues, followers can enhance his or her mindfulness of the moral complexities involved in decision making.

Affective Causal Path

Framing and connecting an issue to the leader's personal concerns can arouse powerful affective reactions, such as guilt or passion. In particular, followers can draw on relevant religious beliefs, personal values or priorities, and responsibilities to direct their leader's attention to ethical issues with which they might not otherwise concern themselves. Senior male executives, for instance, might be more inclined to actively address issues of gender parity if the notion is highlighted that their daughters could suffer from discrimination. Haidt (2001, 2003) demonstrated how moral emotions such as anger and disgust (i.e., other-condemning emotions), shame and guilt (i.e., self-focused emotions), or compassion, empathy, and gratitude (i.e., other-suffering emotions) differentially influence behavior. Reconciliatory or prosocial behaviors, as well as destructive or avoidance behaviors, can be triggered through different emotive paths.

Behavioral Causal Path

Followers can incite their leaders to undertake ethical actions through the provocation or seduction of exemplars. By pointing to behavioral extremes in potential ethically relevant outcomes or portraying actions in starkly ethical terms, followers stimulate an action response that might not otherwise be engendered. Asking a leader, "You don't want to become the next

Ken Lay, do you?" or posing some similarly provocative comparison may push the leader to either forgo an ethically questionable action or undertake a difficult course of action that he or she might have preferred to ignore. Similarly, the seductive power of best practice exemplars (Kaplan, 2003) can be used by followers to legitimate a particular course of action. Thus, examples of how other leaders have behaved in a particular ethical space can be utilized to encourage a specific course of action.

Guiding

Scholars have argued that individuals' ethical judgments may be egocentrically biased through automatic processes (see Epley & Caruso, 2004). Nevertheless, Reynolds (2006) demonstrated that reflexive, intuitive processing of ethical decisions, operating at a subconscious level, is likely only when individuals find prototypes for ethical situations (i.e., an ethical issue stored in memory that matches the current situation). When individuals are faced with a novel situation, a reflective, deliberate process can take place in which the situation is actively reanalyzed, and moral rules are engaged. We posit that followers can prompt leaders to identify or develop different prototypes and draw their attention to particular moral rules, which in turn can influence their biases and, ultimately, their judgment. Thus, when followers guide their leaders, they can shift the trajectory and likelihood of alternative leader ethical actions in particular directions by narrowing real or apparent options. We propose this process can take place in subtle rather than confrontational ways, often without the leader becoming aware of follower intervention.

Cognitive Causal Path

During decision-making processes, followers can influence the prototype set used by the leader by increasing the valance of particular ethical issues. By stressing key aspects of the situation or key action options, followers can focus leaders on prototypes representing particular social prescriptions. In so doing, followers prime (e.g., Bargh & Chartrand, 1999; Bargh, Gollwitzer, Lee-Chai, Barndollar, & Troetschel, 2001) leaders to utilize particular prototypes. After the decisions have been taken, followers may engage in dialogue with leaders aimed at understanding the resulting ethical implications. Through this deliberate processing and analysis, followers can facilitate the creation of new prototypes.

Affective Causal Path

Activating deliberate processing in leaders can also allow followers to make salient the leader's moral identity (e.g., Bergman, 2004). To the extent that leaders believe their actions are in conflict with their moral identities, they may experience cognitive dissonance and emotional discomfort (Festinger, 1957; Treviño, Weaver, & Reynolds, 2006). Followers can prompt such dissatisfaction by emphasizing incongruent elements in the demands of the situation being faced and the outcomes experienced by the leader. Ultimately, producing slight emotional discomfort may allow followers to subtly influence the ethical options open to the leader.

Behavioral Causal Path

Much like a bowling ball travels directly down a lane when child gutters are in place, the social context created by followers can help to channel ethical behavior by constraining the field of options and protecting against ethical pitfalls. Indeed, when followers create a culture of ethics within an organization, they prolong the valence effect of specific prototypes created at the individual level with their leaders. Such social controls can form "ethical infrastructures" (Tenbrunsel et al., 2003) that direct ethical behavior through policies, structures, and procedures designed to promulgate organizational values within employees and the organizational culture. Thus, by collectively behaving according to normative principles within the organizational context, followers can systematically shape how a leader thinks about the situations and challenges confronted.

Sensemaking

Sensemaking is a cognitive process to "structure the unknown" (Waterman, 1990, p. 41). Individuals continuously make sense of experiences both subconsciously and consciously by constructing reality based on their own perceptions, anticipations, and expectations. Sensemaking, however, is not solely an individual activity; it involves a strong social component. As expressed by Karl Weick (1995, p. 6), "Sense may be in the eye of the beholder, but beholders vote and the majority rules." We posit that followers can engage in sensemaking to challenge their leader's interpretation of morally relevant situations.

Cognitive Causal Path

Due to the inherent subjectivity and typical ambiguity involved in applying moral norms across situations, followers often provide explanations or enact processes that help leaders make sense of complex or ambiguous ethical circumstances. Follower sensemaking refers to the follower helping the leader see how action or inaction by a leader, the organization, or other followers might have ethical implications. For example, a leader may be unaware that a particular action could be construed as having ethical implications, instead regarding a decision as an insignificant technical choice. A leader who does not track situational shifts closely may not recognize how a once-benign situation now carries ethical implications. Through persuasive analysis, followers can foster in their leaders an enhanced understanding of the need to stop unethical behavior or discourage it on the part of others within the organization. For instance, followers can articulate a set of procedures, routines, or explicit criteria to which a leader's ethical behavior might adhere. In so doing, the follower can directly confront lapses in the leader's ethicality by explicitly comparing it to broader organizational or social prescriptions.

Affective Causal Path

When followers call into question a leader's understanding of a morally relevant situation, they bring the issue of legitimacy to the forefront. By highlighting how an action (or inaction) is incongruent with social prescriptions, the leader can be made to feel more or less fearful. Followers can fuel this insecurity to accentuate how the leader was unaware or erroneously interpreted morally relevant situational factors or demands in their sensemaking process. Creating such distress, although risky for the leader–follower relationship, may bring to light the defining elements of how a leader is legitimized from a follower perspective. Moreover, the "detection and correction of errors" offers the leader an important organizational learning opportunity (Argyris, 1977; Senge, 1990).

Behavioral Causal Path

A trial-and-error process is sometimes necessary in determining an appropriate course of action in ambiguous and uncertain circumstances. Followers can help a leader make sense of a challenging situation by articulating the benefits and detriments of other organizational members' behavior. Particularly when the leader is new to the organization, followers can provide stories of the past experiences that created the rationales for current organizational policies and processes. In this way, followers explicitly communicate the criteria for leader ethicality that render some behaviors intuitively sensible while others may seem inappropriate or unthinkable within a given organizational context; thus, followers can chart the path for continuing behavioral patterns and routines.

CONCLUSION

Much attention has been paid to how leaders can influence the ethicality of followers, but few have asked "Who is leading the leader?" This is a fundamental question if one takes seriously the notion that leaders do not act in isolation and omnipotence concerning what is ethical. To begin to address this important issue, we have sketched some preliminary theoretical ideas and a framework for understanding how follower behavior can influence leader ethicality. We not only have offered a typology of follower influence behaviors but also have proposed a systematic analytical framework for hypothesizing how those behaviors could affect leader ethicality. The next steps are to further develop and hone the theory and to test it empirically. If we can better understand how leaders can be positively (or negatively) influenced to behave ethically, we will have made a significant step forward in predicting and ameliorating unethical leader behavior.

ACKNOWLEDGMENTS

We thank the participants of the Behavioral Business Ethics Conference and the New Directions in Leadership Conference; we especially appreciate the thoughtful feedback of David Day, Jim Detert, Daan van Knippenberg, and Phil Podsakoff. We also give special thanks to Scott Reynolds for his insightful comments. Finally, we wish to thank David De Cremer and Ann Tenbrunsel for putting together this volume and for their helpful guidance with respect to our chapter.

NOTES

1. It is important to acknowledge that while our focus remains on understanding how followers influence leader ethicality in beneficial ways, followers can cause leaders to go astray, whether intentionally or not. For instance, Offermann (2004) described how followers can become a toxic influence on leaders who are especially susceptible to flattery and ingratiation. By being persuasive and united in a particular course of action, even well-meaning followers can influence a leader's decision making in negative ways. Thus, although we constrain our analysis to how followers positively drive ethical conduct, we wish to note that our framing of follower influence could be applied equally to followers who wish to influence a leader to behave less, as well as more, ethically.

2. Although we examine each type of follower influence behavior and mechanism separately, interactive effects between these elements can exist. In addition, the efficacy of each behavior and mechanism may vary, not only in relation to the leader's openness and receptivity to upward influence, but also in terms of the leader's ethical baseline, as determined, for example, by levels of moral awareness, judgment, and motivation (Rest, 1986; Rest, Narvaez, Bebeau, & Thoma, 1999). Nevertheless, a discussion of the contingencies that can augment or diminish follower influence on leader ethicality is beyond the scope of the current chapter; such an examination is a fruitful area for future ethical inquiry.

REFERENCES

Argyris, C. (1977). Double loop learning in organizations. *Harvard Business Review, 55*(5), 115–126.

Ashford, S. J., Rothbard, N. P., Piderit, S. K., & Dutton, J. E. (1998). Out on a limb: The role of context and impression management in selling gender-equity issues. *Administrative Science Quarterly, 43*(1), 23–57.

Ashkanasy, N. M., & Tse, B. (2000). Transformational leadership as management of emotion: A conceptual review. In N. M. Ashkanasy, C. E. J. Hartel, & W. J. Zerbe (Eds.), *Emotions in the workplace: Theory, research and practice* (pp. 221–235). Westport, CT: Quorum.

Avolio, B. J. (2007). Promoting more integrative strategies for leadership theory-building. *American Psychologist, 62*, 25–33.

Avolio, B. J., Gardner, W. L., Walumbwa, F. O., Luthans, F., & May, D. R. (2004). Unlocking the mask: A look at the process by which authentic leaders impact follower attitudes and behaviors. *Leadership Quarterly, 15*, 801–823.

Bandura, A. (1977). Self-efficacy: Toward a unifying theory of behavioral change. *Psychological Review, 84*(2), 191–215.

Bandura, A. (1986). *Social foundations of thought and action: A social cognitive theory.* Englewood Cliffs, NJ: Prentice Hall.

Bargh, J. A., & Chartrand, T. L. (1999). The unbearable automaticity of being. *American Psychologist, 54*, 462–479.

Bargh, J. A., Gollwitzer, P. M., Lee-Chai, A. Y., Barndollar, K. & Troetschel, R. (2001). The automated will: Nonconscious activation and pursuit of behavioral goals. *Journal of Personality and Social Psychology, 81*, 1014–1027.

Bergman, R. (2004). Identity as motivation: Toward a theory of the moral self. In D. K. Lapsley & D. Narvaez (Eds.), *Moral development, self and identity* (pp. 21–46). Mahwah, NJ: Erlbaum.

Beu, D. S., & Buckley, M. R. (2004). This is war: How the politically astute achieve crimes of obedience through the use of moral disengagement. *Leadership Quarterly, 15*(4), 551–568.

Brown, M. E., & Mitchell, M. S. (2010). Ethical and unethical leadership: Exploring new avenues for future research. *Business Ethics Quarterly, 20*(4), 583–616.

Brown, M. E., & Treviño, L. K. (2006). Ethical leadership: A review and future directions. *Leadership Quarterly, 17*, 595–616.

Brown, M. E., Treviño, L. K., & Harrison, D. A. (2005). Ethical leadership: A social learning perspective for construct development and testing. *Organizational Behavior and Human Decision Processes, 97*, 117–134.

Butterfield, K. D., Treviño, L. K., & Weaver, G. R. (2000). Moral awareness in business organizations: Influences of issue-related and social context factors. *Human Relations, 53*(7), 981–1018.

De Cremer, D., Mayer, D. M., van Dijke, M. H., Schouten, B. C., & Bardes, M. (2009). When does self-sacrificial leadership motivate prosocial behavior? It depends on followers' prevention focus. *Journal of Applied Psychology, 94*(4), 887–899.

Dornbusch, S. M., & Scott, W. R. (1975). *Evaluation and the exercise of authority.* San Francisco: Jossey-Bass.

Dukerich, J. M., Nichols, M. L., Elm, D. R., & Vollrath, D. A. (1990). Moral reasoning in groups: Leaders make a difference. *Human Relations, 43*(5), 473–493.

Dutton, J. E., & Ashford, S. J. (1993). Selling issues to top management. *Academy of Management Review, 18*(3), 397–428.

Epley, N., & Caruso, E. M. (2004). Egocentric ethics. *Social Justice Research, 17*(2), 171–187.

Festinger, L. A. (1957). *A theory of cognitive dissonance.* Stanford, CA: Stanford University Press.

Fry, L. W. (2003). Toward a theory of spiritual leadership. *Leadership Quarterly, 14*(6), 693.

Gardner, W. L., & Avolio, B. J. (1998). The charismatic relationship: A dramaturgical perspective. *Academy of Management Review, 23*, 32–58.

Grant, C. (2002). Whistle blowers: Saints of secular culture. *Journal of Business Ethics, 39*: 391–399.

Greenleaf, R. K. (1977). *Servant leadership: A journey into the nature of legitimate power and greatness.* Mahwah, NJ: Paulist Press.

Haidt, J. (2001). The emotional dog and its rational tail: A social intuitionist approach to moral judgment. *Psychological Review, 108*(4), 814–834.

Haidt, J. (2003). The moral emotions. In R. J. Davidson, K. R. Scherer, & H. H. Goldsmith (Eds.), *Handbook of affective sciences* (pp. 852–870). New York: Oxford University Press.

Hernandez, M. (2008). Promoting stewardship behavior in organizations: A leadership model. *Journal of Business Ethics, 80*(1), 121–128.

Hollander, E. P., & Julian, J. W. (1969). Contemporary trends in the analysis of leadership processes. *Psychological Bulletin, 71*(5), 387–397.

Hollander, E. P., & Webb, W. B. (1955). Leadership, followership, and friendship: An analysis of peer nominations. *The Journal of Abnormal and Social Psychology, 50*(2), 163–167.

Homans, G. C. (1961). *Social behavior, Its elementary forms.* New York: Harcourt, Brace & World.

Johnson, C. E. (2007). *Ethics in the workplace: Tools and tactics for organizational transformation.* Thousand Oaks, CA: Sage.

Jones, T. M., & Ryan, L. V. (1998). The effect of organizational forces on individual morality: judgment, moral approbation, and behavior. *Business Ethics Quarterly, 8*(3), 431–445.

Kaplan, S. (2003). The seduction of best practice: Commentary on "taking strategy seriously." *Journal of Management Inquiry, 12,* 410–413.

Kelley, R. E. (1988). In praise of followers. *Harvard Business Review, 66*(6), 142–148.

Kipnis, D., Schmidt, S. M., & Wilkinson, I. (1980). Intraorganizational influence tactics: Explorations in getting one's way. *Journal of Applied Psychology, 65*(4), 440–452.

Langer, E. J. (1989). *Mindfulness.* Reading, MA: Addison-Wesley.

Langer, E. J. (1997). *The power of mindful learning.* Reading, MA: Addison-Wesley.

Long, C. P. (2010). Control to cooperation: Examining the role of managerial authority in portfolios of managerial actions. In S. B. Sitkin, L. B. Cardinal, & K. M. Bijlsma-Frankema (Eds.), *Control in organizations* (pp. 365–395). Cambridge, MA: Cambridge University Press.

Long, C. P., & Sitkin, S. B. (2006). Trust in the balance: How managers integrate trust-building and task control. In R. Bachmann & A. Zaheer (Eds.), *Handbook of trust research.* Cheltenham, UK: Elgar.

Lord, R. G. (1977). Functional leadership behavior: Measurement and relation to social power and leadership perceptions. *Administrative Science Quarterly, 22*(1), 114–133.

Lord, R. G., Brown, D. J., & Freiberg, S. J. (1999). Understanding the dynamics of leadership: The role of follower self-concepts in the leader/follower relationship. *Organizational Behavior & Human Decision Processes, 78*(3), 167–203.

Lord, R. G., Foti, R. J., & De Vader, C. L. (1984). A test of leadership categorization theory: Internal structure, information processing, and leadership perceptions. *Organizational Behavior & Human Performance, 34*(3), 343–378.

Lord, R. G., Foti, R. J., & Phillips, J. S. (1982). A theory of leadership categorization. In J. G. Hunt, U. Sekaran, & C. Schriesheim (Eds.), *Leadership: Beyond establishment views.* Carbondale: Southern Illinois University Press.

Maister, D. H., Green, C. H., & Galford, R. M. (2000). *The Trusted Advisor.* New York: Free Press.

McCabe, D. L., Treviño, L. K., & Butterfield, K. D. (1996). The influence of collegiate and corporate codes of conduct on ethics-related behavior in the workplace. *Business Ethics Quarterly, 6,* 461–476.

Offermann, L. R. (2004, January). When followers become toxic. *Harvard Business Review,* pp. 55–60.

Pfeffer, J. (1977). The ambiguity of leadership. *Academy of Management Review, 2*(1), 104–112.

Rest, J. (1986). *Moral development: Advances in research and theory.* New York: Praeger.

Rest, J. R., Narvaez, D., Bebeau, M., & Thoma, S. (1999). *Postconventional moral thinking: A neo-Kohlbergian approach.* Mahwah, NJ: Erlbaum.

Reynolds, S. J. (2006). A neurocognitive model of the ethical decision-making process: Implications for study and practice. *Journal of Applied Psychology, 91,* 737–748.

Schein, E. H. (1985). *Organizational culture and leadership.* San Francisco: Jossey-Bass.

Schneider, B. (1990). The climate for service: An application of the climate construct. In B. Schneider (Ed.), *Organizational climate and culture* (pp. 383–412). San Francisco: Jossey-Bass.

Senge, P. M. (1990). *The fifth discipline. The art and practice of the learning organization.* London: Random House.

Sonenshein, S. (2006). Crafting social issues at work. *Academy of Management Journal, 49*(6), 1158–1172.

Sonenshein, S. (2009). The emergence of ethical issues during strategic change implementation. *Organization Science, 20*(1), 223–239.

Suchman, M. C. (1995). Managing legitimacy: Strategic and institutional approaches. *Academy of Management Review, 20*(3), 571–610.

Tenbrunsel, A. E., & Messick, D. M. (1999). Sanctioning systems, decision frames, and cooperation. *Administrative Science Quarterly, 44*, 684–707.

Tenbrunsel, A. E., Smith-Crowe, K., & Umphress, E. E. (2003). Building houses on rocks: The role of ethical infrastructure in organization. *Social Justice Research, 16*, 285–307.

Thaler, R. H., & Sunstein. C. R. (2008). *Nudge: Improving decisions about health, wealth, and happiness.* New Haven, CT: Yale University Press.

Treviño, L. K. (1990). A cultural perspective on changing and developing organizational ethics. *Research in Organizational Change and Development, 4*, 195–230.

Treviño, L. K., & Brown, M. E. (2004). Managing to be ethical: Debunking five business ethics myths. *Academy of Management Executive, 18*, 69–81.

Treviño, L. K., Hartman, L. P., & Brown, M. E. (2000). Moral person and moral manager: How executives develop a reputation for ethical leadership. *California Management Review, 42*, 128–142.

Treviño, L. K., & Weaver, G. R. (2001). Organizational justice and ethics program "follow-through": Influences on employees' harmful and helpful behavior. *Business Ethics Quarterly, 11*(4), 651–671.

Treviño, L. K., Weaver, G. R., Gibson, D. G., and Toffler, B. L. (1999). Managing ethics and legal compliance: What works and what hurts. *California Management Review, 41*(2), 131–151.

Treviño, L. K., Weaver, G. R., & Reynolds, S. J. (2006). Behavioral ethics in organizations: A review. *Journal of Management, 32*(6), 951–990.

Tyler, T. R. (1990). *Why people obey the law.* New Haven, CT: Yale University Press.

Tyler, T. R. (2004). Enhancing police legitimacy. *Annals of the American Academy of Political and Social Science, 593*, 84–99.

Tyler, T. R. (2006). Legitimacy and legitimation. *Annual Review of Psychology, 57*, 375–400.

Tyler, T. R., Boeckmann, R., Smith, H. J., & Huo, Y. J. (1997). *Social justice in a diverse society.* Denver, CO: Westview.

Tyler, T. R., & Huo, Y. J. (2002). *Trust in the law: Encouraging public cooperation with the police and courts.* New York: Russell-Sage Foundation.

Useem, M. (2001). *Leading up: How to lead your boss so you both win.* New York: Three Rivers Press.

Van Dyne, L., Cummings, L. L., & Mclean Parks, J. P. (1995). Extra-role behaviors: In pursuit of construct and definitional clarity. *Research in Organizational Behavior, 17*, 215–287.

van Gils, S., van Quaquebeke, N., & van Knippenberg, D. (2010). The X-factor: On the relevance of implicit leadership and followership theories for leader-member exchange agreement. *European Journal of Work & Organizational Psychology, 19*(3), 333–363.

van Knippenberg, D., van Knippenberg, B., De Cremer, D., & Hogg, M. A. (2004). Leadership, self, and identity: A review and research agenda. *Leadership Quarterly, 15*(6), 825–856.

Victor, B., & Cullen, J. B. (1988). The organizational bases of ethical work climates. *Administrative Science Quarterly, 33*, 101–125.

Waterman, A. S. (1990). Personal expressiveness as a defining dimension of psychosocial identity. In C. Vandenplas-Holper & B. P. Campos (Eds.), *Interpersonal and identity development* (pp. 103–112). New York: New Directions.

Weaver, G. R., Treviño, L. K., & Agle, B. (2005). "Somebody I look up to": Ethical role models in organizations. *Organizational Dynamics, 34*(4), 313–330.

Weick, K. E. (1995). *Sensemaking in organizations*. Thousand Oaks, CA: Sage.

Zey-Ferrell, M., & Ferrell, O. C. (1982). Role-set configuration and opportunity as predictors of unethical behavior in organizations. *Human Relations, 35*(7), 587.

Section 4

Fairness and Morality

5

About Behaving (Un)ethically: Self-Interest, Deception, and Fairness

Eric van Dijk
Leiden University

Erik W. de Kwaadsteniet
Leiden University

and

Lukas Koning
University of Amsterdam

INTRODUCTION

As a scientific field of study, behavioral ethics covers a broad theme and basically refers to all ethical and unethical behaviors. However, when asked to describe the importance of studying behavioral ethics, most people will give examples of *un*ethical behaviors. Many of the articles that focus on behavioral ethics in business settings start off by referring to recent scandals like the Enron case, which involved large-scale deception at the higher managerial levels, and the extreme bonuses higher management (e.g., in the banking sector) allocated to themselves. Apart from the apparent focus on the negative rather than the positive (why not start articles with examples of ethical behavior?), these real-life examples illustrate that people generally feel that the topics of self-benefiting and deception are strongly linked. Moreover, they illustrate that many people feel that unethical behaviors are most likely to be found among those higher in the power hierarchy. In this sense, they seem to fit the general notion that "power corrupts" (Kipnis, 1972).

As an explanatory framework, the characterization of those who commit unethical behaviors as "bad people" or "bad apples" who are mainly to be found in high-power positions is both inadequate and unfortunate. It is inadequate because it fails to acknowledge that many of our social behaviors are as much a function of personality as of the social setting. It is unfortunate because if we want to create ethical organizations we should acknowledge that ethical and unethical behaviors may occur at all levels of organizations and may be performed by all kinds of people, not only by high-power executives. In this chapter, we discuss research showing that unethical behavior is not the exclusive domain of those in power. In doing so, we embrace the framework of the emerging field of behavioral ethics, which acknowledges that "all of us may commit ethical behaviors, given the right circumstances" (De Cremer, 2009, p. 4; for a similar description, see Tenbrunsel & Smith-Crowe, 2008).

SELF-INTEREST, FAIRNESS, AND ETHICS: THE CASES OF SOCIAL DILEMMAS AND ULTIMATUM BARGAINING

In the invitation to contribute to this book (and to the conference on behavioral ethics that provided the basis for the book), authors were asked to write about this new field using their own perspective and research experience. In the current chapter, we take up this challenge by discussing the findings we obtained in two distinct but related fields of research: social dilemmas and bargaining. Both fields depict mixed-motive settings in which self-interest may induce people to act against the interests of others. In social dilemmas, individuals have to decide between furthering their own interests or the interests of the collective to which they belong. In organizational settings, for example, the issue of claiming high bonuses could be considered as a self-interested act that occurs at the expense of one's organization. Bargaining refers to a similar conflict: Individuals may increase their own outcomes at the expense of the outcomes of their opponent.

In both areas, similar issues emerge that bear on the field of behavioral ethics. These issues have to do with the relative importance of the motives

of self-interest and fairness in explaining choice behavior. In both fields, we studied the connection between individual behavior and the social setting, thereby embracing the analytical framework of the emerging field of behavioral ethics.

The Instrumental Use of Fairness in Social Dilemmas

Social dilemmas refer to conflicts people face between their own interests and the collective interest (for overviews on social dilemmas, see, e.g., Komorita & Parks, 1995; Kopelman, Weber, & Messick, 2002; Messick & Brewer, 1983). Well-studied dilemmas concern the consumption of scarce resources and the provision of public goods. As a familiar example of the former type, consider the consumption of scarce resources, such as energy, oil, and water. Despite the collective interest to restrict consumption of these collective resources, it may be in people's individual interest to consume excessively. This dilemma is generally referred to as the "resource dilemma." Although the resource dilemma is typically associated with environmental issues like energy, oil, and water conservation, it should be noted that the dilemma describes a conflict that can basically be observed in any situation or organization in which individuals can draw on collective resources (see also Rutte, 1990). The dilemma of the provision of public goods occurs when individuals can contribute to provide a public good, knowing that they can benefit from the provision even if they do not contribute themselves. As a result, the individual interest may lead to underprovision. This dilemma is generally referred to as the "public good dilemma." Here, also, the collective interest may be situated at different levels, not only at the global level but also at the organizational level (i.e., to what extent should I contribute to the success of my organization?).

It may be clear that both dilemma types present the individual with a potential conflict: to pursue the (immediate) self-interests or the collective interest. With such a conflict, one might expect or fear that people will put their own interests first; that is, that they consume excessively from scarce collective resources and contribute too little to provide public goods. Despite this pessimistic view, however, much of the experimental evidence on both types of dilemmas has shown that self-interest not always wins, and that often people are willing to cooperate in both types of dilemmas. In our own research, we strongly focused on the importance of fairness as an explanation for cooperation.

In particular, we focused on the fact that people often use simple rules of fairness as a basis for their own decisions. For example, in situations of equality, people often rely on the equal division rule (see also Messick, 1993). To give an example: If in a four-person group $12 are needed to provide a public good, individual group members generally decide to contribute one fourth ($3) of the required provision threshold. This basic finding is observed even when decisions have to be made anonymously and privately (i.e., the standard situation in most social dilemma research).

But, what should we conclude if we see people adhering to equality? Initially, the main conclusion in social dilemma research was that if people adhere to equality, they do this because they value fairness (for reviews on the importance of fairness norms in social dilemmas, see, e.g., Kerr, 1995; Schroeder, Steel, Woodell, & Bembeneck, 2003). Indeed, when group members occupy identical positions, and inputs do not differ between group members, theories of fairness (e.g., equity theory, Walster, Walster, & Berscheid, 1978) predict that people would prefer allocations (and contributions) that reflect equality. Equality as a principle is of course strongly related to ethics (for a more elaborate discussion on the relation between equality and Kantian and Rawlsian ethics, see, e.g., Ball, 1987). For the current purpose, it is important to realize that an assumed preference for equality also raises the issue of "equal to what"? In our subsequent studies, we studied which rules people apply when facing asymmetric social dilemmas, in which the group members' positions or endowments are not identical. For example, we studied how people decided when facing a public good dilemma in which some members possessed more endowments than others. In that case, people did not contribute an equal number of endowments, but they applied equality to their *relative* contributions. In other words, group members contributed an equal proportion of their endowments (e.g., Van Dijk & Wilke, 1995, 2000). Again, such a preference could be interpreted in terms of existing theories of justice, such as in terms of equity theory or a general notion of noblesse oblige (Homans, 1974; see also Van Dijk & Wilke, 1994).

The studies cited thus yielded findings that could be interpreted in terms of fairness. This is also how we initially looked at these findings: as evidence showing that people care about fairness and base their behaviors on the fairness norms they value. Later, however, we more and more considered the possibility that there might be an alternative process underlying these findings. In particular, we reasoned that people might "merely" use

the fairness norms to solve the complex social dilemma they face, and that people may use equality for instrumental reasons. This interpretation concurred with Messick's (1993) theorizing when he described the advantages of using equality. Apart from its connection to fairness, Messick also attributed the attractiveness of equality to its simplicity and effectiveness. Equality is simple because you often do not need much information for its application. For example, if group members need to decide how to collectively contribute $100, they only need to know how many group members there are. Furthermore, equality is often effective because it prevents conflict and promotes collective efficiency.

These insights thus suggest that people may base their decisions on equality not only out of a true concern for fairness (*true fairness*) but also out of instrumental reasons (*instrumental fairness*). In this respect, the notion of people anchoring their decisions on equality relates to Schelling's (1960) theorizing on tacit coordination (see also Allison, McQueen, & Schaerfl, 1992). Schelling hinted on the use of equality as a basis for tacit coordination. To illustrate the coordinating potential of equality, he asked participants to divide $100 into two piles, A and B. Participants would only get a prize if they would end up with a similar distribution as their partner. Almost without exception, the participants created two equal piles of $50. Whereas in this context fairness was not an issue—participants only had to divide the money into two piles—equality clearly served as a focal point for tacit coordination.

The distinction between true fairness and instrumental fairness has theoretic appeal. But, how can we distinguish these two motives when the corresponding behavior (adherence to equality) is identical? And, could it be that some people are more driven by true fairness, while others are more motivated by instrumental fairness? To answer this question, Stouten, De Cremer, and Van Dijk (2005) presented their participants with a public good dilemma in which the total contributions should surpass a certain threshold for the public good to become available. Given the previous discussion, it should not come as a surprise that most participants adhered to the equality rule by contributing an equal share. Subsequently, however, they were informed that as a group they had not contributed enough. This would normally mean that the public good would not be provided, and this was indeed what half of the participants learned. Interestingly, however, Stouten et al. informed the other half of the participants that, even though the contributions fell short, the public good would be provided after all. Note that if one would merely adhere to equality for instrumental reasons (i.e., to provide the public good), the message that the public good would be provided after all would imply that things were fine after all. However, if a true concern for fairness would underlie the observed preference for equality, the message that the public good would be provided after all would not do the job as it would not remedy the fact that some members contributed less than others.

To see whether some people are more motivated by true fairness whereas others are more motivated by instrumental fairness, Stouten et al. (2005) assessed the participants' social value orientations. One's social value orientation can be described as stable preference for a certain allocation of outcomes. Many orientations can be distinguished, depending on the weight people assign to their own and others' outcomes, but most people can be classified as prosocials or proselfs (Van Lange, 1999). Prosocials are people who have a preference for maximum joint outcomes and equality in outcomes. In contrast, proselfs prefer to maximize to their own (absolute or relative) outcomes. Based on this distinction, one would expect that prosocials would be more motivated by true fairness, whereas proselfs would be more motivated by instrumental fairness. The results of Stouten et al. (2005) supported this reasoning. Even when learning that the public good was provided after all, the prosocials were angry and unhappy. In contrast, when proselfs learned that the public good would still be provided, they were not angry anymore. This fits with the notion that proselfs primarily rely on equality for instrumental reasons (i.e., to provide the public good). For them, violating equality is not necessarily "wrong" in an ethical or moral sense; if the public good is provided after all, they basically reason that "all is well that ends well."

At the behavioral level, one could of course raise the question of whether we should worry too much about the origin of adherence to equality: After all, the research we discussed so far shows that even those who are instrumentally motivated contribute equally to the collective interest. Note, however, that in some instances—when the conditions for the instrumental use of fairness are not met—the difference between those who are motivated by true fairness and those who are more instrumental in their preference for fairness may surface.

This question was tackled by Van Dijk, De Kwaadsteniet, and De Cremer (2009), who reasoned that the instrumental use of equality hinges on the assumption that others will use equality as well. In more general terms, they reasoned that people should have a common understanding of the situation. This notion resembles Schelling's (1960) argument when he reasoned that, for tacit coordination, people need to "read the same message in the common situation, to identify the one course of action" (Schelling, 1960, p. 54). In one of their studies, Van Dijk et al. (2009) used a very straightforward way to demonstrate the importance of having a common understanding. In a four-person resource dilemma, they manipulated the information participants thought was available to their fellow group members. All participants learned that the group would obtain a group bonus if the group succeeded in harvesting no more than 220 units from a collective resource. However, only half of the participants learned that this was common knowledge. These participants predominantly adhered to equality (and harvested about 55 units). The other half of the participants learned that their fellow group members were not informed about the exact threshold. Note that this asymmetric uncertainty did not affect the possibility for the participants to determine what would be an equal share of the threshold (i.e., 55 units). However, in this case adhering to equality would no longer be instrumental to obtain the bonus, as the participants could not expect that uninformed others would also adhere to equality. So, how would people react who primarily use equality for instrumental reasons (i.e., the proselfs) (Stouten et al., 2005)? As expected, they indeed let go of equality and started harvesting excessively. Prosocials, on the other hand, restricted their harvests, thereby showing their concern for the collective.

In summary, our research on social dilemmas suggests two possible motives for the widespread use of equality: instrumental fairness and true fairness. Acknowledging this difference is important because otherwise one may mistakenly conclude that people are motivated by true fairness when they in fact adhere to equality for instrumental reasons. Also, note that in the context of social dilemmas, adhering to instrumental fairness is not necessarily negative. After all, adhering to instrumental fairness may not hurt the collective interest but even promote the collective interest (e.g., by facilitating the provision of public goods). However, as our discussion of our research on ultimatum bargaining will show, instrumental fairness can also have a darker side to it: Instrumental fairness may be used to further the self-interests *at the expense* of others.

The Instrumental Use of Fairness in Ultimatum Bargaining

Bargaining can be described as "the process whereby two or more parties attempt to settle what each shall give and take, or perform and receive, in a transaction between them" (Rubin & Brown, 1975, p. 2). This definition illustrates that—like the social dilemma—bargaining is a mixed-motive situation (Komorita & Parks, 1995; Pruitt & Carnevale, 1993) in which parties have their own individual interests but need the cooperation of their opponent(s) to secure these interests.

According to the motivated bargaining approach, bargaining behavior can be best understood by assessing what motivates bargainers (De Dreu, Beersma, Steinel, & Van Kleef, 2007; De Dreu & Carnevale, 2003). In this respect, prior research has identified self-interest and fairness as two of the main motives underlying bargaining behavior. To study the relative importance of these two motives, researchers have made extensive use of the ultimatum bargaining game (Güth, Schmittberger, & Schwarze, 1982), which basically portrays the final phase of bargaining, when bargainers make a "take-it-or-leave-it" (ultimatum) offer to their opponent. In the typical ultimatum game, two players—an allocator and a recipient—have to distribute a certain amount of money. The allocator first offers a proportion of the money to the recipient, who then accepts or rejects the offer. If the recipient accepts, the money is distributed in agreement with the allocator's offer. If the recipient rejects, both players get nothing.

With its simple structure, the ultimatum bargaining game is highly suited to study the relative importance of self-interest and fairness concerns. To illustrate this, suppose that the allocator and recipient can divide $10. What would self-interested bargainers do? If the allocator and recipient would only be motivated to maximize their own outcomes, the allocator should only offer 1 cent to the recipient, which should then be accepted by the recipient. After all, this 1 cent would be more than what the recipient would obtain should he or she reject the offer (i.e., nothing). As in our previous discussion of social dilemma research, the prediction of what the bargainers should do if they were only motivated by fairness is simple: The allocator should offer the recipient half of the money (i.e., 5 dollars). In the absence of any differences regarding prior inputs (cf. Walster et al., 1978), such an equal division is clearly the fairest solution (again, see also Messick, 1993).

So, what is the verdict? Is (ultimatum) bargaining all about fairness or all about self-interest? Initially, the research on ultimatum bargaining appeared to favor the fairness explanation: Most allocators in the ultimatum game offered to split the money equally, and hardly anyone made 1-cent offers (for overviews, see, e.g., Camerer & Thaler, 1995; Handgraaf, Van Dijk, & De Cremer, 2003; Thaler, 1988; Van Dijk & Tenbrunsel, 2005). Subsequent studies, however, suggested that here also one runs the risk of mistaking instrumental fairness for true fairness. In particular, research showed that bargainers often only offered the recipient an equal split because they feared that low offers would be rejected. The most convincing evidence came from studies that provided the allocator with more information than the recipient. These studies basically investigated how allocators would decide if—as a result of the information asymmetry—they believed that the recipient would not be able to recognize a low offer as an unfair offer.

Kagel, Kim, and Moser (1996), for example, had participants bargain over a number of chips that were worth three times as much to the allocator as to the recipient. This differential value of the chips was either common knowledge or only known to the allocator. Interestingly, their results showed that when the information was common knowledge, allocators tended to compensate for the differential value by offering the recipient substantially more than half of the chips. In other words, the allocators seemed to be making fair offers. But, were these offers truly fair, or should we interpret them as instrumental fairness? To answer this question, one should consider the offers of allocators who believed that the recipient was not aware of the differential value. Interestingly, these allocators did not seem all that willing to compensate for the differential value; they often offered the recipient an equal split of the chips. In other words, they made an offer that seemed fair to the uninformed recipient, but that was not truly fair and would result in higher outcomes for themselves. They thus primarily seemed to instrumentally use fairness to have their (low) offer accepted. If they would strive for true fairness, they should compensate for the differential value. Similar findings using similar manipulations were obtained by other researchers (e.g., Croson, 1996; Pillutla & Murnighan, 1995; Straub & Murnighan, 1995; Van Dijk & Vermunt, 2000)

Interestingly, the research on ultimatum bargaining also studied the role of social value orientations. Van Dijk, De Cremer, and Handgraaf (2004) studied allocators' offers of prosocials or proselfs in a bargaining situation that was similar to the one discussed: Chips were worth more to the allocator than to the recipient, and this was either common knowledge or only known to the allocator. Corroborating the notion that true fairness is more characteristic of prosocials, and instrumental fairness of proselfs, the results showed that the manipulation of information only affected proselfs. They were the ones who lowered their offers when having the information advantage. In contrast, most prosocials compensated for the differential value even when the recipient was not aware of the differential value.

It thus seems that the distinction between true and instrumental fairness is meaningful not only in social dilemma settings, but also in bargaining settings. There is a difference, however. In the ultimatum bargaining studies we discussed, instrumental fairness basically referred to presenting an unfair distribution as fair. As such, it was used to increase one's own outcomes at the expense of one's opponent. In the social dilemma settings we described, instrumental fairness mainly referred to the extent to which fairness was used to solve the dilemma (e.g., to provide the public good). In social dilemmas, adherence to instrumental fairness was thus not used at the expense of others.

In this sense, the instrumental use fairness we revealed in ultimatum bargaining has a darker connotation, and one would probably be more inclined to describe it as unethical behavior. This darker side is even more apparent if one considers the connection between information exchange and deception. In the studies discussed, allocators with an information advantage could not communicate the value of the chips to their opponent; that is, they could not share their information advantage with their opponent. So, what if they could—before making their offer to the recipient—inform the recipient about the alleged value of the chips? Would they truthfully inform their opponent about the differential value? Or would they, for example, inform the other that all chips were of equal value and thus deceive their opponent?

As Tenbrunsel (1998, p. 330) noted, "Negotiations are asserted to be breeding grounds for unethical behavior, with deception positioned as a common bargaining tactic." In agreement with this assertion, Pillutla and Murnighan (1995) showed that bargainers lied about the fairness of their offers to get lower offers accepted (see also Boles, Croson, & Murnighan, 2000). However, this does not mean that bargainers will always try to deceive others, or that all bargainers use deception as a bargaining strategy.

That bargainers do not uniformly turn to deception as a bargaining strategy was demonstrated by Van Dijk, Van Kleef, Steinel, and Van Beest (2008). Whereas these authors more broadly aimed to study how bargainers respond to others' emotions, one of their studies (experiment 2) is of special relevance here. In this experiment, an ultimatum bargaining setting was used to investigate how allocators responded to anger versus happiness expressed by the recipient. Using an asymmetric value setting, with chips being worth more to the allocator than to the recipient, they manipulated the information level: The asymmetry was either common knowledge or only known to the allocator. In this respect, the setup thus resembled that of other studies on asymmetric information. This time, however, participants with an information advantage could send a message to the recipient before making their offer and either truthfully reveal the value asymmetry or state that the chips were of equal value to both parties. So, did the participants deceive their opponent? Yes, they did, but primarily when facing an angry recipient (as opposed to a happy recipient). Additional data showed that this high willingness to use deception was primarily due to the allocator's fear of the angry opponent. These findings not only suggest that fear may be an instigator of deception but also suggest that people may use fairness to reach their own personal goals. At this point, it may be noted that we obtained similar findings when studying bargainers' reactions to threats and promises (Van Dijk, Van Kleef, Van Beest, & Reinders-Folmer, 2010). Threats, more than promises, are likely to elicit deception.

Whereas these studies showed that the behavior of others (anger, threats) may evoke deception, and that people may strategically use equality for this purpose, we also collected data showing the role of personality. Koning, Van Dijk, Steinel, and Van Beest (2010) studied how social value orientations affect the willingness to deceive. They used an ultimatum game setting in which participants learned that chips were worth more to themselves than to their opponents. Again, this value difference was either common knowledge or only known by oneself. The setup thus resembled Van Dijk et al.'s (2004) study on social value orientations that we discussed, but now people had the additional opportunity to deceive the recipient. The results showed that proselfs, more than prosocials, deceived the recipient, making their opponents believe that the values were more equal than they actually were. Moreover, people who had deceived their opponents, most of whom were proselfs, were also the ones who made lower offers. Thus, especially proselfs appeared to instrumentally use deception and tried to appear fair to have their low offers accepted.

At this point, it may be noted that there may be multiple ways to appear fair. In all of our studies we presented thus far, participants received a higher value for their chips and could deceive their opponent by downplaying the alleged value of their chips. For example, when receiving 10 cents per chip while their opponent would only receive 5 cents per chip, they could inform the other that they also only received 5 cents per chip. Downplaying the own outcomes is only one strategy, however. An alternative deceptive strategy would be to exaggerate the other's outcomes (e.g., letting the other believe that he or she would also receive 10 cents).

Koning, Van Dijk, Steinel, and Van Beest (2010) investigated whether people would prefer one strategy over the other. For this purpose, participants could distribute two envelopes between themselves and their opponent, knowing that one envelope contained 5 euros, while the other contained only 1 euro. Similar to the ultimatum game, participants learned that their opponent could either accept or reject their offer. If their opponent would reject the offer, both would receive nothing. Not surprisingly, almost all participants preferred to allocate the envelope with 5 euros to themselves. The problem, of course, was how they would make such a 5–1 distribution acceptable to their opponent? To study the use of deception, we informed all participants that their opponent was unaware of the fact that one envelope contained 5 euros and the other only 1 euro, and that they could inform their opponent of the alleged content of the envelopes. It is here that we introduced the possible strategies of deception. The participants could truthfully inform their opponent of the content, but they could also deceive their opponent. If they chose to deceive their opponent, they could downplay their own outcomes and inform the opponent that both envelopes contained 1 euro. As an alternative strategy, they could also exaggerate the outcomes of their opponent by informing him or her that both envelopes contained 5 euros. The results not only showed that many participants were willing to deceive their opponent, but also that they preferred downplaying the own outcomes to exaggerating the other's outcomes. In other words, many participants instrumentally used fairness to deceive their opponent but preferred to do this by downplaying their own outcomes. From an instrumental point of view, this differential preference may be surprising, as one would expect that—if one would expect any difference at all—a 5–5 distribution would seem more attractive to the opponent than a 1–1 distribution. Additional data suggested that people generally refrained from exaggerating other's outcomes because they felt it would be unethical to falsely let the other believe that he or she would receive a high outcome. Such findings can be understood in terms of the idea that inflicting losses on others is deemed less appropriate than withholding gains (i.e., the "do no harm principle"; Baron, 1995, 1996; see also Leliveld, Van Beest, Van Dijk, & Tenbrunsel, 2009).

As said, the picture emerging from the research on bargaining appears darker than that of the research on social dilemmas. When it comes to the deception data, the research seems to reveal the downsides of instrumentality, with bargainers being prepared to deceive their opponent; instrumental fairness appears to be the vehicle that brings the self-interested bargainer the outcomes he or she values. But even here, however, we should note that deception is not uniformly used. Some elements appear to be needed for people to resort to deception. The behavior of one's opponent (showing anger, ushering threats) seems to act as a catalyst for deception. Personality is another element to consider, with prosocials being less inclined to deceive their opponent.

IMPLICATIONS FOR BEHAVIORAL ETHICS

Taken together, the findings we presented here underscore the benefits of taking both personality and situational characteristics into account when studying behavioral ethics. As such, they fit the direction the field has taken. In this chapter, we discussed many issues that are typically associated with unethical behavior. We talked about putting the self-interests first (and collective interests second), and we talked about deception and misrepresentation. To many, these behaviors are almost synonyms for unethical behavior.

Note, however, that our discussions were more nuanced. The primary insight was not that self-interested behavior would be unethical. Even when distinguishing true fairness from instrumental fairness, our main conclusion was not that instrumental fairness should be seen as more unethical than true fairness. Especially when discussing our social dilemma research, we did not mean to argue that basing decisions on instrumental fairness—using fairness as a means rather than as a goal—would be less ethical. What the research on social dilemmas in our opinion does show is that what on first sight may seem as highly ethical or fair behavior (furthering the collective interest; adhering to fairness norms) can sometimes be explained in instrumental terms. In the beginning of this chapter, we argued that when it comes to business ethics, most people immediately provide examples of unethical behavior. Although this focus on the negative is understandable, the current studies showed that it may be equally relevant for the field to take a broader perspective, in this case to try understand seemingly fair behaviors.

The distinction between instrumental and true fairness not only helped us to understand decisions in social dilemmas but also provided a fruitful framework for understanding bargaining behavior. Here, we did address behaviors that are generally considered unethical, such as deception. But, even while the research on bargaining did show some of the darker sides of instrumental fairness, it should be noted that the main contribution lies in identifying the factors that promote such behaviors, and not in identifying deception as being unethical. This, in our opinion, is the ultimate conclusion of taking a psychological perspective that acknowledges the situational determinacy of moral judgments and behaviors. As an emerging field that embraces the empirical approach, the main strength lies in understanding the processes that underlie ethical and unethical conduct. It is with this in mind that we distinguished between true fairness and instrumental fairness. By examining the processes that determine the relative importance of both motives, we hope to have contributed to the further development of the field.

As a final note, the field may wish to further explore the relative importance of instrumental and true fairness. In the current chapter, we related the relative strength of both forms of fairness to social value orientations. It is conceivable that other personality differences may also be related. A likely candidate would be moral identity. Moral identity describes the extent to which "being moral" is a central aspect of someone's self-concept and is generally seen as a personality trait (Aquino & Reed, 2002). If true fairness would be considered as more moral than instrumental fairness, it seems likely that true fairness would be more important for people with a high moral identity. In addition to more studies on personality, the field of business ethics could also benefit from more studies on the impact of the situation on the relative importance of true versus instrumental fairness. How, for example, do the relative weights relate to the ethical climate of an organization (Martin & Cullen, 2006; Victor & Cullen, 1988)? Does an ethical climate evoke a greater concern for true fairness? Together, studies like this not only would provide new insights but also would again underscore the importance of taking both personality and situation into account when trying to explain ethical and unethical behaviors.

REFERENCES

Allison, S. T., McQueen, L. R., & Schaerfl, L. M. (1992). Social decision making processes and the equal partitionment of shared resources. *Journal of Experimental Social Psychology, 28*, 23–42.

Aquino, K., & Reed, A. (2002). The self-importance of moral identity. *Journal of Personality and Social Psychology, 83*, 1423–1440.

Ball, S. W. (1987). Choosing between choice models of ethics: Rawlsian equality, utilitarianism, and the concept of persons. *Theory and Decision, 22*, 209–224.

Baron, J. (1995). Blind justice: Fairness to groups and the do-no-harm principle. *Journal of Behavioral Decision Making, 8*, 71–83.

Baron, J. (1996). Do no harm. In D. M. Messick & A. Tenbrunsel (Eds.), *Codes of conduct: Behavioral research into business ethics* (pp. 197–213). New York: Russell Sage Foundation.

Boles, T. L., Croson, R. T. A., & Murnighan, J. (2000). Deception and retribution in repeated ultimatum bargaining. *Organizational Behavior and Human Decision Processes, 83*, 235–259.

Camerer, C., & Thaler, R. H. (1995). Ultimatums, dictators and manners. *Journal of Economic Perspectives, 9*, 209–219.

Croson, R. T. A. (1996). Information in ultimatum games: An experimental study. *Journal of Economic Behavior & Organization, 30*, 197–212.

De Cremer, D. (2009). Psychology and ethics: What it takes to feel unethical when being unethical. In D. De Cremer (Ed.), *Psychological perspectives on ethical behavior and decision making* (pp. 3–13). Charlotte, NC: Information Age.

De Dreu, C. K. W., Beersma, B., Steinel, W., & van Kleef, G. A. (2007). The psychology of negotiation: Principles and basic processes. In A. W. Kruglanski & E. T. Higgins (Eds.), *Social psychology: Handbook of basic principles* (2nd ed., pp. 608–629). New York: Guilford Press.

De Dreu, C. K. W., & Carnevale, P. J. (2003). Motivational bases of information processing and strategy in conflict and negotiation. *Advances in Experimental Social Psychology, 35*, 235–291.

Güth, W., Schmittberger, R., & Schwarze, B. (1982). An experimental analysis of ultimatum bargaining. *Journal of Economic Behavior & Organization, 3*, 367–388.

Handgraaf, M. J. J., Van Dijk, E., & De Cremer, D. (2003). Social utility in ultimatum bargaining. *Social Justice Research, 16*, 263–283.

Homans, G. (1974). *Social behavior: Its elementary forms.* New York: Harcourt, Brace.

Kagel, J. H., Kim, C., & Moser, D. (1996). Fairness in ultimatum games with asymmetric information and asymmetric payoffs. *Games and Economic Behavior, 13*, 100–111.

Kerr, N. L. (1995). Norms in social dilemmas. In D. Schroeder (Ed.), *Social dilemmas: Social psychological perspectives* (pp. 31–47). New York: Pergamon.

Kipnis, D. (1972). Does power corrupt? *Journal of Personality and Social Psychology, 24*, 33–41.

Komorita, S. S., & Parks, C. D. (1995). Interpersonal relations: Mixed-motive interaction. *Annual Review of Psychology, 46,* 183–207.

Koning, L., Van Dijk, Steinel, & Van Beest, I. (2010). *Deception and misrepresentation in bargaining: Downplaying the own outcomes versus exaggerating other's outcomes.* Unpublished manuscript.

Koning, L., Van Dijk, E., Van Beest, I., & Steinel, W. (2010b). An instrumental account of deception and reactions to deceit in bargaining. *Business Ethics Quarterly, 20,* 57–73.

Kopelman, S., Weber, J. M, & Messick, D. M. (2002). Factors influencing cooperation in commons dilemmas: A review of experimental psychological research. In E. Ostrom, T. Dietz, N. Dolšak, P. Stern, S. Stonich, & E. U. Weber (Eds.), *The drama of the commons* (pp. 113–156). Washington, DC: National Academy Press.

Leliveld, M. C., Van Beest, I., Van Dijk, E., & Tenbrunsel, A. E. (2009). Understanding the influence of outcome valence in bargaining: A study on fairness accessibility, norms and behavior. *Journal of Experimental Social Psychology, 45,* 505–514.

Martin, K. D., & Cullen, J. B. (2006). Continuities and extensions of ethical climate theory: A meta-analytic review. *Journal of Business Ethics, 69,* 175–194.

Messick, D. M. (1993). Equality as a decision heuristic. In B. A. Mellers & J. Baron (Eds.), *Psychological perspectives on justice* (pp. 11–31). New York: Cambridge University Press.

Messick, D. M., & Brewer, M. B. (1983). Solving social dilemmas. In L. Wheeler & P. R. Shaver (Eds.), *Review of personality and social psychology* (Vol. 4, pp. 11–44). Beverly Hills, CA: Sage.

Pillutla, M., & Murnighan, J. K. (1995). Being fair or appearing fair: Strategic behavior in ultimatum bargaining. *Academy of Management Journal, 38,* 1408–1426.

Pruitt, D. G., & Carnevale, P. J. (1993). *Negotiation in social conflict.* Oxford, UK: Oxford University Press.

Rubin, J. Z., & Brown, B. (1975). *The social psychology of bargaining and negotiations.* New York: Academic Press.

Rutte, C. G. (1990). Solving organizational social dilemmas. *Social Behaviour, 5,* 285–294.

Schelling, T. C. (1960). *The strategy of conflict.* Oxford, UK: Harvard University Press.

Schroeder, D. A., Steel, J. E., Woodell, A. J., & Bembeneck, A. F. (2003). Justice within social dilemmas. *Personality and Social Psychology Review, 7,* 374–387.

Stouten, J., De Cremer, D., & Van Dijk, E. (2005). All is well that ends well, at least for proselfs: Emotional reactions to equality violation as a function of social value orientation. *European Journal and Social Psychology, 35,* 767–783.

Straub, P. G., & Murnighan, J. K. (1995). An experimental investigation of ultimatum games: Information, fairness, expectations, and lowest acceptable offers. *Journal of Economic Behavior and Organization, 27,* 345–364.

Tenbrunsel, A. E. (1998). Misrepresentation and expectations of misrepresentation in an ethical dilemma: The role of incentives and temptation. *Academy of Management Journal, 41,* 330–339.

Tenbrunsel, A. E., & Smith-Crowe, K. (2008). Ethical decision making: Where we've been and where we're going. *Academy of Management Annals, 2,* 545–607.

Thaler, R. H. (1988). Anomalies: The ultimatum game. *Journal of Economic Perspectives, 2,* 195–206.

Van Dijk, E., De Cremer, D., & Handgraaf, M. J. J. (2004). Social value orientations and the strategic use of fairness in ultimatum bargaining. *Journal of Experimental Social Psychology, 40,* 697–707.

Van Dijk, E., De Kwaadsteniet, E. W., & De Cremer, D. (2009). Tacit coordination in social dilemmas: The importance of having a common understanding. *Journal of Personality and Social Psychology, 96,* 665–678.

Van Dijk, E., & Tenbrunsel, A. (2005). The battle between self-interest and fairness: Evidence from ultimatum, dictator, and delta games. In S. W. Gilliland, D. D. Steiner, D. P. Skarlicki, & K. Van den Bos (Eds.), *What motivates fairness in organizations?* (pp. 31–48). Greenwich, CT: Information Age.

Van Dijk, E., Van Kleef, G. A., Steinel, W., & Van Beest, I. (2008). A social functional approach to emotions in bargaining: When communicating anger pays and when it backfires. *Journal of Personality and Social Psychology, 94,* 600–614.

Van Dijk, E., Van Kleef, G. A., Van Beest, I., & Reinders-Folmer, C. (2010). *When promises may work, and threats may backfire in bargaining.* Unpublished manuscript.

Van Dijk, E., & Vermunt, R. (2000). Strategy and fairness in social decision making: Sometimes it pays to be powerless. *Journal of Experimental Social Psychology, 36,* 1–25.

Van Dijk, E., & Wilke, H. (1994). Asymmetry of wealth and public good provision. *Social Psychology Quarterly, 57,* 352–359.

Van Dijk, E., & Wilke, H. (1995). Coordination rules in asymmetric social dilemmas: A comparison between public good dilemmas and resource dilemmas. *Journal of Experimental Social Psychology, 31,* 1–27.

Van Dijk, E., & Wilke, H. (2000). Decision-induced focusing in social dilemmas: Give-some, keep-some, take-some and leave-some dilemmas. *Journal of Personality and Social Psychology, 78,* 92–104.

Van Lange, P. A. M. (1999). The pursuit of joint outcomes and equality in outcomes: An integrative model of social value orientation. *Journal of Personality and Social Psychology, 77,* 337–349.

Victor, B., & Cullen, J. B. (1988). The organizational bases of ethical work climates. *Administrative Science Quarterly, 33,* 101–125.

Walster, E., Walster, G. W., & Berscheid, E. (1978). *Equity: Theory and research.* Boston: Allyn & Bacon.

6

Deonance: Behavioral Ethics and Moral Obligation

Robert Folger
University of Central Florida

The concept of Ought is the basic concept of the whole of ethics.

—Ernst Mally[1]

In applying behavioral ethics to business, a definition of behavioral ethics needs to come first. The catch is the combination of the words *behavioral* and *ethics*. Even without adding the behavioral part, there are questions about what a subject called ethics is all about. The answer is that ethics is what philosophers of ethics say it is, at least in the way it is often taught. The definition of behavioral ethics is thus not unlike the famous remark by Supreme Court Justice Potter Stewart about pornography: "I know it when I see it." Ethics is in the eye of the beholder.

One place we see it is that certain kinds of *illegal* corporate conduct are also *un*ethical. Current articles on ethics often start, for example, by mentioning the Enron and MCI WorldCom accounting–fraud scandals. Sadly, that may be just the tip of the iceberg, as suggested by a study of 10 years of incidents of illegal practices recorded in data from regulatory agencies, corporations' own documents, and other publicly available sources. The results showed that almost two-thirds of the *Fortune* magazine's top 500 industrial corporations had engaged in one or more forms of illegal activity that included patent infringements, price-fixing, falsified tax records, and various forms of fraud (Etzioni, 1985). Nor is it just egregious behavior at the corporate level that we recognize as unethical when we see it, as indicated by the investigations into such now-familiar research topics as *abusive supervision* (e.g., Tepper, 2007) and *workplace deviance* (Bennett & Robinson, 2000).

So, here is one way of talking about behavioral ethics: We know hard-core unethical conduct when we see it, and I think we can gain some insight into its nature (and that of the less-hardcore kind, as well as ethical conduct) by using the tools of the behavioral sciences. I think social psychology and social cognition are the areas of behavioral science that have made the greatest contribution so far, which means that the focus has been largely at the individual level. When I first referred to behavioral ethics in print,[2] however, I had not run across that term in the literature, so it meant something a little bit different to me—at the individual level, yes, pretty much (in the beginning?); exclusively in terms of psychology, no.

Put another way, I think that the *behavioral* in behavioral ethics should extend to any scientific approach (research and empirically oriented theory) when it is used to gain a better understanding of ethical and unethical behavior. Strictly speaking, a wide variety of scientific disciplines can contribute when people apply the outlook of a given field (e.g., its methodology) to the subject matter of behavioral ethics. When people bring a scientific perspective to bear on the antecedents and consequences of (un)ethical behavior, that is when I "see" it (e.g., Chugh, Banaji, & Bazerman, 2005; De Cremer, Tenbrunsel, & Dijke, 2011; Grover, 1993; Schminke, Ambrose & Neubaum, 2005; Treviño, Weaver, & Reynolds, 2006; Tyler & Blader, 2005).

The precedent for *behavioral* is another newly minted term, *behavioral economics*. The study of behavioral economics provides not only an apposite descriptive label but also an illustration of a well-established field benefitting from an interdisciplinary melding. Behavioral ethicists should also look for such benefits. I originally thought, and still do, that the disciplines relevant to research in behavioral ethics should include not only psychology (social and social-cognitive) but also anthropology (McElreath, Boyd, & Richerson, 2003) and primatology (e.g., de Waal, 1991) as behavioral sciences. Other disciplines make contributions when they deal with human behavior; these include neuroscience (e.g., for a review, see Salvador & Folger, 2009); biology (e.g., Bingham, 1999); evolutionary theory and research (e.g., Boehm, 1999; Cosmides & Tooby, 1994); and an emerging experimental philosophy (e.g., Nichols & Mallon, 2006).

We can benefit from using the tools of those sciences to study moral obligations: "Ethics is ... about deciding how we *ought to behave* with others. It's about our *obligations* and rights with respect to others" (Gini,

2010, p. 738, emphasis added). As put in the title of a major work on moral philosophy, ethics is *What We Owe to Each Other* (Scanlon, 1998). I like that succinct definition of ethics. We can use it to define *behavioral business ethics* as a scientific approach for studying perceptions of how we ought to treat one another in business-related matters and how such perceptions influence behavior. Referring to how we ought to treat one another implies restrictions or constraints on behavior and notions of responsibility and accountability, as various business ethicists noted in essays on the 20th anniversary of *Business Ethics Quarterly*:

> Business decisions ... carry moral implications, hence *accountability.* (Hartman, 2010, p. 742, emphasis added)
>
> It may be tempting for a video game company to disclaim responsibility for negative social effects on youth because *other* factors also contribute (e.g., parents, TV networks, Hollywood). But. ... Is there not an obligation to *make an effort* to collaborate for the common good? (Goodpaster, 2010, p. 741, emphasis in original)
>
> Both business and business persons are required to ask the question: What *ought to be* done in regard to those who we work with, work for, and come to work to serve? (Gini, 2010, pp. 738–739)

These ethicists are saying that ethical business practices involve norms of obligation. The theory I discuss in this chapter focuses on perceptions of obligation and their influence on behavior.

BEHAVIORAL BUSINESS ETHICS AND PERCEIVED MORAL DUTY: TOWARD A THEORY OF DEONANCE

I have tried to develop a metaperspective on philosophy and psychology— deonance theory (DT)—that takes an empirical approach (descriptive rather than prescriptive) to studying business conduct with tools derived from the behavioral sciences. (Other treatments of aspects of the deonance construct include Folger & Cropanzano, 2010; Folger, Cropanzano, & Goldman, 2005; Folger & Skarlicki, 2008.) *Deonance* (a neologism) is derived from the Greek *deon*, referring to duty or obligation. The significance for morality comes from the additional translation as that which is binding or proper, thereby also implying accountability.

This DT approach is consistent with Fritz Heider's chapter on "Ought and Value": "oughts or obligations … play a major role … in the evaluation and determination of behavior and its consequences," given a person's "sense of duty" (Heider, 1958, p. 218). The perceived "ought" of a situation indicates "that people in general should concur in its directives" (Heider, 1958, p. 222); empirically "the meaning of ought … can be defined by investigating the functional role it plays in our thinking and our reactions" (Heider, 1958, p. 222).

DT cuts across philosophical traditions but remains neutral about their content. Studying the psychological *processes* whereby moral norms influence behavior (empirically investigating the role of ought) is independent of the *content* of such norms—just as the study of underlying linguistic processes applies equally to the content of any given language. DT is a process theory that proposes a hypothetical construct, the psychological state of deonance, whose arousal occurs when a situation brings to bear beliefs about the relevance of moral directives (even if not a perception at the conscious level). The arousal of the psychological state of deonance represents the instigation of an "ought force" (Heider, 1958, p. 234) that calls for self-restraint rather than unfettered choice. Ethical philosophy suggests what those oughts should be; DT addresses their psychology in a neutral way, not adopting any specific philosophical perspective.

Similarly, *deontic* is used as a philosophically neutral adjective in some areas of research. Linguists, for example, classify certain auxiliary verbs (e.g., ought to, must, may, should) as expressing a *deontic mood*. Cognitive psychologists (e.g., Bucciarelli & Johnson-Laird, 2005) study people's reasoning about *deontic conditionals* (if … then statements or their equivalents), which indicate "what a person may do, must not do, must do, or need not do" (Beller, 2008, p. 305). They "direct people's actions by defining rights, duties, and bans" (Beller, 2010, p. 123). These obviously have a key role to play in business organizations: "Rules for the financial markets might determine, for example, the rights of investors to deposit insurance if a bank collapses, the equity ratio that banks are obliged to keep, or the types of financial products and transactions that are forbidden" (Beller, 2010, p. 123).

As a philosophically neutral theory, DT holds that people *can* be influenced by "ought to" norms—even if outside conscious awareness—but does not hold that people *are* always influenced by them (e.g., Boesky, Milken). DT instead considers moral judgments in light of another psychological state, *reactance*. Reactance theory (discussed in the next section) addresses conditions under which people resist perceived reductions to, or elimination of, the freedom to choose any of the options available in a given situation. Obviously, such a theory would be unnecessary unless people sometimes allow their freedom to be curtailed because they *accept* (or on an even more internalized basis, *endorse*) those restrictions as morally warranted.

DEONANCE, REACTANCE, AND BOUNDED AUTONOMY

Reactance theory assumes that "for a given person at a given time, there is a set of behaviors any one of which he could engage in" (Brehm, 1966, p. 3), or *free behaviors*, and that "most of the time people will feel that they are relatively free to engage in a variety of different behaviors and that they can select among these as they please" (Brehm, 1966, p. 1). Moreover, they are inclined to protect that freedom. Deonance, on the other hand, applies to *nonfree* behaviors. As cognitive psychologists who study deontic reasoning put it, the logic (and psycho-logic) of moral norms is that they exist "to restrict the freedom of individuals to do as they please" (Bender & Beller, 2003, p. 133). Deonance is the motivational force of those norms, so it picks up where reactance theory leaves off. The theories are complementary to one another in that respect.

DT, however, emphasizes a broader perspective. Free behaviors and nonfree behaviors exist within the set of all behaviors, separated by the same criteria: "Behaviors may become free in a variety of ways … [including] by experience, by general custom, or by formal agreement" (Brehm, 1966, pp. 3–4), which are the same elements that establish boundary lines between the free and the not-free. Deonance (cf. Heider's ought force) is an experienced psychological state made possible because of the existence of such boundaries. Where the boundary line involves a moral norm, it "has binding force, as a consideration that the agent has to take into account, to the extent that she accepts it as offering criticism from an interpersonal standpoint that she is in no position to set aside unilaterally" (Greenspan, 2010, p. 204). Actual behaviors, therefore, are determined by the strength of one force (reactance) relative to the other (deonance).

Bounded autonomy (Folger, 1998) is a DT term about free behaviors morally curtailed as the resultant of those forces. Simon (1947) famously referred to *bounded rationality*: We have limited cognitive capacities. Our autonomy is also circumscribed, in ways necessary for social life: We are constrained by others to behave as they think we should or should not, and we exercise self-restraint according to what we ourselves consider to be right and wrong.[3] These are the contours of our free behaviors, the area of autonomy bounded by its socially allowable (legitimately justifiable) limits (cf. Folger, 1998; Scanlon, 1998; Simon, 1951). In that sense, the experience of deonance varies with the extent to which people do or do not experience reactance.

DT focuses on behaviors that are commonly perceived as reasonable and appropriate (legitimate, justifiable, and so forth) to regard as bounded rather than free. This type of bound behaviors reflects restrictions and constraints accepted routinely as part of the normal (and normative) interrelations among people in a well-ordered society. The person whose domain of free behaviors is thus circumscribed will ordinarily act in a manner consistent with those limitations, but his or her reactions can include internalized acceptance, mere compliance, or resistance because of the belief that these should be treated as free behaviors.

Thus, DT motivations contrast with reactance motivations, which are "directed against any loss of freedom … and toward the re-establishment of … freedom … threatened" (p. 2). The motivational arousal of deonance is directed against the unauthorized loosening of the relevant bounds. Just as one influence on the strength/magnitude of reactance is the importance of the free behaviors that are in jeopardy, for example, deonance is experienced to a greater or lesser degree based on the relative importance of the duty-related considerations activated at the time. Moreover, reactance *increases* with the extent of the threat aligned against free behaviors; deonance mirrors this effect, in that the greater the perceived moral validity and weight of the relevant duties that confine the area of bounded autonomy are, the *less* reactance there is.

Bounded autonomy refers to justified or legitimate restrictions on freedom. Concerning the nature of reactance, however, justification and legitimacy received only the briefest of treatments as factors "affecting the magnitude of reactance" (Brehm, 1966, p. 8). Reactance experiments were thus designed to have "justification and legitimacy held constant" because "their total effects are complicated" (Brehm, 1966, p. 9). The discussion of those factors was limited to an example about Mr. Brown, who wanted

Betty Smith as a babysitter on a particular evening. The context implied that having Betty babysit was a normal part of Brown's free-behavior set.

A threat to that free behavior was the following: "If Mr. Smith says to Mr. Brown, 'You cannot have Betty for babysitting this evening,' ... then Brown should experience reactance" (Brehm, 1966, p. 7). Brehm's point was that Brown experiences reactance if he thinks that Smith had no right to determine what Betty did or did not do. If Smith is Betty's father and she is a young teenager, however, "then Smith can legitimately control Betty's activities and ... Brown is not likely to show a strong negative reaction" (Brehm, 1966, p. 7). Legitimacy thus refers to governing certain kinds of activities (behaviors). Similarly, "if Smith adds that Betty's mother has gone to the hospital for an emergency operation, thus justifying the restriction, Brown will not show a strong negative reaction" (Brehm, 1966, p. 7). Justification thus refers to the importance of certain kinds of outcomes.

DT relates legitimacy and justification to deontological and consequentialist ethics. To deontologists, categories of *behaviors* (such as "virtues" and "vices") must be subject to bounded autonomy based on a given category's moral *legitimacy*. Consequentialists focus on *outcomes*: the greater the extent of certain outcomes, the greater the moral *justification* (e.g., "the greatest good for the greatest number"; "the ends justify the means"). DT conceptualizes legitimacy and justification in terms of duties, which thereby puts the free behaviors of reactance in a new light. Legitimacy directly stipulates specific categories of behavior as not-free (required or forbidden); these are behavior-based duties. Justification allows free behaviors consistent with the provision for certain kinds of outcomes to the greatest degree possible; these are outcome-based duties.

Sometimes, a behavior-based duty makes it hard for a person to meet his or her obligations vis-à-vis some justifiable outcome. If a behavior-based duty is perceived as threatening to certain free behaviors that might foster the outcome, reactance can be aroused ("a loss of freedom no matter how legitimate, can also result in reactance"; Brehm, 1966, p. 8). The DT analysis indicates that justifiability as a variable can affect how someone might look to reassert those freedoms: To the extent that the outcome-based obligations can be fulfilled more completely (e.g., a larger amount of those outcomes), the person will be increasingly inclined to perceive those behaviors as justified—and so the person will be more likely to engage in them.

This analysis applies readily to behavioral ethics in a business context. Managers want free behaviors that can influence business outcomes (e.g., staying afloat; being positioned to go public). Norms of moral legitimacy can act as boundary conditions restricting free behaviors, however, perhaps limiting the ways that managers can seek what they believe are justifiable outcomes as corporate goals. Such goals might seem especially justifiable if the manager believes that they also constitute moral obligations (e.g., higher dividends for stockholders). Milton Friedman famously brought this idea to the forefront in an essay entitled "The Social Responsibility of Business Is to Increase Its Profits": "[The corporate executive's] responsibility ... generally will be to make as much money as possible while conforming to the basic rules of the society ... embodied in law and ... in ethical custom" (Friedman, 1970). His comment illustrates the potential conflict between the outcome-based duty to make "as much money as possible" and the behavior-based duty of "ethical custom." DT provides a framework for investigating how this tension plays itself out, which is the subject of the next section.

THE DT APPROACH TO TRADE-OFFS AMONG DUTIES

DT brings the empiricism of behavioral ethics to bear on major philosophical positions and the substantive issues characteristic of organizational settings. As the first part of a two-step process, DT takes an outcome-based duty approach to managerial decision making, analogous to consequentialist ethics. Business goals such as increased revenue, market share, stock price, and so forth can be conceptualized as outcome-based duties. Gauging successful results in terms of economic efficiency, such as according to a cost–benefit analysis, can also be justified that way—as can efforts relevant to corporate social responsibility measures, customer satisfaction, or product defects. DT classifies all such activities as efforts to meet outcome-based obligations, usually based on the interests of some party or parties (e.g., shareholders)—that is, in terms of perceived responsibilities to those parties. In organizational behavior, various stakeholder theories (e.g., Donaldson & Preston, 1995) deal with the implications of such responsibilities.

The first step of the DT analysis addresses how perceived outcome duties can influence management actions in line with Kahneman and Tversky's prospect theory (1979). According to prospect theory, decision makers are influenced more by the motive to avoid losses than by the motive to seek gains; losses loom larger than gains. These are outcome-based categories applicable when managers worry about potential losses or hope for gains. The loss/gain, negative/positive asymmetry relating to the outcomes is an example of an effect prevalent across a wide variety of psychological phenomena: Negative stimuli elicit stronger reactions than positive stimuli (Baumeister, Bratslavsky, Finkenauer, & Vohs, 2001). DT proposes that this asymmetry influences the perceived ethicality of decisions regarding such issues as company policies toward the environment, given the costs and benefits of various options.

The second step in building this DT conceptual framework addresses deontological (e.g., Kantian) ethics as another source of a negative/positive asymmetry, namely, the Kantian distinction between *perfect* duties and *imperfect* duties. The psychological implications of those categories can be expressed for convenience in behavior-based terms: "eschewing vice" as an analog to perfect duties (with a strong motivational impact like loss-avoidance), and "endorsing virtue" as an analog to imperfect duties (like gain seeking as a weaker motivation). As psychological (perceived) oughts, prohibitions that call for eschewing vice-like behavior (e.g., the moral principles of not committing murder, not stealing, not cheating) carry more weight than positively framed exhortations for virtuous behavior (e.g., the Golden Rule, which endorses the principle of treating others as you would want to be treated).

Janoff-Bulman, Sheikh, and Hepp (2009) obtained evidence for a similar distinction about behavior-based duties, indicating that moral constraints on categories of behavior framed *pro*scriptively ("don't," vis-à-vis vice) have more influence than those framed *pre*scriptively ("do," vis-à-vis virtue); the former are "harsher, more demanding" and "more mandatory," so there is "a stronger motivation to avoid 'errors'" construed as "bad, immoral behaviors" (Janoff-Bulman et al., 2009, p. 524). Conversely, prescriptive priorities involve obligations with some wiggle room across situations, just as imperfect duties lack specificity and allow discretion according to ethicists (Greenspan, 2010; Rainbolt, 2000). It is virtuous to be charitable, for example, but we have some free behaviors regarding when, how, to whom, and to what degree we are charitable. To eschew vice is thus a stronger motivation than to act virtuously, which makes *not* acting in accord with the duty of virtue a more situation-specific option.

DT links asymmetric virtue/vice psychology with the philosophical characterization that "moral obligations ... rest on criticism from the standpoints of other persons" (Greenspan, 2010, p. 183); hence, they are duties that a decision maker will "lack the authority to discount unilaterally" (Greenspan, 2010, p. 183) and "consideration[s] that the agent has to take into account" (Greenspan, 2010, p. 204). DT thus derives the psychological implication that to justify having an outcome-based duty override a behavior-based duty, framing the latter in terms of virtue allows decision makers to convince themselves and others that they have taken both duties into account and appropriately discounted the latter one relative to the former. The same psychology applies, therefore, to the gain/loss asymmetry: It is easier to justify having an outcome-based duty override a behavior-based duty when the former is framed in terms of losses to be avoided rather than as gains to be achieved.

DT thus proposes a 2 × 2 matrix that has psychological implications—the prediction of two main effects—for the behavioral ethics of managerial decision making (see Table 6.1). First, the authority of managers to pursue a given project does not constitute an unfettered right to discount moral norms of virtue and vice unilaterally, but discounting the situational importance of virtue is more likely to dampen criticism from others (and placate one's own conscience). Second, managers can also have legitimate obligations to pursue certain projects based on the extent of the gains that might result or the extent of the losses that might be avoided. The greater impact of loss avoidance might justify overriding either type of behavior-based duty on a specific occasion, perhaps because of perceived obligations to stakeholders—in other words, a justification based on the outcome-based duty of a consequentialist ethic.

TABLE 6.1

Dilemma: Whether an Outcome-Based Duty Can Override a Behavior-Based Duty

Category of Behavior-Based (Potentially Overridden) Duty	Category of Outcome-Based (Potentially Overriding) Duty	
	Gains Achieved	Losses Avoided
Imperfect/do virtue (encouraged)	Cell 1	Cell 2[a]
Perfect/not do vice (banned)	Cell 3[b]	Cell 4

[a] More than in any other cell, the perception of the outcome-based duty in this one might justify overriding the behavior-based duty (i.e., the manager might refrain from helping his or her colleague by submitting a letter that gave him the credit he deserved).

[b] More than in any other cell, the perceived justifiability of the outcome-based duty in this one might not be enough to override the behavior-based duty (i.e., the manager might not try to discredit his or her colleague).

The Appendix, in conjunction with Table 6.1, gives a 2 × 2 matrix based on DT analysis.[4] The scenarios describe a decision involving an outcome—funds for product development—with prospects framed either as potential gains (text in italics) or losses to be avoided (regular font style). The situation also involves the possibility of a decision inconsistent with a behavior-based duty: an option to discredit (text in bold) or not to give credit (underlined text). The former goes against "don't harm" as a perfect duty, and the latter goes against "do help" as an imperfect duty.

Two main effects would make Cells 2 and 3 the most different from one another. More than in any of the other three situations, the perception of the outcome-based duty in Cell 2 might justify overriding the behavior-based duty. Here, the way the two factors combine would tend to make the manager perceive that he could justify refraining to help his colleague (not send a letter that gave him the credit he deserved) because that way the manager could try to prevent a budget cut and thereby not lose the opportunity to develop a worthwhile project. To refrain from helping does not seem so bad (relative to discrediting); to avoid a loss seems especially significant.

Cell 3 illustrates the opposite kind of situation. This cell represents a situation in which the manager is the least likely to perceive that the outcome-based duty justifies overriding the behavior-based duty. Discrediting the colleague violates a "do no harm" moral norm regarding how to behave, and this "eschew vice" duty has a high degree of seriousness. To violate it would take some considerable justification, and the prospect of gains (added funds) might not manifest itself as demonstrably, with sufficient gravity, as the prospect of avoiding losses.

Scenarios such as this could be accompanied by many different kinds of dependent variables. Research participants could be asked whether they would choose to override the virtue/vice imperatives, for example, and the entries of the cells would be percentages. Another format could end each scenario with the statement that the manager chose the option of discrediting/not crediting (i.e., overriding the behavior-based duty for the sake of outcomes). The possible dependent variables include ratings of the morality of such a decision, as well as ratings of the manager's ethics (along with ratings on a number of adjectives descriptive of behavior, such as likable, trustworthy, good, despicable, contemptible, disreputable, and so on).

Experiments on "taboo values" by Lichtenstein, Gregory, and Irwin (2007) demonstrated this kind of adaptability to various measurement approaches. One of their 22 vignettes in Experiment 1, for example, referred to a life insurance company and setting different rates for whites and blacks. Two questionnaire items measured agreement and approval with such decisions (or proposals or plans, depending on the vignette), and eight assessed reasons why the participant might disapprove (e.g., anger about the action; disgust toward it; belief that it would be unethical). Each of the vignettes was designed to create disapproval despite offering a potential benefit, and the experimenters wanted to see whether the potential for benefit might offset the potential disapproval and what degree of benefit would be required in that case.

One vignette described a utility company that could save rate payers money if it reduced expenditures on the pollution controls it used, for example, and respondents were asked the following question: "What is the SMALLEST reduction in your yearly costs for electricity that you would require to approve of this proposal to reduce expenditures on pollution controls? My saving would have to be at least $_____ per year to approve of this proposal" (Lichtenstein et al., 2007, p. 174). Two other questions were directly relevant to that one: "I don't think it's right to put a dollar value on something like this," and "You couldn't pay me enough to approve of this proposal" (p. 174), followed by 5-point agree/disagree ratings.

DT studies could easily adapt these kinds of items. They are often used in research traditions that deal with such concepts as protected values (Baron & Leshner, 2000; Baron & Spranca, 1997; Irwin & Baron 2001), moral mandates (Mullen & Skitka, 2006), sacred values (Tanner, Ryf, & Hanselmann, 2009), and various kinds of trade-offs such as *taboo* and *tragic*, as well as other value conflicts that violate spheres of justice (e.g., Fiske & Tetlock, 1997; Tetlock, Peterson, & Lerner, 1996). These terms essentially involve states of affairs that some people will not consider any deviation from—a personal value so absolute that it "precludes comparisons, tradeoffs, or indeed any other mingling with … sacred values" (Tetlock, Kristel, Elson, Green, & Lerner, 2000, p. 853), "particularly [tradeoffs with] economic values" (Lichtenstein et al., 2007, p. 170).

Nonetheless, DT is significantly distinguishable from the underlying research questions motivating these paradigms. The difference stands out when comparing definitions. *Sacred values*, for example, are "those values that a moral community treats as possessing transcendental significance that preludes comparisons, trade-offs, or indeed any mingling with secular values" (Tetlock, 2003, p. 320). *Protected values* are "those that resist tradeoffs with other values, particularly economic values" (Baron & Spranca, 1997,

p. 1). *Moral mandates* "are selective expressions of values that are central to people's sense of personal identity" (Skitka, 2002, p. 588). The typical study focuses on identifying people who hold values that are infinitely important and hence simply refuse to answer any questions about trade-offs. The DT distinction between perfect and imperfect duties, however, does not require associating the more extreme (perfect) with infinite value. In fact, a key point of the DT approach is the examination of situations in which people have at least some latent inclination *not* to act in accord with behavior-based duties, thereby making it possible to assess at what point the gain or loss frames are compelling enough to cause the abandonment of support for behavior-based duties. Also, the concept of behavior-based duties is much broader than that of sacred or protected values.

DT also does not require that the situation being assessed involve a deep-seated moral conviction that is central to a person's own self-identity and self-definition, which contrasts with moral mandate research. Rather than being a self-defining value, a perfect behavior-based duty (e.g., don't lie) might be considered universal rather than individuating.

More generally, DT studies could examine reactions to different kinds of *procedures*, from the standpoint of behavior-based duties, along with the gain and loss frames of outcome-based duties. DT studies might create manipulations of—or use measures of—decision procedures (pretested to frame them as perfect or imperfect duties) in conjunction with manipulations or measures of gain-framed versus loss-framed outcomes attainable by undermining those procedures. With this kind of paradigm as well as others, measuring behavior-based duty would mean that the perfect/virtue and imperfect/vice dimension could be treated as a continuous variable, which contrasts with the very nature of existing value-conflict research. This feature illustrates that DT not only is a conceptually broad theory of behavioral ethics but also lends itself to a wide range of measurement and design approaches.

DT AND OTHER TOPICS

DT has been applied to shed new light on the nature of moral emotions, such as the distinction between shame and guilt. For example, the DT perspective can be applied to an emotional experience that otherwise seems particularly odd, namely, *survivor guilt* as "first used to describe the guilt that people may feel when literally surviving the death of another ... [and currently] expanded to include guilt about any advantage a person believes they have when compared with others, such as success, superior abilities, or a greater degree of health and well-being" (O'Connor, Berry, & Weiss, Schweitzer, & Sevier, 2000). Guilt as an imperfect duty also relates to Boehm's (1999, 2000) evolutionary analysis of sharing (see Folger & Cropanzano, 2010). Moreover, DT has already begun to play a significant role as a construct adopted in the organizational justice literature (see Cropanzano, Byrne, Bobocel, & Rupp, 2001). It contrasts with two standard approaches to procedural justice in particular—one based on procedures as a means to increase the chances of desirable outcomes for oneself (Thibaut & Walker, 1975), and the other based on procedures as sources of information about one's acceptability to the members of desirable groups (e.g., Lind & Tyler, 1988; Tyler & Lind, 1992). DT relates to moral considerations about fairness more generally, however, which transcend self-interest regarding outcomes or relationships with groups. For example, third-party evaluation—a perspective uniquely highlighted by DT—applies to the fairness of decision makers and to procedures themselves, in ways that can have nothing to do with the self-interest of those evaluators (for a review of third-party reactions to injustice from a DT perspective, see Skarlicki & Kulik, 2005).

CONCLUDING REMARKS

As a conceptual framework for studying behavioral business ethics, DT proposes the construct of psychological deonance in contrast with psychological reactance. Reactance causes people to resist the *presence* of restrictions on autonomy; they try to reassert being able to do as they please. Deonance involves perceived moral obligations as legitimate limits to autonomy and how people react to the "ought force" of such restrictions and their *absence*.

DT explains, for example, why third parties might punish violations of moral norms (such as justice) but does not claim that punishment (e.g., involving self-sacrifice) always will occur (self-interest might prevail) or predict which norm applies (e.g., equity vs. equality vs. need). Misinterpretations characterize DT as advocating "that people value justice in society ... and therefore are convinced that just and fair interaction is a principle of moral duty" or suggest "that such a view [viz. DT] is too narrow. ... We *also* need a behavioral approach that examines how individuals make actual decisions and engage in real actions when faced with ethical dilemmas" (De Cremer, 2010, p. 112, emphasis added). DT does adopt a behavioral ethics approach about dealing with actual ethical dilemmas, applicable to *any* norm perceived as morally legitimate—including those endorsed by a Nazi (e.g., obedience to der Führer), by socialist ideologies, or by free-market capitalist ideologies. Kantian and consequentialist ethical theories, for example, represent attempts to specify ideal kinds of moral obligations. A DT analysis can use a 2 × 2 matrix of those ideals to predict how people might respond to their competing obligations as a function of situational factors (e.g., gain or loss framing).

In short, DT is a broad framework for taking into account one source of motivation that can influence behavior—ethically or unethically—in business contexts, namely, an ought force.

People can feel moral obligations of various types and in various ways, and DT looks to bring a greater understanding of the results that those influences can have.

NOTES

1. From an entry on Mally's Deontic Logic in the online *Stanford Encyclopedia of Philosophy*.
2. Sometime before 2000, I began calling myself a "behavioral ethicist," and discussions with various people about this idea (e.g., with Roy Lewicki at the 2003 Academy of Management meeting) eventually led to my proposal for a caucus that appeared in the 2005 program of the Academy of Management as "Behavioral Ethics and Organizations." Of course, David Messick and Ann Tenbrunsel had already edited *Codes of Conduct: Behavioral Research Into Business Ethics* (Messick & Tenbrunsel, 1996), which dealt with some of the same issues I had in mind (although I was thinking about behavioral ethics not just in business contexts).
3. Bounded autonomy and another recently introduced concept, bounded ethicality (Chugh et al., 2005; Kern & Chugh, 2009), should be differentiated. Each plays off Simon's original phrase, but in different ways. Simon's phrase applies to capabilities, such as our limited span of memory and limited capacity for processing information. Similarly, bounded autonomy refers to how moral norms place constraints (limits) on our freedom to do certain kinds of things in the domain of social conduct. In contrast, bounded ethicality deals with the cognitive deficiencies (biased tendencies) that in some sense interfere with our desire to be ethical: We think of ourselves as ethical when actually we apply the relevant criteria in a distorted way because the

exact, correct basis for doing so is "unavailable" to us. Bounded autonomy thus applies to social constraints, whereas bounded ethicality refers to cognitive constraints (i.e., deficiencies).

4. This scenario is merely illustrative, so nothing about the specific operationalization (e.g., questions about construct or internal validity) has a bearing on the fundamental analysis itself. For example, suppose the gain-framed version actually is perceived as providing greater justification than the loss-framed version, which would be opposite to the DT analysis. The point is simply that the same outcome-based duties *can* be framed differently (as illustrated by the scenario), regardless of whether this particular example has any problematic features vis-à-vis the possible *effects* of framing as operationalized in this scenario.

APPENDIX

You are a department head in a manufacturing company. Recently, you took part in an effort to revise the training program at the company. There was some unevenness of contribution among the project members (another department head, as well as with supervisors from various other departments), and it affected the time it took to accomplish the final result. You thought that you and the other department head were the best contributors, and that he performed at least as well as you did. Now, you have an opportunity to write a letter of support on his behalf. It is somewhat customary, but not mandatory, to write a letter commenting on a colleague's work under such circumstances. The letter would go to his boss, the chief financial officer (CFO).

The CFO (who is also your boss) is planning the department budgets for the upcoming year. Your team has been developing a new production method for the company. In order not to have to abandon the project and render the work a waste of time [*in order to continue working on it and benefit from the work done on it so far*], you cannot afford to lose any company allocations for this work [*you will need the current level of company allocations for this work*] in next year's budget. The budgets are limited, and the CFO has to split the budget between your department and the department of your colleague.

You believe that if the project were abandoned [*not continued*] the company might be put at a disadvantage as far as performance against competitors [*might not be able to take advantage of an opportunity to outperform competitors*].

You know that if you write a strong letter of support for your colleague, the funds for your project would be lost from [*not be kept in*] your budget for next year.

If you do not send a letter acknowledging the other department head's contributions to revising the training program, knowing that it is not a requirement [*if you send a letter that denies any contributions of the other department head in revising the training program*], it would be because that is what it would take not to lose some of your budget for next year [*to keep your budget the same for next year*].

THIS TEXT = loss

THIS TEXT = gain

THIS TEXT = imperfect

THIS TEXT = perfect

REFERENCES

Baron, J., & Leshner, S. (2000). How serious are expressions of protected values? *Journal of Experimental Psychology-Applied, 6*(3): 183–194.

Baron, J., & Spranca, M. (1997). Protected values. *Organizational Behavior and Human Decision Processes, 70,* 1–16.

Baumeister, R. F., Bratslavsky, E., Finkenauer, C., & Vohs, K. D. (2001). Bad is stronger than good. *Review of General Psychology, 5,* 323–370.

Beller, S. (2008). Deontic norms, deontic reasoning, and deontic conditionals. *Thinking & Reasoning, 14,* 305–341.

Beller, S. (2010). Deontic reasoning reviewed: Psychological questions, empirical findings, and current theories. *Cognitive Processing, 11,* **123–132.**

Bender, A., & Beller, S. (2003). Polynesian tapu in the "deontic square": A cognitive concept, its linguistic expression and cultural context. In R. Alterman & D. Kirsh (Eds.), *Proceedings of the Twenty-Fifth Annual Conference of the Cognitive Science Society* (pp. 133–138). Mahweh, NJ: Erlbaum.

Bennett, R. J., & Robinson, S. L. (2000). Development of a measure of workplace deviance. *Journal of Applied Psychology, 85,* 349–360.

Bingham, P. M. (1999). Human uniqueness: A general theory. *Quarterly Review of Biology, 74,* 133–169.

Boehm, C. (1999). *Hierarchy in the forest: The evolution of egalitarian behavior.* Cambridge, MA: Harvard University Press.

Boehm, C. (2000). Conflict and the evolution of social control. In L. D. Katz (Ed.), *Evolutionary origins of morality: Cross-disciplinary perspectives* (pp. 79–101). Bowling Green, OH: Imprint Academic.

Brehm, J. W. (1966). *A theory of psychological reactance*. New York: Academic Press.

Bucciarelli, M., & Johnson-Laird, P. N. (2005). Naive deontics: A theory of meaning, representation, and reasoning. *Cognitive Psychology, 50*, 159–193.

Chugh, D., Banaji, M., & Bazerman, M. (2005). Bounded ethicality as a psychological barrier to recognizing conflicts of interest. In D. Moore, D. Cain, G. Loewenstein, & M. Bazerman. (Eds.), *Conflicts of interest: Challenges and solutions in business, law, medicine, and public policy*. New York: Cambridge University Press.

Cosmides, L., & Tooby, J. (1994). Beyond intuition and instinct blindness: Toward an evolutionarily rigorous cognitive science. *Cognition, 50*(1–3), 41–77.

Cropanzano, R., Byrne, Z. S., Bobocel, D. R., & Rupp, D. R. (2001). Moral virtues, fairness heuristics, social entities, and other denizens of organizational justice. *Journal of Vocational Behavior, 58*, 164–209.

De Cremer, D. (2010). On the psychology of preventing and dealing with ethical failures: A behavioral ethics approach. In M. Schminke (Ed.), *Managerial ethics: Managing the psychology of morality* (pp. 111–125). New York: Routledge.

De Cremer, D., Tenbrunsel, A. & van Dijke, M. H. (2011). Regulating ethical failures: Insights from psychology. *Journal of Business Ethics*.

de Waal, F. (1991). The chimpanzee's sense of social regularity and its relation to the human sense of justice. *American Behavioral Scientist, 34*, 335–349.

Donaldson, T., & Preston, L. E. (1995). The stakeholder theory of the corporation: Concepts, evidence, and implications. *Academy of Management Review, 20*, 65–91.

Etzioni, A. (1985, November 15). Shady corporate practices. *The New York Times*.

Fiske, A. P., & Tetlock, P. E. (1997). Taboo trade-offs: Reactions to transactions that transgress the spheres of justice. *Political Psychology, 18*, 255–297.

Folger, R. (1998). Fairness as a moral virtue. In M. Schminke (Ed.), *Managerial ethics: Morally managing people and processes* (pp. 13–34). Mahwah, NJ: Erlbaum.

Folger, R., & Cropanzano, R. (2010). Social hierarchies and the evolution of moral emotions. In M. Schminke (Ed.), *Managerial ethics: Managing the psychology of morality* (pp. 207–234). Mahwah, NJ: Erlbaum.

Folger, R., Cropanzano, R., & Goldman, B. (2005). What is the relationship between justice and morality? In J. Greenberg & J. A. Colquitt (Eds.), *Handbook of organizational justice* (pp. 215–245). Mahwah, NJ: Erlbaum.

Folger, R., & Skarlicki, D. P. (2008). The evolutionary basis of deontic justice. In S. Gilliland, D. Steiner, & D. Skarlicki (Eds.), *Research in social issues in management: Justice, morality, and social responsibility* (pp. 29–62). Greenwich CT: Information Age.

Friedman, M. (1970). The social responsibility of business is to increase its profits. *The New York Times Magazine*, September 13.

Gini, A. (2010). On being a generalist. *Business Ethics Quarterly, 20*(4): 738–740.

Goodpaster, K. E. (2010). Business ethics: Two moral provisos. *Business Ethics Quarterly, 20*(4): 740–742.

Greenspan, P. (2010). Making room for options: moral reasons, imperfect duties, and choice. *Social Philosophy & Policy, 27*(2): 181–205.

Grover, S. (1993). Why professionals lie: The impact of professional role conflict on reporting activity. *Organizational Behavior and Human Decision Processes, 55*, 251–272.

Hartman, E. M. (2010). Ending the separation. *Business Ethics Quarterly, 20*(4): 742–743.

Heider, F. (1958). *The psychology of interpersonal relations.* New York: Wiley.

Irwin, J. R., & Baron, J. (2001). Response mode effects and moral values. *Organizational Behavior and Human Decision Processes, 84*(2): 177–197.

Janoff-Bulman, R., Sheikh, S., & Hepp, S. (2009). Proscriptive versus prescriptive morality: Two faces of moral regulation. *Journal of Personality and Social Psychology, 96*, 521–537.

Kahneman, D., & Tversky, A. (1979). Prospect theory: Analysis of decision under risk. *Econometrica, 47*, 263–291

Kern, M., & Chugh, D. (2009). Bounded ethicality: The perils of loss framing. *Psychological Science, 20*(3), 378–384.

Lichtenstein, S., Gregory, R., & Irwin, J. (2007). What's bad is easy: Taboo values, affect, and cognition. *Judgment and Decision Making Journal, 2*(3): 169–188.

Lind, E. A., & Tyler, T. R. (1988). *The social psychology of procedural justice.* New York: Plenum Press.

McElreath, R., Boyd, R., & Richerson, P. J. (2003). Shared norms can lead to the evolution of ethnic markers. *Current Anthropology, 44*(1): 122–130.

Messick, D. M., & Tenbrunsel, A. E. (1996). *Codes of conduct: Behavioral research into business ethics.* New York: Russell Sage.

Mullen, E., & Skitka, L. J. (2006). Exploring the psychological underpinnings of the moral mandate effect: Motivated reasoning, group differentiation, or anger? *Journal of Personality and Social Psychology, 90*, 629–643.

Nichols, S., & Mallon, R. (2006). Moral dilemmas and moral rules. *Cognition, 100*, 530–542.

O'Connor, L. E., Berry, J. W., Weiss, J., Schweitzer, D., & Sevier, M. (2000). Survivor guilt, submissive behaviour and evolutionary theory: The down-side of winning in social comparison. *British Journal of Medical Psychology, 73*, 519–530.

Rainbolt, G. (2000). Perfect and imperfect obligations. *Philosophical Studies, 98*, 233–256.

Salvador, R., & Folger, R. (2009). Business ethics and the brain. *Behavioral Ethics Quarterly, 19*, 1–31.

Scanlon, T. M. (1998). *What we owe to each other.* Cambridge, MA: Harvard University Press.

Schminke, M., Ambrose, M. L., & Neubaum, D. O. (2005). The effect of leader moral development on ethical climate and employee attitudes. *Organizational Behavior and Human Decision Processes, 97*(2): 135–151.

Simon, H. A. (1947). *Administrative behavior.* New York: Free Press.

Simon, H. A. (1951). A formal theory of the employment relation. *Econometrica, 19*, 293–305.

Skarlicki, D. P., & Kulik, C. 2005. Third party reactions to employee mistreatment: A justice perspective. In B. Staw & R. Kramer (Eds.), *Research in organizational behavior* (Vol. 26, pp. 183–230). Greenwich, CT: JAI Press.

Skitka, L. (2002). Do the means always justify the ends, or do the ends sometimes justify the means? A value protection model of justice reasoning. *Personality and Social Psychology Bulletin, 28*, 588–597.

Tanner, C., Ryf, B., & Hanselmann, M. (2009). Sacred Value Measure (SVM): Construction and validation of an instrument to assess sacred values. *Diagnostica, 55*, 174–183.

Tepper, B. J. (2007). Abusive supervision in work organizations: Review, synthesis and research agenda. *Journal of Management, 33*, 261–289.

Tetlock, P. E. (2003). Thinking the unthinkable: sacred values and taboo cognitions. *Trends in Cognitive Sciences, 7*, 320–324.

Tetlock, P. E., Kristel, O., Elson, B., Green, M., & Lerner, J. (2000). The psychology of the unthinkable: Taboo trade-offs, forbidden base rates, and heretical counterfactuals. *Journal of Personality and Social Psychology, 78*, 853–870.

Tetlock, P. E., Peterson, R., & Lerner, J. (1996). Revising the value pluralism model: Incorporating social content and context postulates. In C. Seligman, J. Olson, & M. Zanna (Eds.), *Ontario symposium on social and personality psychology: Values.* Hillsdale, NJ: Erlbaum.

Thibaut, J., & Kelley, H. H. (1959). *The social psychology of groups.* New York: John Wiley & Sons.

Thibaut, J., & Walker, L. (1975). *Procedural justice: A psychological analysis.* Hillsdale, NJ: Erlbaum.

Treviño, L. K., Weaver, G. R., & Reynolds, S J. (2006). Behavioral ethics in organizations: A review. *Journal of Management, 32,* 951–990.

Tyler, T. R., & Blader, S. L. (2005). Can businesses effectively regulate employee conduct? The antecedents of rule following in work settings. *Academy of Management Journal, 48,* 1143–1158.

Tyler, T., & Lind, E. A. (1992). A relational model of authority in groups. In M. Zanna (Ed.), *Advances in experimental social psychology* (Vol. 25, pp. 115–191). New York: Academic Press.

7

Moral Foundations at Work: New Factors to Consider in Understanding the Nature and Role of Ethics in Organizations

Gary R. Weaver
University of Delaware

and

Michael E. Brown
Pennsylvania State University

INTRODUCTION

Recent research rooted in a mix of anthropology, sociology, and evolutionary and social psychology has highlighted the fact that the social psychological study of ethics typically takes a relatively narrow view of the domain of morality (e.g., Haidt & Graham, 2007, 2009). Conventional scholarship conceptualizes morality in terms of matters of harm, welfare, fairness, or equality with respect to individuals—core ideals of various forms of the dominant Western tradition of ethical, political, and social thought. Conventional treatments of ethical behavior in organizations often appear similarly focused. But this focus ignores the possibility that, anthropologically speaking, a preeminent concern for welfare and fairness is a minority position in the world and is not even the only moral outlook expressed in modern Western cultures. If so, organizational research not only needs to focus on matters of welfare and fairness, but also attend to other categories of moral thought and behavior. In what follows, we summarize a recent alternative, empirically founded account of the scope of human moral intuitions—moral foundations theory—and develop its implications specifically for behavior in organizations.

MORAL FOUNDATIONS THEORY

Recent research on moral behavior increasingly notes that persons' moral responses to situations (e.g., judging something right or wrong; responding to a wrong) often (even usually) occur in rapid, unintentional, and largely automatic fashion, more along the lines of intuitive, emotionally laden reactions of (for example) fear or disgust (Haidt, 2001, 2003), quick heuristic judgments (Sunstein, 2005), or rapidly triggered schematic cognition (Lapsley & Narvaez, 2004) than as the outcome of conscious, intentional reasoning processes (as in Kohlberg-type moral reasoning models, e.g., Kohlberg, Levine, & Hewer, 1983; see Lapsley & Hill, 2008, for a review). Conscious, intentional reasoning does sometimes occur vis-à-vis moral questions and situations and does influence behavior. But, moral thought and behavior best are explained in terms of a dual process (Haidt, 2001; Reynolds, 2006b): automatic, intuitive responses with respect to familiar situations (or familiar sources of opinion, such as trusted friends) and conscious reasoning in response to situations for which no repertoire of intuitive responses has developed (or with regard to moral advice proffered by strangers).

Moral foundations theory (Graham, Haidt, & Nosek, 2009; Haidt & Graham, 2007, 2009; Haidt & Joseph, 2007; Haidt & Kesebir, 2010; Haidt, Seder, & Kesebir, 2008) proposes that humans have intuitive, nondeliberative moral responses to situations, and that those intuitive responses reflect innate sensitivities to multiple categories of moral concern that, in human history, developed out of different kinds of individually or collectively adaptive challenges (see, for example, Fiske, 1991; Fiske & Haslam, 2005; Shweder, Much, Mahapatra, & Park, 1997). Persons' intuitive responses to particular moral situations and issues originate in one or another of these innate response categories, although the particular behavioral form a response category takes varies across different cultures and times.

In its current state of empirical and theoretical development, moral foundations theory identifies five categories of moral responses (Haidt &

Kesebir, 2010). The *fairness* foundation is based on the demands of gaining the benefits of cooperation but with diligence regarding cheaters or others who fail to reciprocate altruistic behavior. Judgments of unfairness, in effect, are responses to breakdowns in reciprocity, and the adaptive process over time made this kind of response innate, or intuitive. A foundation oriented toward avoiding *harm* (or, put positively, ensuring *care*) reflects adaptive pressures to provide for or protect children or other near relations and is related to emotional reactions of empathy.

But, in addition to the foregoing moral concerns, moral foundations theory attends to anthropological and other evidence indicating the innate importance of concerns for one's collective (an in-group-oriented response), for authority (and with it, hierarchy), and for purity (or sanctity) (Graham et al., 2009; Haidt & Joseph, 2004, 2007). The *in-group* foundation reflects the adaptive difficulties of establishing and maintaining cohesion and cooperation in large groups in contexts of intergroup competition, such that solidarity with, loyalty to, and protection of one's group are important protections against the actions of free riders and cheaters in competitive struggles with other collectives. The *authority* foundation, and the *hierarchical* social structures that embody it, involves a two-directional relationship in which lower-status individuals show deference toward higher-status persons, and higher-status persons provide protection or in other ways assume responsibility for lower-status persons, resulting in a social collective that enforces an orderly cohesion among its members that can be advantageous in intergroup competition. (Hierarchical authority, in this sense, is not simply equivalent to the idea of power because hierarchical authority incorporates both upward allegiance and downward responsibility; Haidt & Graham, 2009; cf. Nisbet, 1993). And, the *purity/sanctity* foundation is rooted in an adaptive concern for preventing the corruption of people by those who might have had contact with unclean things (e.g., disease-carrying persons or illness-generating nonpersons, such as certain edibles). As the basis of prohibitions on certain behavior, this is related to reactions such as disgust and avoidance, and such reactions can be applied both to literal disease sources and dangers and symbolically to people, practices, and things associated with disease or danger. But, it also can appear positively, as an intuitive expectation that one ought not merely eschew the unclean but actively seek what is considered pure, noble, or sacred (as in the aspirations of various religious cultures) in contrast to what is base, merely utilitarian, or self-interested (Haidt & Graham, 2009; Haidt & Joseph, 2007).

Why Moral Foundations Theory Matters

Moral foundations theory implies that much organizational research, especially regarding ethical behavior, has been too narrow in focus, ignoring key elements of the moral domain as experienced by many people. To grasp the implications of this, consider a parallel critique in the more narrowly defined world of organizational justice research. Cropanzano and Stein (2009) argued that organizational justice research in fact is far removed from considering justice in its full sense because organizational justice research—with its roots in equity theory—understands justice largely in terms of self-interested outcomes (see also Folger, Cropanzano, & Goldman, 2005). This understanding of justice is quite different from the sense of impartiality embodied, for example, in accounts of justice rooted in philosophical and political theory. According to Cropanzano and Stein's criticism, the oft-studied distributive, procedural, and interactional justice—as typically articulated in organizational justice research—matter to individuals and to researchers because those forms of justice affect valued outcomes for people, most notably, material welfare and social standing (2009, p. 197), and not because of some intrinsic moral quality. Cropanzano and Stein contrast this with behavioral ethics research, which focuses on moral convictions (p. 194) as ends in themselves rather than as phenomena in the service of some perhaps nonmoral or self-interested end. Recognizing a larger conception of justice in turn generates more research issues and a better understanding of justice-related phenomena (as in recent deontic justice research; e.g., Folger et al., 2005).

Shifting venues, Haidt and Kesebir (2010) argue that social justice research also is characterized by a narrow focus with regard to what justice incorporates. They argue that social justice research typically focuses only on matters of harm and fairness, and that this is part of a general pattern of emphasis in social psychology, captured well in Turiel's definition of morality as involving "prescriptive judgments of justice, rights and welfare" (Turiel, 1983, p. 3; cf. Haidt & Kesebir, 2010). The relevant issues and debates in the field, then, are essentially in-house struggles within the context of this definition (e.g., Kohlberg [justice; Kohlberg et al., 1983] vs. Gilligan [welfare, or, more specifically, care; Gilligan, 1993]), implicitly or explicitly mirroring more philosophical debates among various kinds of deontological and social welfare-based utilitarian forms of ethical inquiry. Left out is the large array of phenomena and concerns that many individuals and cultures experience as essentially moral, and that moral foundations theory tries to incorporate.

Much research on ethics in organizations fits a harm-and-fairness framework. For example, Jones's (1991) widely applied account of moral intensity—a characteristic of moral issues held to influence individuals' awareness of and responses to moral issues—states that "a moral issue is present when a person's actions, when freely performed, may harm or benefit others. … In other words, the action or decision must have consequences for others" (p. 367). Following this definition, Jones's model of moral intensity articulates that concept in terms of the magnitude, temporal immediacy, probability, proximity, and concentration of harm or benefit from a contemplated decision or issue, along with the degree of social consensus regarding which outcomes are to be avoided or sought. Cognitively oriented empirical research focused on the ethical predispositions of actors exemplifies another fairness-and-harm approach, in that ethical predispositions are understood as commitments to either ethical formalism (deontology and related notions of fairness) or consequentialism (e.g., utilitarianism or other harm/benefit calculi) (Reynolds, 2006a; also see the review of this general line of research in Reynolds & Ceranic, 2007). Compared to Jones's moral intensity construct, the ethical predispositions approach broadens the realm of morality from one outlook only to two.

Apart from those studies and approaches that explicitly adopt a harm/welfare or fairness framework for understanding morality, a different set of work generally defers the issue of commitment to a particular moral framework. Thus, for example, Treviño, Weaver, and Reynolds's 2006 review of behavioral ethics research on organizations defined the field as focusing on "individual behavior that is subject to or judged according to generally accepted norms of moral behavior" or "individual behavior that occurs in the context of larger social prescriptions" (a position echoed in Kish-Gephart, Harrison, & Treviño's 2010 meta-analysis of ethical choice research), while remaining agnostic regarding just what those "larger social prescriptions" entail. Aquino and Reed's (and colleagues') multiple studies involving moral identity frame morality in terms of certain paradigmatic traits (e.g., honesty) that presumably hold across multiple moral outlooks (e.g., both utilitarians and formalists might assent to the general propriety of honest behavior, even if they differ with regard to why honest behavior is morally proper or with regard to other forms of behavior that might or might not be viewed as morally proper) (e.g., Aquino & Reed, 2002). Brown, Treviño, and Harrison's (2005) work on ethical leadership also defined that behavior as "promoting normatively appropriate conduct to followers" without specifying what such conduct involves. These kinds of noncommittal approaches avoid overly narrow specification of the realm of ethics, but such refusals to specify fail to encourage consideration of accounts of moral behavior beyond the usual range of harm and fairness perspectives.

Moral foundations theory's combination of behavioral ethics research on moral intuition with attention to the realities of variance in the lived moral experience of people both across and within cultures provides an alternative way of thinking about behavioral research on ethics in organizations. Its intuitionist element provides an alternative to the heavily cognitivist approaches of much, if not most, mainstream organizational ethics research, and its anthropological element opens the door to considering a wider range of stances toward the subject content at hand: morality. What, then, might this combination mean for thinking about organizations? What new questions and research topics does it generate for the study of organizations?

MORAL FOUNDATIONS IN ORGANIZATIONS

In this section, we specifically consider how our understanding of behavior in organizations might change or expand were researchers and theorists to include in-group, authority/hierarchy, and purity/sanctity dimensions as elements of morality alongside the usual harm and fairness aspects typically used to delineate the realm of the moral in organizational research. (We grant that authority and in-group phenomena are frequently considered in organizational research but generally not from the perspective that they are *foundational* to morality rather than either amoral phenomena or sources of immoral behavior.)

The Purity/Sanctity Foundation

Treviño, Brown, and Hartman's 2003 study of ethical leadership found that matters of personal morality—such as involved in the President Clinton-Monica Lewinski scandal (their specific example)—are widely viewed as a relevant components of a multidimensional understanding of ethical leadership (see also Brown & Treviño, 2006). That the Clinton-Lewinski episode was sexual in character (in addition to whatever other issues it might have raised, e.g., truthfulness) suggests that, at least for some of the interview subjects in that study (American executives), something like purity/sanctity concerns were at work (even if not all persons would have the same reaction).

Attending to the purity/sanctity intuition (or any other moral intuition) can help explain why ethical cognitions and behaviors, such as moral awareness (Butterfield, Treviño, & Weaver, 2000), are, in fact, issue contingent—but not quite in the way Jones's (1991) issue-contingent moral awareness model envisioned—because people are reacting to different aspects of a situation in light of the different combinations of moral foundations held to by those people. Where some people might intuitively react to the Clinton-Lewinski situation negatively, due to its departure from an intuitive purity standard, others who score low on the purity/sanctity foundation might not sense a moral issue at all or sense a very different issue (e.g., one of harm to a particular individual or of disrespect to the authority of the office of president). More generally, the purity foundation is related closely to disgust (with disgust constituting, in effect, the characteristic affective response to impurity) (Rozin, Lowery, Imada, & Haidt 1999). This kind of reaction incorporates tendencies toward avoiding or cutting off the actor or entity thought to be impure (Rozin & Fallon 1987), just as one would avoid impure food. So, can purity concerns, understood as intuitive moral reactions, help to explain organizational phenomena?

Purity intuitions could undergird exclusionary and "purifying" behavior, including the stigmatizing of dirty work (Ashforth & Kreiner, 1999; Ashforth, Kreiner, Clark, & Fugate, 2007) and, more generally, persons' disgust and avoidance reactions to those engaged in behaviors that, in a given social or organizational culture, are considered degrading or polluted. Research by Zhong and colleagues (Liljenquist, Zhong, & Galinsky, 2010; Zhong, Strejcek, & Sivanathan, 2010) has shown that physical cleanliness is closely linked to both moral behaviors (e.g., charity) and the quality of moral evaluations (e.g., harsh vs. lenient judgments of others). Others have noted how people will avoid even remote association with persons seen as evil; Rozin, Markwith, and McCauley (1994) found people unwilling to associate themselves even with items of clothing previously worn by persons perceived to be morally tainted. So, research could consider whether "private" behaviors, such as marital infidelity, that violate a sense of purity/sanctity can have an impact on informal dimensions of organization life, such as personal reputation, trust, and collaboration (at least among employees who rank high on the purity/sanctity foundation), and even informally enter into decisions such as promotions that formally might be supposed to disregard such extraorganizational matters. Even associating with stigmatized individuals can have repercussions for those who associate with them (Kulik & Roberson, 2008), so one need not be seen as engaging in impure actions directly to be affected by them.

If the purity side of the purity/sanctity foundation involves reactions against or avoidance of something, the sanctity side of it represents an intuitively favorable reaction toward nonbase actions and motives— a kind of aspirational rather than avoidance response. Obviously, this can include conventionally religious impulses (toward particular beliefs, behaviors, attitudes, or emotions), but as articulated in moral foundations theory, it also could take the form of a more secular concern for "higher" or ennobling things. Empirical research on specifically religious attitudes and behavior in work organizations has been sparse even though (for example) a recent Gallup survey found 81% of American respondents claiming that religion is at least fairly important in their lives (Gallup, 2009). It seems at least prima facie important in explaining behavior. For example, Vitell and colleagues (2009) found that internalized religious beliefs are related to an individual's moral identity and self-control, while Parboteeah, Hoegl, and Cullen (2009) found that national religious context affects individuals' sense of their obligations in the workplace, and Weaver and Agle (2002) theorized factors that would moderate linkages between religious identity and organizational outcomes. On a more macrosociological level, Putnam's (2007) study of the negative impact of ethnic diversity on civic engagement and on both interethnic and intraethnic trust found that, of a wide range of factors studied (e.g., education, age, crime level, income level, etc.), only religious involvement seemed to mitigate the civic withdrawal and general lack of inter- and intraethnic trust associated with higher levels of neighborhood diversity. With regard to the more secular version of the sanctity intuition (i.e., positive responses toward nonsectarian views of ennobling and "higher" beliefs, attitudes, and behaviors), note how research on organizational ethics initiatives has found stronger impacts to arise from initiatives that appeal to employees' ethical aspirations than for programs that focus on rules, controls, and rewards (Weaver & Treviño, 1999).

Purity reactions might help to explain variations in employees' willingness to get involved in "messy" situations in the workplace (e.g., willingness to help a substance-abusing coworker; willingness to assist a victim of abusive supervision or sexual harassment). But how? An intuitive concern for purity might undermine intervention, insofar as intervention involves proximity to "dirty" individuals (e.g., a substance abuser or harasser). But, the same concern for purity might foster intervention insofar as intervention helps to rid the organization of a perceived impurity (e.g., an abusive supervisor). Besides these behavioral reactions, however, a strong purity foundation could have cognitive effects, influencing how employees make sense of organizational situations. For example, varying strength on the purity/sanctity foundation might influence how employees view organizational politics. If internal political maneuvering and deal making is intuitively viewed as undignified or impure, might individuals strong on that moral foundation be less likely to be involved in it? Or, would they be more likely to be involved as organizational politics are viewed as simply a means toward an ultimately pure aim that, due to its perceived purity and ennobling character, is not to be compromised as though it were simply a matter of negotiable personal self-interest (i.e., when an issue is seen as moral, not pragmatic, cooperation and negotiation are less likely) (Skitka, Bauman, & Sargis, 2005; Wright, Cullum, & Schwab, 2008).

At a more macrolevel, managers' purity/sanctity intuitions might have implications for understanding stakeholder management. Conventional research argues that stakeholder legitimacy, power, and urgency will influence the extent to which stakeholders are accommodated by an organization (Mitchell, Agle, & Wood, 1997). But, might managers' reactions to stakeholders' purity/sanctity also play a role, either in managers' perceptions of stakeholder legitimacy or in other responses to stakeholders? Does a "dirty work" stakeholder group (e.g., a cleaning/janitorial/sanitation employees' union) receive less-solicitous attention and willing engagement than does a stakeholder group seen as purer? Do stakeholder groups perceived as engaged in ennobling or sanctifying endeavors (e.g., charities) gain preferential treatment because managers (or even employees) intuitively perceive their work as of higher moral status? And, just as importantly, do managers' own varying degrees of strength on the purity/sanctity dimension lead them to differential treatment of stakeholder groups (i.e., a manager with low purity/sanctity makes decisions about a given stakeholder group differently than a manager with high purity/sanctity)? How do managers' own strength on the purity/sanctity dimension mesh with the moral intuitions of others whom they serve? For example, to what extent do differentials in investment behaviors vis-à-vis "sin stocks" (e.g., gambling companies, alcoholic beverage companies; e.g., Hong & Kacperczyk, 2009) reflect the purity/sanctity stances of decision makers at institutional investors versus the decision makers' perceptions of more general, societally shared purity intuitions about sin stocks or nonpurity factors such as concerns about the harms of gambling addiction or the unfairness of negative externalities generated by alcoholism?

Differences regarding the purity/sanctity foundation within a group or organization can be sources of conflict; individuals sometimes have negative views of others who strongly hold opposing beliefs about morality or religion that are closely related to the purity/sanctity foundation (Haidt, Rosenberg, & Hom, 2003). But, are typical workplace accommodations of religious differences—such as in work scheduling or cafeteria menus or in sponsorship of religious or moral-issue affinity groups—effective at avoiding tension or satisfying employees' expression of their moral intuitions (or related religious views)? Purity/sanctity intuitions also might be linked, for example, to individuals' choices of dress (given that clothing could, in some contexts, constitute a type of moral identity symbolization). To what degree does clothing have an impact on other employees who share or lack the same purity/sanctity intuitions as the wearer? And what, if anything, can managers do to address such tension? This situation could manifest itself in a variety of ways—from an employee who wears an article of clothing that has important religious significance, to an employee whose provocative clothing triggers negative assessments by colleagues who score differently on a purity/sanctity foundation. Similarly, attempts at humor in the workplace have the potential to make salient key differences in purity and sanctity (jokes about sex, religion, etc.). In short, there is a wealth of research and practice questions raised by recognition of the role of a purity/sanctity moral foundation in the behavior of individuals in organizations.

The Authority/Hierarchy Foundation

Moral foundations theory implies that many people intuitively view authority and hierarchy as essentially moral phenomena or intrinsic moral goods, and not merely means to other ends (and thus also might view other phenomena as problematic insofar as they undermine authority and hierarchy). As a *moral* foundation, an intuitive and favorable stance toward authority/hierarchy is not viewed merely as a preference or attitude (and thus is distinct from social dominance orientation, a possibly related but conceptually distinct construct over which individuals vary; Pratto, Sidanius, Stallworth, & Malle, 1994). The intuition of authority relationships in hierarchy as, ceteris paribus, moral goods (i.e., barring conflicts with other intuitive moral foundations) might help explain oft-noted tendencies for people to defer to authority, even in Milgram-type situations and even without the authority figure promising to take responsibility, exercise expertise, offer rewards, or otherwise display conventional elements of authority or power (cf. French & Raven, 1959). Put differently, the authority-subordinate relationship in a hierarchy might receive a kind of "innocent until proven guilty" "benefit of the doubt" in the minds of people, with violations of hierarchical structures and authority relationships inherently suspect and in need of a strong basis in one of the other moral foundations. From a moral foundations standpoint, conventional conceptualizations of power and influence are not adequate for explaining why "followership" can be seen by many as an ethical duty. In what follows, we use the authority/hierarchy foundation as a means for rethinking leadership research.

Conventional research on organizational ethics generally makes two negative assumptions about authority that do not rest easily with an intuitive recognition of hierarchical authority as good. First, conventional writing often views authority—specifically the authority of organizational leaders—with suspicion. Organizational ethicists often have focused on the dark side of leader power, influence, and behavioral styles (Ciulla, 2004). Scholars have noted the corrupting potential of leader power (Hollander & Offerman, 1990; Kipnis, 1976) and have specified how leaders ought to use their power fairly, with minimal harm to followers. Leaders use power negatively when they seek "power over" followers for personal gain, while positive leaders desire "power with" followers to benefit the greater good (Follett, 1940; Howell, 1988; McClelland, 1975). Transformational leadership, which engages and inspires followers by appealing to shared values and beliefs (Bass & Steidlmeier, 1999; Burns, 1978; Kanungo & Mendonca, 1996), generally is preferred because it is viewed as less likely to generate excessive and harmful leader power and influence.

A second assumption has to do with follower compliance. Generally, follower obedience to authority is seen negatively (Milgram, 1974). Obedience to authority can cause followers to lose their individuality and engage in ethically bad acts (Treviño & Weaver, 2003). Even transformational leadership has critics concerned that the power of transformational leaders to build shared values destroys followers' independence. According to Keeley (2004), followers should maintain their own visions and values instead of accepting the vision and values of their leader, and this independence is thought to provide a check against leader power. Allowing a diversity of perspectives to flourish is seen as protecting against the harm that can come from dogmatic adherence to a single vision set forth by a leader. Expectations of obedience to authority also have been criticized for fostering a sense of displaced responsibility among followers (Kelman & Hamilton, 1989; Milgram, 1974), with resultant higher risks of improper behavior.

But, if hierarchy and authority constitute a core moral foundation for many people, we need to consider how a generally negative view of follower compliance misses an important element driving actual obedience in organizations. Rather than focusing on followers as somewhat hapless targets or victims of an authority's power and control, research needs to consider how followers conceptualize their obedience in positive ways: as appropriate deference (or respect) or as the living out of a moral obligation. This positive conceptualization of obedience to authority in turn has implications for how we understand leadership phenomena. For example, research on ethical leadership (Brown et al., 2005) has conceptualized it in terms of a social learning process (Bandura, 1986). This means that leaders must be seen as attractive and credible to be effective ethical models. And, according to the role-modeling literature, attractive models are those that are nurturing (Yussen & Levy, 1975; see Weaver, Treviño, & Agle, 2005, specifically regarding ethical role models). But, if hierarchical authority is seen as a positive good by some followers, with leaders due a degree of deference out of a intuitive moral duty, then just how important is it that an effective ethical leader be seen as attractive, credible, and nurturing?

From a moral foundations standpoint, authority relationships are perceived by people as involving reciprocal duties—of deference to authority and of responsibility for those under authority. At least some leader influence arises because a leader's position in a hierarchy itself is viewed as worthy of deference and not because of the instrumental power that position provides or because of a leader's attributes or behavior. However, the leader in that position—regardless of any traits or other behaviors—is expected to exercise leadership in reciprocal fashion, such that notions of servant leadership (in which employees follow in part because leaders serve; Greenleaf, 1977; cf. Hollander 1958) might best capture the daily implementation of authority relationships. Followers also have a duty to respect hierarchy and the authority of their leaders. Thus, functioning leader–follower relationships, from a moral foundations standpoint, rest in part on a mutual recognition of the moral nature of hierarchy and the reciprocal exchange of leader stewardship and follower obedience.

By contrast, transactional leadership ignores, and perhaps risks violating, the essentially moral way in which many people view hierarchical relationships because it makes the leader–follower relationship one primarily based on self-interested calculation (e.g., reward). If we assume a moral foundations view of hierarchical authority, transactional leadership behaviors might undermine a leader's position, similar to how extrinsic rewards can undermine behaviors that are viewed as morally good in themselves (e.g., Reed, Aquino, & Levy, 2007), by divorcing followers' behavior from the moral motivation for it. Future research could examine how transactional leader behaviors interact with followers' intuitive commitment to authority and hierarchy as moral goods.

Transformational leadership also might face problems if organization members view authority and hierarchy as embodiments of a foundational moral stance. Literally, transformational leaders are thought to "transform" followers into leaders (Burns, 1978), thereby reducing the need for leadership. By suggesting that the goal of leadership is, ultimately, to turn followers into self-motivated leaders themselves, transformational leadership can run afoul of persons' tendencies to view the existence of an authoritative hierarchy structure as a good in itself; if hierarchical authority is a good, why ought it be eliminated or distributed among many people? Transformational leadership, in effect, loses sight of the sense of positive good that people may attach to being in a leader–follower relationship, regardless of what side of that relationship they are on.

One new leadership research direction indicated by moral foundations theory is to examine what it means for leaders and followers to see themselves and their responsibilities in intrinsically moral terms. For example, leader power orientation is an important aspect of leadership. Do persons with a strong authority/hierarchy moral foundation perceive their power as "power with" or "power over," so that foundational moral intuitions constitute an important type of leader trait (Howell, 1988; McClelland, 1975)? And, what happens if obligations to accomplish organizational performance goals—perhaps a kind of group welfare outcome—interfere with the concept of reciprocity or stewardship toward specific followers? And to what degree do other factors—such as other managers' behavior, organizational ethical climate, and leaders' individual differences—influence a leader's strength of moral intuition and resulting reciprocity? New constructs and measures to tap into leaders' intuitions specifically with regard to their reciprocal responsibilities would be useful in answering these questions.

Incorporating moral foundations theory into research on followers also opens new avenues of investigation. How and why do followers intuit foundationally moral authority in specific ways in specific contexts? Because of cultural norms? Individual personality differences? Demographic factors such as age, education, and experience? And, if failing to follow a leader's directives is not only a pragmatic failure but also a moral failure, what implications does that failure have for the individuals involved and overall for the morally endowed hierarchy structure? What kinds of events, circumstances, and behaviors violate persons' intuitions about the moral status of authority in hierarchy, and what are the outcomes of such violations?

Cross-cultural research on ethical leadership indicates that specific dimensions of ethical leadership are more highly valued in some cultures rather than others. For example, obedience to authority is more highly valued in Middle Eastern cultures in comparison to Nordic cultures (Resick, Hanges, Dickson, & Mitchelson, 2006). Might this be because of differences in the relative strength of moral foundations, with Nordic cultures perhaps displaying lower levels of the authority/hierarchy foundation? From the standpoint of practice, the variance across settings in the authority/hierarchy foundation indicates that successful ethical leadership might require more in the way of inspiration and motivation of followers in some settings and less in others (with more simple reliance on the obligating power of an intuition of authority as a positive good in those latter settings).

Finally, if some people intuit authority in hierarchy as good, might this occur in part because of its outcomes? Answering this question in the context of moral foundations theory might appear somewhat paradoxical, insofar as a positive answer would, in effect, undergird the status of one foundation by its outcomes with respect to other foundations (as in an argument that hierarchical authority reduces harm, enhances fairness, or promotes purity and sanctity). But, could mutually supportive relationships not hold among various embodiments of the various moral foundations, and does not moral foundations theory hold that foundations develop because of their mutually adaptive value? So, it is reasonable to consider how attention to the authority/hierarchy foundation—that is, understanding authority in hierarchy as intuitively good—might be linked to a variety of positive outcomes.

The absence of order and structure, and the expectations on behavior that they embody, often are associated with problems of *anomie* (i.e., normlessness; Durkheim 1897/1951). Anomie typically is associated with both individual and collective stresses and problems—for example, suicide at the individual level (Durkheim, 1897/1951), corruption within organizations (Cohen, 1993; Martin, Johnson, & Cullen, 2009), and tendencies toward unrestrained or anarchic behavior at the societal level (Durkheim, 1897/1951; Messner & Rosenfeld, 1997). Thus, in a general way the presence of authority in hierarchy provides order and can reduce individual stresses and social problems. But how, and to what other ends?

The presence of authority in hierarchy can enhance the predictability and stability of norms and practices. Having one authoritative set of standards and values to follow in an organization could eliminate confusion and idiosyncratic responses to ethical challenges—as long as organization members embody similar levels of this moral foundation (and noting that the elimination of confusion and idiosyncratic responses does not necessarily imply ethically proper behavior in some objective or extraorganizational sense). The presence of a reciprocal sense of authority also might protect followers from blame when things go wrong (i.e., it might prevent blame shifting onto those with less power in an organization). Possession of a strong authority/hierarchy foundation might motivate leaders to engage in active moral management (Treviño et al., 2003) and create a stronger ethical context because doing so prevents follower misconduct for which leaders might have to pay the price.

The In-Group Foundation

According to moral foundations theory, unity in, solidarity with, preference for, and loyalty to an in-group are intuited as inherently good by many people. Associating and cooperating with fellow group members, defending the group from outside threats, and sacrificing for the good of the group are seen as noble activities. Individuals from the same in-group are joined by strong ties of mutual trust and admiration. A predisposition to develop such ties is "hard-wired" in people, and the social integration these ties provide has psychological benefits for many individuals and potential benefits for the group itself; developmentally, this differential treatment is an adaptive response. Those outside the group, however, may be viewed with distrust, suspicion, or in other cautious ways. Although grouping phenomena often have been studied, moral foundations theory adds the recognition that group members not only behave in these ways but also intuitively view in-group commitments as moral goods.

To some degree, conventional organizational research has touched on the benefits of in-group commitments, such as increased cooperation and satisfaction (see Williams & O'Reilly, 1998). In terms of prosocial behavior, research has shown that groups can positively influence individual ethical outcomes (Zey-Ferrell, Weaver, & Ferrell, 1979), at least toward others in the group. And, in some cases, the group context can encourage group members to turn against each other (e.g., report improper behavior) if it means protecting the greater good of the group (Treviño & Victor, 1992).

However, much conventional organizational research has identified negative aspects of the in-group experience, such as groupthink (Janis, 1972), the moral exclusion of outsiders (Opotow, 1990; Treviño et al., 2006), and the social learning of unethical behaviors from peers (Robinson & O'Leary-Kelly, 1998). This research views preference toward one's group not as a foundation for moral action, but as producing favoritism among colleagues (cast negatively as nepotism or cronyism) and discrimination and bias toward outsiders (Tajfel & Turner, 1985)—all morally bad things from the standpoint of harm and fairness concerns.

Thus, according to moral foundations theory, persons' moral views of some in-group commitments are to some degree at odds with how such phenomena typically are conceived in group-related research. Broad expressions of in-group commitments (e.g., unity, solidarity, and preference with regard to one's in-group) are intuited as virtuous or admirable by people, according to moral foundations theory. By contrast, much traditional theory and research on in-group behavior and attitudes suggested that such preferential commitment is a form of bias (i.e., unfair/unethical treatment of outsiders).

In considering in-group phenomena, it is important to distinguish among the many kinds of groups that exist in the workplace. Employees can be members of multiple groups, such as formal groups based on job assignment (e.g., employees who report to a common supervisor or work in the same department) or organizational membership (e.g., employees from the organization) and identity groups based on demographics (e.g., race, gender), values/beliefs (e.g., religious and political affiliation), and profession (e.g., engineer, accountant), all of which imply some degree of homogeneity across at least one identifying dimension. But then, any dimension on which group identity, and in-group identification, is based could form the focus of in-group commitment phenomena and thus the locus of preferential biases and fairness problems. But, if group phenomena such as loyalty, solidarity, unity, and preference are intuited as moral goods according to persons' in-group moral foundation, then identification with the group entails the likelihood of such preferential attitudes and behaviors in accord with the group's defining homogeneous features.

In-group commitments, and the problematic behaviors and biases they might generate, in short, are to some degree rooted in homogeneity across the defining characteristics of a group. Research on intergroup bias has been extensive (Pearson, Dovidio, & Gaertner, 2009), and suggested remedies to help group members overcome their biases have been developed (Gaertner & Dovidio, 2000). Insofar as in-group commitments pose problems (e.g., of fairness, groupthink, etc.), one response is to weaken homogeneity across whatever dimensions are problematic (e.g., weaken ethnicity-based commitments by increasing ethnic homogeneity; weaken groupthink effects by increasing educational or professional heterogeneity). Thus, diversity and broad inclusiveness often are recommended, and actions that maintain in-group homogeneity with regard to some sources of group identity (e.g., ethnicity, age) are advised against on grounds that they are morally problematic (according to a harm/benefit or fairness criterion) or not task related (and even perhaps task undermining) in workplace contexts (Page, 2007; see also Bell, Connerley, & Cocchiara, 2009, Kulik & Roberson, 2008).

Empirical research, however, shows that the relationships among group heterogeneity, group processes, and performance are complex and often do not match the positive assessment of heterogeneity derived from normative harm and fairness-based perspectives (Klein & Harrison, 2007; see van Knippenberg & Schippers, 2007, for a review). In the workplace, people categorize themselves and others according to important social identities such as race, gender, and functional area (Ashforth & Mael,

1989; Tajfel & Turner, 1985). Research indicates that people are attracted to (Brewer, 1979; Byrne, 1971; Jackson, 1992), network with (Ibarra, 1992), and more readily accept influence from similar others (Cialdini, 2001) due to shared social identities. Even persons who consciously and sincerely see themselves as tolerant and inclusive of others nevertheless can display implicit prejudices characteristic of homophily (Pearson et al., 2009), and at the macrosociological level, some demographic research indicates that increases in ethnic heterogeneity are associated not with greater tolerance and acceptance but with withdrawal by persons into essentially private worlds (Putnam, 2007). Research old and new has also shown that homogeneity can provide important benefits; Durkheim (1897/1951) observed that suicide levels were higher in societies characterized by more social isolation (i.e., less group identification), and Williams and O'Reilly (1998) noted that homogeneity yields benefits such as enhanced communication and decreased conflict.

Thus, uniformly positive assessments of diversity, like uniformly positive assessments of in-group loyalty, oversimplify a complex phenomenon (Klein & Harrison, 2007), and more research is needed. From a moral foundations standpoint, this should not be surprising, given the inclusion of in-group commitment in the theory as a foundational stance deeply rooted in persons' moral intuitions, with deep origins in human history. To some extent, the mixed outcomes of homogeneity and heterogeneity, and the strength of people's commitments toward in-groups, can be explained by the individual and group-level benefits conferred, whether in a long-term developmental perspective or with regard to immediate contexts. What moral foundations theory adds, however, is the recognition that many people intuit group loyalty as something morally proper. And, if group commitment and related phenomena have a foundational moral quality, rather than merely being the source of pragmatic benefits, it is not surprising that any negative aspects of it are difficult to overcome. Assigning a moral quality to something such as loyalty to one's group likely makes it more difficult for people to willingly negotiate it away or replace it with a substitute. For example, persons' reluctance to "snitch" or "blow the whistle" on coworkers is not simply a matter of fear of consequences for oneself or for one's group, but rather might function as an intuitive moral wrong in people's minds (perhaps in tension with the intuitive moral wrong of standing aside when in a position to prevent someone else from acting harmfully or unfairly). It also has implications for practice;

defenses of whistle-blowing that appeal to in-group preferences might be more effective than other defenses when dealing with people with strong in-group loyalty intuitions (e.g., defending whistle-blowing as protecting the welfare of the entire group by taking action against misbehavior or by framing the misbehavior as an affront to the group). More generally, the relative strength of individuals' in-group intuitions will affect their responsiveness to different kinds of appeals, just as in the case of the purity/sanctity foundation. Thus, research is needed to consider how different mixes of appeals succeed and fail at motivating people toward ethically important behavior in organizations.

Research relating to moral foundations also indicates the value of attending to multiple categories of heterogeneity and persons' varying degrees of willingness to identify with those categories. For example, multiple studies (Haidt et al., 2003; Skitka et al., 2005; Wright et al., 2008) found that individuals more easily associated with others who were demographically different compared to morally or politically different (i.e., heterogeneity in ideas about what is right and wrong). And although it often is assumed the surface-level diversity corresponds with deep-level diversity, this connection is not well supported (Harrison, Price, & Bell, 1998; Harrison, Price, Gavin, & Florey, 2002). Furthermore, variation in deep-level diversity is related (positively and negatively) to individual and group outcomes (Harrison et al., 1998, 2002; Jehn, Northcraft, & Neale, 1999). Thus, researchers might need to adopt a more complex view of group homogeneity (e.g., homogeneity or heterogeneity across moral foundations) and probe how this influences behavior.

What does this mean for the workplace? Would moral diversity regarding practices such as whistle-blowing, social loafing, or lying to the boss be disruptive and detrimental? Do some kinds of deep-level heterogeneity make it harder or easier for people to work together? If affection for and allegiance to an in-group is treated as illegitimate or deviant, will this be seen itself as a kind of moral offense by some people because it conflicts with an in-group-oriented foundational intuition? What reaction would that generate? If those who see in-group loyalty as intuitively good, and perhaps in conflict with one or another positive characterization of workplace diversity, do not feel it is safe to voice their dissenting opinions, then efforts to promote inclusion might be seen as a different form of exclusion with its own negative outcomes (Stewart, Crary, & Humberd, 2008). Paradoxically, might there be a need to frame workplace harm or fairness goals, such as concerns for bias-free diversity, in the language of moral foundations other than harm and fairness, appealing instead to purity/sanctity intuitions (e.g., ennobling aspirations) or to respect for the judgments of hierarchical authorities who request inclusive behavior from subordinates? Should such efforts be presented by means of an alternative vision of group identity that transcends (or perhaps sanctifies) one kind of heterogeneity (e.g., ethnicity) by relegating it to secondary status in comparison to some other kind of homogeneity (e.g., identification with a company), in keeping with research highlighting the role of social categorization and framing processes in persons' responses to social dilemmas involving nested group relationships (Polzer, Stewart, & Simmons, 1999)? Finally, new research might consider whether the negative outcomes (vis-à-vis harm and unfairness) of in-group commitments or homophily might be mitigated or prevented in some way by group-level heterogeneity. This would, of course, raise new questions and potential problems with regard to *intergroup* rivalry, but explicit attention to potential interactions among individual-level and group-level homogeneity and heterogeneity might generate insightful findings.

MORAL FOUNDATIONS AND ORGANIZATIONAL ETHICS: NEW ISSUES AND INTERACTIONS

In addition to the specific implications that each of the purity, authority/hierarchy, and in-group foundations generate, those foundations together (and moral foundations theory generally) can help to illuminate a variety of ethical issues and situations—and responses to them—in organizations. Behaviorally, the internalization of various sets of moral foundations (to varying degrees) is linked to the kinds of intuitive reactions persons have to particular kinds of moral situations—including both "that's wrong/right" responses and the potential for persons to become aware of particular situations as posing moral issues (cf. Butterfield, Treviño, & Weaver, 2000) and their potential to let those issues fade from view (Tenbrunsel & Messick, 2004). For example, someone strong on the purity foundation might see a moral issue regarding an executive's extramarital affairs, while someone low on the purity foundation sees no issue or instead an issue of fairness or harm vis-à-vis an aggrieved spouse. This means, in short, that the varying foundations likely are linked to different kinds and degrees of emotional responses, cognitive schemas, and behavioral scripts regarding the extent to which people see situations as embodying morally significant issues. Might a stronger harm foundation make individuals more likely to notice negative outcomes in organizations and less likely to notice other aspects of an issue? Might differences in strength of the in-group foundation yield more solicitous behavior toward coworkers and more disinterested behavior toward customers? Might high levels of in-group, authority, and purity foundations lead people to be more concerned with organizational well-being (i.e., system survival) rather than individual well-being (i.e., increased benefits for specific individuals within the organization)? And, if moral awareness is in part a function of issue characteristics (Jones, 1991), do we need a broader vocabulary and measures to assess issue characteristics vis-à-vis authority/hierarchy, preference for an in-group, and purity/sanctity?

In addition, what are we to make of the relationships among various moral foundations? Strong levels of the in-group foundation might, in effect, change the relevant venue for developing reactions based on a given level of concern for fairness (e.g., more intuitive concern for fair treatment of one's group); low levels of the authority/hierarchy foundation might change the focal point of reactions rooted in concerns to avoid harm (lowered intuitive reactions toward actions that might undermine hierarchy). Different combinations of moral foundations, then, might be equifinal; one person might have strong intuitive reactions regarding fair treatment of a group because of high levels of the fairness foundation despite lower levels of the in-group foundation—thus being attuned to even small acts of unfairness—whereas another person might respond similarly in behavior due to low levels of the fairness foundation combined with very high levels of the in-group foundations—thus being attuned to any action against the in-group, regardless of how slight it might be. More generally, high levels on any one foundation provide a potential influence on (i.e., interaction with) any of the other foundations. Thus, high levels on the harm foundation in combination with authority/hierarchy could yield a focus on harm to hierarchy or concern that authority be used to mitigate harm; in combination with strong in-group intuitions, a focus on harm to and within the group; or in combination with purity/sanctity, a focus on those particular forms of pure or ennobling behavior that minimize harm or promote care. In short, the foundations do not necessarily work independently of each other, and they might not act together in simply additive fashion. These complexities require elaboration in additional research.

The multifaceted complexities of moral foundations theory have implications specifically for organizational policies and practices regarding ethics. For example:

Ethical differences and conflicts: Ethical disputes within and between organizations (e.g., between businesses and their stakeholders) can seem intractable. Attention to moral foundations can help explain why. Welcomer, Gioia, and Kilduff, for example (2000), analyzed a dispute between a business and community over siting for a toxic waste facility. Rhetoric in the dispute pitted a focus on economic benefit (a harm/welfare issue and, distributively, a fairness issue) against a rural/pastoral community self-identity (arguably a mix of in-group and purity foundations). A temptation in such disputes is to dismiss opposing opinions as merely rationalizations for self-interest (or for dim-wittedness or other flaws). Moral foundations theory casts those disputes in a different light, however, portraying them as disputes about genuinely held moral positions. But, besides providing a framework for understanding such disputes, might moral foundations theory also indicate the value of enabling key organizational decision makers to better grasp the nature of all five foundations? Is this possible, and if so, how could this be done? And, does this have implications for staffing decisions within organizations? What implications would this have for the way we study and approach significant cultural differences in the workplace?

Organizational ethical infrastructure: Organizations engage in many and varied initiatives to foster ethical behavior in the workplace, including both formal policies and programs (e.g., monitoring systems, training and communication efforts, punishments and rewards) and informal practices (e.g., organizational culture and climate development, managerial behavioral modeling) (Tenbrunsel, Smith-Crowe, & Umphress, 2003; Treviño & Weaver, 2003). These efforts have varying success. A moral foundations approach to ethics in organizations potentially can identify a larger basis on which to build such initiatives, depending on the range of foundations common among the workforce. Organizational ethics initiatives might need to be framed in ways that appeal to multiple moral foundations to have maximal effect. For example, the need to avoid conflicts of interests might be presented not only in terms of avoiding harm (e.g., legal penalties) or fairness (e.g., to customers) but also in terms of in-group concern (e.g., bringing penalties or shame onto one's group), purity (e.g., not sullying oneself with practices common among disreputable organizations), or authority (e.g., respecting the orderly arrangements and procedures within one's organization). Similarly, the need for honesty and the avoidance of deception could be framed as unfair (appealing to the fairness foundation) and as behavior that criminals engage in (thus framing them as dirty work and engaging the purity/sanctity foundation). Thus, managers might need to learn to speak in multiple moral languages (i.e., fairness, harm, purity/sanctity, etc.) to reach all employees with any kind of message about ethics; talking about right and wrong without reference to purity/sanctity might be relatively ineffective for some employees.

More generally, greater recognition of the authority, in-group, or purity dimensions of many persons' moral outlooks could lead to deeper forms of moral commitment in organizational contexts and less alienation or anomie of the sort sometimes attributed to more narrowly contractual social settings (Haidt & Graham, 2009; Martin et al., 2009). This in turn might have implications for other important phenomena, such as job satisfaction, perceived organizational support, and trust in leaders. Attention to moral foundations, in short, provides a greater array of moral motivations to appeal to in fostering ethical workplace behavior.

━━━━━━━━━━

EXPANDING THE MORAL FOUNDATIONS PERSPECTIVE

As much as moral foundations theory can expand our understanding of ethical behavior, behavioral and organizational research on ethics also can be used to further develop moral foundations theory. Although the existence of, and persons' internalization of, moral foundations is well established, less clear are the factors that influence that process, and that might lead to greater or lesser activation of one or another foundation in particular circumstances. Contextual triggers have been proposed as influences on the salience and activation of persons' identities (e.g., Aquino,

Freeman, Reed, Lim, & Felps, 2009; Weaver & Agle, 2002). Might contextual triggers—such as the presence of absence of others who have internalized a similar set of moral foundations or the use of particular moral language—likewise yield temporary rises and falls in the influence of a moral foundation on behavior? Do organizational influences—culture, workforce heterogeneity, rewards, and so on—moderate the extent to which moral foundations are operative? Do organizational factors influence the form that particular moral foundations take in behavior? We know what purity might mean in one or another sociocultural context with regard to dietary and cleanliness practices, for example, but what might it mean in an organizational context (specifically a business context)? Would that context give different meaning to the idea, or would extraorganizational, sociocultural foundational responses manifest themselves easily within organizations regardless of organizational conditions?

MORAL FOUNDATIONS IN ORGANIZATIONS: A CONCLUDING EXAMPLE

We conclude our review by providing an example of how moral foundations theory might influence the way we conceptualize important ethics constructs. Moral identity research (e.g., Aquino & Reed, 2002; Aquino et al., 2009; Shao, Aquino, & Freeman, 2008) has produced an impressive stream of behavioral ethics research. Aquino and Reed's moral identity construct is conceptualized and measured by assessing the self-importance of nine moral traits: caring, compassionate, fair, friendly, generous, hardworking, helpful, honest, and kind. These traits appear to draw heavily from the harm and fairness foundations—note the absence of adjectives such as "respectful" (authority foundation), "loyal" (in-group), "self-controlled" or "noble" (purity), and so on. Although the standard moral identity list is not meant to be exhaustive of all possible moral traits (Aquino & Reed, 2002), might a primary emphasis on two of the five moral foundations create a skewed understanding of moral identity, biased toward individuals who are high on the harm and fairness foundations? In other words, if presented with a list of moral traits based almost exclusively on harm and fairness, would an individual who strongly embodies all five foundations appear to rate those traits lower in importance than someone who strongly embodies just those two, because the former individual holds fairness and harm concerns in tension with other moral foundations not included in the moral identity measure, whereas for the latter individual no other foundational concerns compete with harm and fairness? So, on the conventional moral identity measure, this person might appear to have a weaker moral identity than others, but only because the measure used does not incorporate this person's entire deeply and sincerely held foundational moral positions. In reality, harm and fairness traits might be very important to someone with broad moral foundations, but only when held in balance with traits that reflect the in-group, authority, and purity moral foundations. Future research, then, should consider broadening the list of moral traits used to measure moral identity to include the in-group, authority and purity foundations (and, for that matter, whatever other moral foundations might be discovered through future research). Such traits might include adjectives such as loyal, respectful, dutiful, faithful, noble, honorable, temperate, reverent, etc.

Moral identity also currently is assessed along two broad dimensions, internalization ("these traits are an important part of who I am") and symbolization (traits as expressed in behavior). However, incorporating the purity, in-group, and hierarchy dimensions might require an expanded view of how the self-importance of traits is expressed (and therefore measured), perhaps based on social/relational dimensions. For example, would the purity foundation imply that someone with a strong moral identity would avoid engagement with persons who lack particular moral traits? The in-group foundation suggests that membership in certain organizations is desirable not because it communicates an individual's possession of certain moral characteristics to others (one of the items used to measure the symbolization dimension of moral identity; Aquino & Reed, 2002), but because associating with others who share the same characteristics intuitively is the right and proper thing to do. Our intention here is not to criticize the fine work of Aquino, Reed, and their colleagues, but to highlight how attending to five moral foundations calls for an expansion of much current thinking. By incorporating all five moral foundations into our research agendas, we believe we can capture a more complete picture of the impact and inner processes of ethics in organizational behavior.

REFERENCES

Aquino, K., Freeman, D., Reed, A., II, Lim, V. K. G., & Felps, W. (2009). Testing a social-cognitive model of moral behavior: The interactive influence of situations and moral identity centrality. *Journal of Personality and Social Psychology, 97,* 123–141.

Aquino, K., & Reed, A., II. (2002). The self-importance of moral identity. *Journal of Personality and Social Psychology, 83*(6), 1423.

Ashforth, B. E., & Kreiner, G. E. (1999). How can you do it? Dirty work and the challenge of constructing a positive identity. *Academy of Management Review, 24,* 413–434.

Ashforth, B. E., Kreiner, G. E., Clark, M. A., & Fugate, M. (2007). Normalizing dirty work: Managerial tactics for countering occupational taint. *Academy of Management Journal, 50,* 149–174.

Ashforth, B. E., & Mael, F. (1989). Social identity theory and the organizations. *Academy of Management Review, 14*(1), 20–39.

Bandura, A. (1986). *Social foundations of thought and action.* Englewood Cliffs, NJ: Prentice Hall.

Bass, B. M., & Steidlmeier, P. (1999). Ethics, character, and authentic transformational leadership behavior. *Leadership Quarterly, 10,* 181–218.

Bell, M. P., Connerley, M. L., & Cocchiara, F. K. (2009). The case for mandatory diversity education. *Academy of Management Learning & Education, 8*(4), 597–609.

Brewer, M. B. (1979). In-group bias in the minimal intergroup situation: A cognitive-motivational analysis. *Psychological Bulletin, 86,* 307–324.

Brown, M. E., & Treviño, L. K. (2006). Ethical leadership: A review and future directions. *Leadership Quarterly, 17,* 595–616.

Brown, M. E., Treviño, L. K., & Harrison, D. A. (2005). Ethical leadership: A social learning perspective for construct development and testing. *Organizational Behavior and Human Decision Processes, 97,* 117–134.

Burns, J. M. (1978). *Leadership.* New York: Harper Row.

Butterfield, K., Treviño, L. K., & Weaver, G. R. (2000). Moral awareness in organizations: Influences of issue-related and social context factors. *Human Relations, 53,* 981–1018.

Byrne, D. (1971). *The attraction paradigm.* New York: Academic.

Cialdini, R. B. (2001). *Influence: Science and practice* (4th ed.). Boston: Allyn & Bacon.

Ciulla, J. B. (Ed.). (2004). *Ethics, the heart of leadership* (2nd ed.). Westport, CT: Praeger.

Cohen, D. V. (1993). Creating and maintaining ethical work climates: Anomie in the workplace and implications for managing change. *Business Ethics Quarterly, 3,* 343–358.

Cropanzano, R., & Stein, J. H. (2009). Organizational justice and behavioral ethics: Promises and prospects. *Business Ethics Quarterly, 19,* 193–234.

Durkheim, E. (1951). *Suicide.* New York: Free Press. (Original work published 1897)

Fiske, A. P. (1991). *Structures of social life: The four elementary forms of human relations.* New York: Free Press.

Fiske, A. P., & Haslam, N. (2005). The four basic social bonds: Structures for coordinating interaction. In M. W. Baldwin (Ed.), *Interpersonal cognition* (pp. 267–298). New York: Guilford Press.

Folger, R., Cropanzano, R., & Goldman, B. (2005). Justice, accountability, and moral sentiment: The deontic response to "foul play" at work. In J. Greenberg & J. Colquitt (Eds.), *Handbook of organizational justice* (pp. 214–245). Mahwah, NJ: Erlbaum.

Follett, M. P. (1940). *Dynamic administration: The collected papers of Mary Parker Follett.* New York; London: Harper Brothers.

French, J. R. P., & Raven, B. (1959). The bases of social power. In D. Cartwright & A. Zander (Eds.), *Group dynamics* (pp. 150–167). New York: Harper & Row.

Gaertner, S. L., & Dovidio, J. F. (2000). *Reducing intergroup bias: The common ingroup identity model*. Philadelphia: Psychology Press.

Gallup. (2009). Retrieved from http://www.gallup.com/poll/1690/religion.aspx

Gilligan, C. (1993). *In a different voice: Psychological theory and women's development*. Cambridge, MA: Harvard University Press.

Graham, J., Haidt, J., & Nosek, B. A. (2009). Liberals and conservatives rely on different sets of moral foundations. *Journal of Personality and Social Psychology, 96,* 1029–1046.

Greenleaf, R. K. (1977). *Servant leadership: A journey into the nature of legitimate power and greatness*. New York: Paulist Press.

Haidt, J. (2001). The emotional dog and its rational tail: A social intuitionist approach to moral judgment. *Psychological Review, 108,* 814–834.

Haidt, J. (2003). The moral emotions. In R. J. Davidson, K. R. Scherer, & H. H. Goldsmith (Eds.), *Handbook of affective sciences* (pp. 852–870). Oxford, UK: Oxford University Press.

Haidt, J., & Graham, J. (2007). When morality opposes justice: Conservatives have moral intuitions that liberals may not recognize. *Social Justice Research, 20,* 98–116.

Haidt, J., & Graham, J. (2009). Planet of the Durkheimians, where community, authority, and sacredness are foundations of morality. In J. Jost, A. C. Kay, & H. Thorisdottir (Eds.), *Social and psychological bases of ideology and system justification* (pp. 371–401). Oxford, UK: Oxford University Press.

Haidt, J., & Joseph, C. (2004). Intuitive ethics: How innately prepared intuitions generate culturally variable virtues. *Daedalus, 133*(4), 55–66.

Haidt, J., & Joseph, C. (2007). The moral mind: How five sets of innate moral intuitions guide the development of many culture-specific virtues, and perhaps even modules. In P. Carruthers, S. Laurence, & S. Stich (Eds.), *The innate mind* (Vol. 3, pp. 367–391). Oxford, UK: Oxford University Press.

Haidt, J., & Kesebir, S. (2010). Morality. In S. T. Fiske & D. Gilbert (Eds.), *Handbook of social psychology*. New York: Wiley.

Haidt, J., Rosenberg, E., & Hom H. (2003). Differentiating diversities: Moral diversity is not like other kinds. *Journal of Applied Social Psychology, 33,* 1–38.

Haidt, J., Seder, J. P., & Kesebir, S. (2008). Hive psychology, happiness, and public policy. *Journal of Legal Studies, 37,* S133–S156.

Harrison, D. A., Price, K. H., & Bell, M. P. (1998). Beyond relational demography: Time and the effect of surface- versus deep-level diversity on group cohesiveness. *Academy of Management Journal, 41,* 96–107.

Harrison, D. A., Price, K. H., Gavin, J. H., & Florey, A. T. (2002). Time, teams, and task performance: Changing effects of diversity on group functioning. *Academy of Management Journal, 45,* 1029–1045.

Hollander, E. P. (1958). Conformity, status, and idiosyncrasy credit. *Psychological Review, 65,* 117–127.

Hollander, E. P., & Offerman, L. R. (1990). Power and leadership in organizations: Relationships in transition. *American Psychologist, 45*(2): 179–189.

Hong, H., & Kacperczyk, (2009). The price of sin: The effects of social norms on markets. *Journal of Financial Economics, 93,* 15–36.

Howell, J. M. (1988). Two faces of charisma: Socialized and personalized leadership in organizations. In J. A. Conger & R. N. Kanungo (Eds.), *Charismatic leadership* (pp. 213–236). San Francisco: Jossey-Bass.

Ibarra, H. (1992). Homophily and differential returns: Sex differences in network structure and access in an advertising firm. *Administrative Science Quarterly, 37,* 422–447.

Jackson, S. E. (1992). Team composition in organizational settings: Issues in managing an increasingly diverse work force. In S. Worchel, W. Wood, & J. A. Simpson (Eds.). *Group process and productivity* (pp. 136–180). Newbury Park, CA: Sage.

Janis, I. (1972). *Victims of groupthink: A psychological study of foreign policy decisions and fiascoes.* Boston: Houghton Mifflin.

Jehn, K. A., Northcraft, G. B., & Neale, M. A. (1999). Why differences make a difference: a field study of diversity, conflict, and performance in workgroups. *Administrative Science Quarterly, 44,* 741–763.

Jones, T. M. (1991). Ethical decision making by individuals in organizations: An issue-contingent model. *Academy of Management Review, 16,* 366–395.

Kanungo, R., & Mendonca, M. (1996). *Ethical dimensions of leadership.* Thousand Oaks, CA: Sage.

Keeley, M. (2004). The trouble with transformational leadership: Toward a Federalist ethic for organizations. In J. B. Ciulla (Ed.), *Ethics, the heart of leadership* (pp. 149–174). Westport, CT: Sage.

Kelman, H. C., & Hamilton, V. L. (1989). *Crimes of obedience.* New Haven, CT: Yale University Press.

Kipnis, D. (1976). *The powerholders.* Chicago: University of Chicago Press.

Kish-Gephart, J. J., Harrison, D. A., & Treviño, L. K. (2010). Bad apples, bad cases, and bad barrels: Meta-analytic evidence about sources of unethical decisions at work. *Journal of Applied Psychology, 95*(1), 1–31.

Klein, K. J., & Harrison, D. A. (2007). On the diversity of diversity: Tidy logic, messier realities. *Academic of Management Perspectives, 21*(4), 26–33.

Kohlberg, L., Levine, C., & Hewer, A. (1983). *Moral stages: A current formulation and a response to critics.* New York: Karger.

Kulik, C. T., & Roberson, L. (2008). Common goals and golden opportunities: Evaluations of diversity education in academic and organizational settings. *Academy of Management Learning & Education, 7*(3), 309–331.

Lapsley, D. K., & Hill, P. L. (2008). On dual processing and heuristic approaches to moral cognition. *Journal of Moral Education, 37,* 313–332.

Lapsley, D. K., & Narvaez, D. (2004). A social-cognitive approach to moral personality. In D. K. Lapsley & D. Narvaez (Eds.), *Moral development, self and identity* (pp. 189–213). Mahwah, NJ: Erlbaum.

Liljenquist, K. A., Zhong, C.-B., and Galinsky, A. D. (2010). The smell of virtue: Clean scents promote reciprocity and charity. *Psychological Science, 21*: 381–383.

Martin, K. D., Johnson, J. L., & Cullen, J. B. (2009). Organizational change, normative control deinstitutionalization, and corruption. *Business Ethics Quarterly, 19,* 105–130.

McClelland, D. C. (1975). *Power: The inner experience.* New York: Irvington.

Messner, S. F., & Rosenfeld, R. (1997). Political restraint of the market and levels of criminal homicide: A cross-national application of institutional-anomie theory. *Social Forces, 75,* 1393–1416.

Milgram, S. (1963). Behavioral study of obedience. *Journal of Abnormal and Social Psychology, 67,* 371–378.

Milgram, S. (1974). *Obedience to authority: An experimental view.* New York: Harper and Row.

Mitchell, R. K., Agle, B. R., & Wood, D. J. (1997). Toward a theory of stakeholder identification and salience: Defining the principle of who and what really counts. *Academy of Management Review, 22,* 853–996.

Nisbet, R. A. (1993). *The sociological tradition.* New Brunswick, NJ: Transaction.

Opotow, S. (1990). Moral exclusion and injustice: An introduction. *Journal of Social Issues, 46*(1), 1–20.

Page, S. E. (2007). Making the difference: Applying a logic of diversity. *Academy of Management Perspectives, 21*(4), 6–20.

Parboteeah, K. P., Hoegl, M., & Cullen, J. (2009). Religious dimensions and work obligation: A country institutional profile model. *Human Relations, 61*(1), 119–148.

Pearson, A. R., Dovidio, J. F., & Gaertner, S. L. (2009). The nature of contemporary prejudice: Insights from aversive racism. *Social and Personality Psychology Compass, 3,* 2–25.

Polzer, J., Stewart, K., & Simmons, J. (1999). A social categorization explanation for framing effects in nested social dilemmas. *Organizational Behavior and Human Decision Processes, 79*: 154–178.

Pratto, F., Sidanius, J., Stallworth, L. M., & Malle, B. F. (1994). Social dominance orientation: A personality variable predicting social and political attitudes. *Journal of Personality and Social Psychology, 67,* 741–763.

Putnam, R. (2007). E Pluribus Unum: Diversity and community in the twenty-first century. *Scandinavian Political Studies, 31,* 137–174.

Reed, A., II, Aquino, K., & Levy, E. (2007). Moral identity and judgments of charitable behaviors. *Journal of Marketing, 71,* 178–191.

Resick, C. J., Hanges, P. J., Dickson, M. W., & Mitchelson, J. K. (2006). A cross-cultural examination of the endorsement of ethical leadership. *Journal of Business Ethics, 63,* 345–359.

Reynolds, S. J. (2006a). Moral awareness and ethical predispositions: Investigating the role of individual differences in the recognition of moral issues. *Journal of Applied Psychology, 91*(1), 233–243.

Reynolds, S. J. (2006b). A neurocognitive model of the ethical decision-making process: Implications for study and practice. *Journal of Applied Psychology, 91,* 736–748.

Reynolds, S. J., & Ceranic, T. (2007). The effects of moral judgment and moral identity on moral behavior: An empirical examination of the moral individual. *Journal of Applied Psychology, 92,* 1610–1624.

Robinson, S., & O'Leary-Kelly, A. (1998). Monkey see, monkey do: The influence of work groups on antisocial behavior of employees. *Academy of Management Journal, 41*(6), 658–672.

Rozin, P., & Fallon, A. (1987). A perspective on disgust. *Psychological Review, 95,* 228–239.

Rozin, P., Lowery, L., Imada, S., & Haidt, J. (1999). The moral-emotion triad hypothesis: A mapping between three moral emotions (contempt, anger, disgust) and three moral ethics (community, autonomy, divinity). *Journal of Personality and Social Psychology, 76,* 574–586.

Rozin, P., Markwith, M., & McCauley, C. (1994). Sensitivity to indirect contacts with other persons: AIDS aversion as a composite of aversion to strangers, infection, moral taint, and misfortune. *Journal of Abnormal Psychology, 103,* 495–504.

Shao, R., Aquino, K., & Freeman, D. (2008). Beyond moral reasoning: A review of moral identity research and its implications for business ethics. *Business Ethics Quarterly, 18*(4), 513–540.

Shweder, R. A., Much, N. C., Mahapatra, M., & Park, L. (1997). The "big three" of morality (autonomy, community, divinity) and the "big three" explanations of suffering. In A. Brandt & P. Rozin (Eds.), *Morality and health* (pp. 119–169). New York: Routledge.

Skitka, L. J., Bauman, C. W., & Sargis, E. G. (2005). Moral conviction: Another contributor to attitude strength or something more? *Journal of Personality and Social Psychology, 88*, 895–917.

Stewart, M. M., Crary, M, & Humberd, B. K. (2008). Teaching value in diversity: On the follow of espousing inclusion, while practicing exclusion. *Academy of Management Learning & Education, 7*(3), 374–386.

Sunstein, C. R. (2005). Moral heuristics. *Behavioral and Brain Sciences, 28*, 531–573.

Tajfel, H., & Turner, J. C. (1985). The social identity theory of intergroup behavior. In S. Worchel & W. Austin (Eds.), *Psychology of intergroup relations* (pp. 7–24). Chicago: Nelson-Hall.

Tenbrunsel, A., & Messick, D. (2004). Ethical fading: The role of self-deception in unethical behavior. *Social Justice Research, 17*(2): 223–236.

Tenbrunsel, A., Smith-Crowe, K., & Umphress, E. (2003). Building houses on rocks: The role of ethical infrastructure in organizations. *Social Justice Research, 16*(3): 285–207.

Treviño, L. K., Brown, M., & Hartman, L. (2003). A qualitative investigation of perceived executive ethical leadership: Perceptions from inside and outside the executive suite, *Human Relations, 56*(1), 5–37.

Treviño, L. K., & Victor, B. 1992. Peer reporting of unethical behavior: A social context perspective. *Academy of Management Journal, 35*(1), 38–64.

Treviño, L. K., & Weaver, G. R. (2003). *Managing ethics in business organizations*. Stanford, CA: Stanford Business Books.

Treviño, L. K., Weaver, G. R., & Reynolds, L. K. (2006). Behavioral ethics in organizations: A review. *Journal of Management, 32*, 951–990.

Turiel, E. (1983). *The development of social knowledge: Morality and convention*. Cambridge, UK: Cambridge University Press.

van Knippenberg, D., & Schippers, M. C. (2007). Work group diversity. *Annual Review of Psychology, 58*, 515–541.

Vitell, S. J., Bing, M. N., Davison, H. K., Ammeter, A. P., Garner, B. L., & Novicevic, M. M. (2009). Religiosity and moral identity: The mediating role of self-control. *Journal of Business Ethics, 88*(4), 601–613.

Weaver, G. R., & Agle, B. R. (2002). Religiosity and ethical behavior in organizations: A symbolic interactionist perspective. *Academy of Management Review, 27*(1), 77–97.

Weaver, G. R., & Treviño, L. K. (1999). Compliance and values oriented ethics programs: Influences on employees' attitudes and behavior. *Business Ethics Quarterly, 9*, 315–337.

Weaver, G. R., Treviño, L. K., & Agle, B. R. (2005). "Somebody I look up to": Ethical role modeling in organizations. *Organizational Dynamics, 34*, 313–330.

Welcomer, S. A., Gioia, D. A., & Kilduff, M. (2000). Resisting the discourse of modernity: Rationality versus emotion in hazardous waste siting. *Human Relations, 53*, 1175–1205.

Williams, K. Y., & O'Reilly, C. A. (1998). Demography and diversity in organizations: A review of 40 years of research. *Research in Organizational Behavior, 20*, 77–140.

Wright, J. C., Cullum, J., & Schwab, N. (2008). The cognitive and affective dimensions of moral conviction: Implications for attitudinal and behavioral measures of interpersonal tolerance. *Personality and Social Psychology Bulletin, 34*, 1461–1476.

Yussen, S. R., & Levy, V. M., Jr. (1975). Effects of warm and neutral models on the attention of observational learners. *Journal of Experimental Child Psychology, 20*, 66–72.

Zey-Ferrell, M. K., Weaver, M., & Ferrell, O. C. (1979). Predicting unethical behavior among marketing practitioners. *Human Relations, 32*(7), 557–569.

Zhong, C.-B., Strejcek, B., & Sivanathan, N. (2010). A clean self can render harsh moral judgment. *Journal of Experimental Social Psychology, 46*: 859–862.

8

Defining Behavioral Business Ethics: The Role of Morality in Business Organizations[1]

Tom R. Tyler
New York University

DO MANAGEMENT VALUES MATTER?

The purpose of this chapter is to define the parameters of the area of behavioral ethics in the context of business organizations. I think that this first requires us to define the core elements of behavioral ethics and to then consider the implications of those elements for business practices and organizations. I argue that behavioral business ethics should be different in its focus from the topics traditionally studied in the field of ethics.

Ethics has traditionally been defined as the study of how people reason about and make decisions concerning right and wrong. A number of examples of ethics and of the difficulties of ethical reasoning about complex problems in all realms of life are provided in the highly popular book *Justice: What's the Right Thing to Do?* written by Michael Sandel and published in 2009. Sandel describes the reasoning processes through which philosophers, political theorists, and those involved in everyday reasoning seek to make the right decisions when resolving conflicts between moral principles or between morality and other societal concerns ranging from lowering costs to ensuring survival or simply following social rules. However people reason, ethics is concerned with the rightness or wrongness of decisions they make about what to do, for instance, with achieving desirable ends.

And, of course, psychologists like Lawrence Kohlberg have made the study of how people reason ethically central to their discussions about the

evolution of values across the life span. In one particularly famous example, Kohlberg asks people to think about what they would do if they needed
a drug to help cure their spouse of an illness but could not afford to buy it
(see Kohlberg, 1981; Rest, Narvaez, Bebeau, & Thoma, 1999). As in other
ethical dilemmas, the issue in Kohlberg's work is not primarily with what
people decide to do, but with the issues they consider and principles they
evoke when making the decision. However, its focus is on the morality of
ends: whether what people do is consistent with moral principles. The process is one of reasoning about what is right and wrong to obtain a desired
end. We do not know, for example, whether it is really more ethical to obey
the law or steal a drug to save one's spouse, but we can evaluate the quality
of the reasoning that goes into deciding what to do.

Behavioral ethics uses the results of empirical studies to illuminate ethical reasoning. For example Appiah (2008) explored the implications of
recent research on emotion for understanding how people resolve conflicts
in ethical dilemmas such as the trolley problem, in which differences in
people's willingness to engage in active versus passive harm to others is used
to understand the nature of reasoning about moral dilemmas (Kamm, 1989;
Thomson, 1985). Research suggests that the differences between decisions
involving actions that require people to act to cause harm versus not to act
and thereby allow harm are different because deciding to cause harm activates more emotional areas of the brain in decision making (Haidt, 2007).

The issue of concern here is not behavioral ethics but behavioral business
ethics. In contrast to the approaches to ethics outlined in their extension to
the field of behavioral ethics, I suggest that behavioral ethics should have a
distinct focus. That focus should be on our understanding of the role that
values and ethical principles play in the social dynamics of groups. Here,
the question is whether values matter because a person's values shape their
behavior. This includes the values of chief executive officers (CEOs) and others in management and the ethical values of everyday employees. This focus
is what Treviño, Weaver, and Reynolds (2006) refer to as moral motivation,
which Rest describes as a person's "degree of commitment to taking the
moral course of action, valuing moral values over other values, and taking
personal responsibility for moral outcomes" (Rest et al., 1999, p. 101).

While I endorse this general motivational perspective, I suggest that the
values of concern in behavioral business ethics are broader in scope than
just the moral values that are discussed by Rest et al.. When Rest et al. discusses moral values they were concerned with people's views concerning

what is right or wrong, that is, with the ethicality of the decisions made and with the way that people use their reasoning skills to obtain those ends. So, for example, in the already-noted moral dilemma originally utilized by Kohlberg (1981), a man must decide whether to break the law to steal a drug for his sick wife or follow the law and see her illness worsen. More recently, studies of moral reasoning have presented people with the trolley problem. A person can take an action (diverting a runaway trolley) that kills one person but saves several, or the person can take no action and allow the several endangered people to die. Here, the moral question is whether it is right to take action in which one person is hurt or killed to save the lives of many.

All of the moral dilemmas noted focus on decisions about what conduct is right or wrong—on the morality of the decisions made about what to do. This is the morality of ends. I believe ethics is broader than whether the actions taken are consistent with principles of right or wrong (i.e., whether moral ends are achieved). I think it also concerns the morality of means. Two aspects of the morality of means are important: the ethicality of management conduct during the decision-making process and the general procedural fairness of organizational culture and management actions.

My view of behavioral business ethics is, as Treviño et al. (2006) suggest, motivational in nature. It asks whether ethics matters in the sense that it shapes what people do. In contrast, traditional ethics has focused primarily on how people reason their way to desirable solutions (i.e., outcomes) when confronted with ethics-related problems. My concern is with the influence of such solutions on employee actions. In other words, once people have a view about what is right or wrong, are they motivated to act in accordance with this judgment of appropriateness? I suggest that this motivation is shaped by the ethics of both means and ends.

In contrast to Kohlberg, who asked whether people will break rules to uphold principles of right and wrong, I suggest that in business environments the question is whether people's motivation to avoid punishment or gain material reward will be tempered by their desire to make their behavior congruent with values. In particular, I am concerned with employee willingness to defer to the policies, practices, and rules of work organizations because those organizations are being managed in ways they view as moral, ethical, or just.

Why focus on employee behavior? I suggest that to be of utility behavioral business ethics needs to focus on concerns that matter in the management context. One key concern is whether values shape the viability of work organizations. And, a large literature suggests that the willingness of employees to abide by rules is a key driver of effectiveness because it is central to the ability of companies to conform to legal and ethical standards of appropriate conduct. Such value-based employee behavior is more effective than is compliance based on the threat of sanctions.

From this perspective, two empirical questions are important. The first is whether employee judgments about the moral values of management shape employee behaviors in work organizations. Are employees, for example, motivated by whether they believe that the policies and practices of management are consistent with their own moral values? For the second, which aspects of the ethical culture (Treviño et al., 2006) of business organizations shape the behavior of employees within those organizations?

The contrasting perspective to a value-based model is the traditional rational choice model, which links behavior to promised incentives or threatened punishments. Within the legal arena, a number of studies supported the value-based perspective (Tyler, 2007, 2008). Tyler and Blader (2005) compared the instrumental model to a model based on values in two management settings and found that values are a stronger influence on behavior than incentives. Their findings are consistent with those of other studies conducted in work, political, and regulatory settings. Cooperation is primarily responsive to values and not incentives and sanctions (Tyler, 2011).

LEVEL OF ANALYSIS

In many of the corporate scandals in recent years, a key issue in the scandal has been that upper management was unethical. Hence, one important issue is why CEOs or other higher-level managers would behave ethically. However, I focus my attention on lower-level employees. I do so not because that focus is more appropriate in terms of addressing overall ethical issues but rather because there is more readily accessible empirical data. In particular, my own work has focused on employees at various levels of management, but not on CEOs or boards of directors. Hence, I discuss motivating employees within organizations, rather than focus on leaders at the CEO level.

FORMS OF COOPERATION

As part of my argument about the importance of morality, ethics, and justice, I want to draw on the literature on cooperation (Tyler, 2011) to make a distinction between two forms of cooperative behavior. That distinction is between behavior that is under the control of incentives and behavior that is voluntary in the sense that it is not motivated by expected gains or feared losses. My suggestion is that organizations gain to the degree that they can motivate their members to engage in voluntary cooperation because then people self-regulate, for example, engage in the behavior because of their internal desires to behave in ways that are moral, ethical, and just.

The distinction between economically driven behavior and voluntary behavior can be made concerning two core types of cooperation: rule following and productivity. *Rule following* refers to bringing one's behavior into line with rules and policies. *Productivity* involves making positive contributions to the workplace and work tasks. Rule following can refer to compliance, which is often motivated by fear of punishment. But, voluntary compliance is deference and occurs for internally motivated reasons. Productivity can be in-role behavior (e.g., doing one's assigned job), or it can involve additional, not required, actions that are not rewarded in material terms. These types of cooperative behaviors are often labeled extrarole behaviors.

Businesses can gain great advantage by emphasizing self-regulatory approaches that motivate employees to follow rules based on their internal desires. Similarly, internally motivated employees engage in voluntary extrarole behavior, which also benefits their organization. Hence, a focus on morality, ethics, and justice is central to a strategy of management that is desirable for work organizations. The key empirical issue is whether people can be motivated by appeals to their values.

These comments are part of a broader argument concerning the value of self-regulatory approaches in groups, organizations, and communities (see Tyler, 2007, 2009; Tyler & Fagan, 2008). This approach suggests that we need to change our goals regarding the behavior we want from the members of groups. The second is that this change in behavioral objectives leads to a change in the tactics that we should employ to obtain our goals. The key suggestion is that there are tremendous benefits to shifting our focus toward voluntary acceptance of decisions and, beyond that, toward voluntary cooperation with legal authorities.

Such a shift in behavioral focus requires a shift in motivational strategy away from sanctions or incentives and toward the creation and activation of values, that is, toward a self-regulatory approach to generating law-abiding behavior. The first aspect of such a model is the argument that people are motivated by their values. It is to this issue, which is an empirical question, that I direct this chapter.

QUESTION 1. DO EMPLOYEE'S VALUES SHAPE BEHAVIOR IN WORK ORGANIZATIONS?

If either managers or employees only act out of their simple economic self-interest, then the values that employees attribute to management are not particularly important in the business context. Rather, what would then be important are the judgments made about the likely short- and long-term costs and benefits associated with conduct. In such a case, regulation of behavior by either upper management or the government would have to take the form of creating threats of punishment for rule-breaking behavior or incentives for rule-following behavior. However, if the behavior of employees is shaped by their values, then moral values, ethical decisions, and management via procedural justice are important and can potentially be the basis for designing organizations.

Moral Values

The first value-based motivation is linked to moral values. Does it matter if management is pursuing moral ends? In considering the role of moral values in work settings, I distinguish between moral values and legitimacy. Both moral values and feelings of obligation to obey legitimate rules and authorities are values that involve acting based on a sense of appropriateness. The difference is that moral values indicate a correct course of conduct, that is, the right course of action to take. People are motivated to act in ways that are consistent with their evaluations of the rightness or wrongness of different behaviors. In contrast, legitimacy involves obligation: The correct course is to act based on responsibility to defer to the directives of others. Three types of obligation to one's work organization are potentially important: the obligation to follow rules and policies; the obligation to work well;

and feelings of loyalty to the company that lead people to stay with the company when given other alternatives.

Legitimacy is a general obligation to defer to authorities, and a number of studies indicated that it is linked to voluntary rule following (see Tyler, 2006a, 2006c). Morality, on the other hand, only works if the actions involved are consistent with people's own moral values. The issue of concern here is the influence of such moral evaluations on employee conduct distinct from evaluations of legitimacy. In other words, from an ethical perspective the issue is whether employees are influenced by their evaluations of the morality of management policies and practices. And, the assumption is that they make such judgments by comparing those policies and practices to their own moral values—that they make judgments of moral value congruence.

Recent empirical research strongly supported the suggestion that employees are influenced by their views about whether management is acting in moral ways, and that the influence of such moral evaluations is distinct from that of legitimacy. For example, Tyler and Blader (2005) show that both obligation and moral value congruence shape employee's rule-related behavior, including their compliance with organizational policies, their voluntary deference to such policies, and their rule-breaking behavior. These value-based influences are further shown to be distinct from the influence of promised rewards or expected punishments on rule-related behavior. The Tyler and Blader study looked at two distinct groups: corporate bankers and a broad sample of employees. In both groups, moral values had a distinct influence on employee behavior. Tyler and Blader (2000) also linked moral value congruence to employee extrarole behavior in a study that considered a different sample of employees based in New York City.

In considering these findings, two caveats are important. First, the survey-based approach used by Tyler and Blader (2000, 2005) looks at evaluations of general moral values. That is, it does not focus on a particular issue of morality. Employees are asked whether management generally shares their values and whether they are rarely or often asked to do things that they think are morally wrong. This general approach makes sense given that the studies look at the general climate of organizations. For example, the second study in Tyler and Blader (2005) looks at a random sample of American employees and suggests that, within the range of the policies and practices these employees encounter in their work environments, behavior is linked to the perceived relationship of those policies and practices and the moral values of management they reflect to the employee's own moral values.

Tyler, Callahan, and Frost (2007) considered similar issues in samples of law enforcement and military personnel. Interestingly, they found evidence that, as expected, moral value congruence shaped voluntary deference to policies among both groups, but did not shape compliance with organizational rules. This is consistent with the general argument that compliance, as opposed to deference, is more likely to be instrumentally motivated. It is interesting that, even in the relatively highly structured environments represented by the military and the police, views about the moral values reflected in management practices were found to be important.

These findings do not mean that there are no situations in which morality is so weak or self-interest so strong that the influence of general morality outlined based on these findings changes. It could be that when self-interest is a very strong motivation the role of morality diminishes. However, the results suggest that in general the degree to which employees act is based on their judgments about whether management has moral values similar to their own. Employees are motivated to cooperate with a management that shares their values.

Second, the approach to morality I outline here accepts a common assumption of psychology: that moral values are difficult to change among adults (Tyler, 2006b). Therefore, it asks about consistency with existing values. I am not suggesting that management should or could reeducate employees by altering their moral values. Rather, I am asking whether it facilitates employee motivation when employees perceive that their own values are consistent with the policies and practices of management.

We can compare this to a parallel issue in law: Does law change attitudes? When a law is passed, it may change behavior irrespective of whether it changes attitudes. People can bring their behavior into line with the new law but still think the new behavior is morally wrong. Does the law actually change what people think they ought to do, and therefore what they do willingly and voluntarily? Studies suggest that it can but does not necessarily (Muir, 1967). The parallel management question is whether management can change what employees believe is moral by enacting a new policy. For example, if management decided to open a factory on Sunday, would employees consequently come to believe that working on Sunday is a morally appropriate action? And, as with law, that question is not

TABLE 8.1

Moral Value Congruence and Voluntary Behavior

	Compliance		Deference	
Values	.37***	—	.66***	—
Legitimacy		.32***		.46***
Moral value congruence		.07***		.17***
Risk-benefit analysis	.69***	—	.38***	—
	26%	—	36%	—

Note: The data used in this analysis are described in more detail in Tyler & Blader (2005), study 2.

addressed here. Instead, the underlying assumption is that employees will employ their existing moral values to evaluate policies.

As noted, the data outlined indicate that moral value congruence matters. The second issue is whether moral value congruence is especially important in the case of voluntary behavior. This issue can also be examined in the case of rule following using the data considered by Tyler and Blader (2005, Study 2). The results shown in Table 8.1, which is drawn from Tyler and Blader (2005), suggest that, while moral value congruence is important with both compliance and deference, it is especially important when voluntary deference is the focus. This makes sense. Employees will more voluntarily accept and follow those decisions, rules, and policies that accord with their own values concerning appropriateness. But, it also indicates that employees respond to moral judgments in work settings.

Organizational Implications

The core of my own argument for the value of ethics is that an awareness of how employees think about ethics is the key to understanding how to motivate voluntary behavior. And, I further argue that voluntary behavior is better for organizations (Tyler, 2011). If organizations do not need to incentivize or conduct surveillance of their employees, they have the capacity to deploy resources to more productive uses. This is a major consideration in all conditions, but especially so during times of difficulty and crisis when organizations need to be able to focus their available resources on building new opportunities.

Further, employees are often best able to understand local conditions, and if they are motivated to exercise discretion and to make judgments about how to solve problems and improve task productivity, organizations can be national or international in scope, but still benefit from local opportunities and potential for gain. For this reason, there has been a general recognition in the area of law of the value of "soft law," which encourages public cooperation in the development and implementation of legal and regulatory rules, hoping to take advantage of the public's awareness of the best ways to manage local problems and conditions.

QUESTION 2. DOES THE ETHICAL NATURE OF THE ACTIONS OF LEADERS AND MANAGEMENT MATTER?

Like evaluations of moral value, congruence evaluations of the ethicality of management decisions asks employees to compare the decisions made by management to their own ethical standards. Some discussions of ethics treat morality and ethics as interchangeable terms (see, e.g., Treviño et al., 2006). In this chapter, I argue for the value of treating ethical decision making (means) as distinct from acting in ways consistent with moral values (ends). I do so because I believe that an important issue concerning moral values is the degree to which management can influence an employee's views about the congruence of management values to the employee's own values. In other words, is there anything that management can do to communicate to employees that they are moral? One thing that management could do is to make decisions in fair ways.

An important empirical question is whether employee judgments about the ethical quality of management decision making shapes views about the morality of management or cooperative behavior? And, consistent with the value-based approach of behavioral business ethics, it is especially important that it is the ethics of management decision making that matters. For example, if employees reacted to management competence rather than management ethicality, that would suggest that their orientation toward management is instrumental, and they are concerned with their gains and losses. From such an instrumental perspective, it is the competence of management (i.e. their ability to keep the company profitable) that should matter to employees and not whether they are ethical.

If moral values are not related to the ethicality of the actions of management, then values are exogenous to organizations. Of course, this does not make values irrelevant. For example, selection is still a potentially viable organizational strategy. Management can hire employees who share their moral values. This has been the case, for example, in efforts to select honest employees via mechanisms such as integrity testing (Ones & Viswesvaran, 1998). However, this is at best a second-rate strategy. Consider the difference between a bullet and a missile. A bullet, once fired, continues on its course, while a missile can be altered by later signals as the target moves. Hiring employees with one set of moral values and hoping that those will fit management policies and practices throughout their life course of employment is problematic. It would clearly be desirable for management to be able to shape employee beliefs about management morality by the manner in which management makes decisions and establishes policies and practices.

Consistent with the general line of argument in this chapter, I first want to describe what I think is key to an ethical approach to evaluating management. This view is that employees seek to evaluate the intentions, motivations, and character of managers. It has long been recognized that when people are evaluating others, a key issue they focus on is the underlying character of that person (Heider, 1958). This involves their values, as well as their attitudes and other dispositions that shape future behavior. But, inferences about character and values have always been central to efforts to understand others because people believe they are stable and therefore provide a guide to understanding future actions. For example, research shows that people in all types of social settings focus their evaluations of authorities on the character of those authorities more than on their competence (see Tyler & Degoey, 1996).

I think that ethical decision making is distinct from shared moral values because inferences about the ethicality of decision making focus on intentions. It is true that intentions reflect underlying character and values, so ethicality in decision making should be a reflection of underlying moral values. However, I think it is useful to view them as distinct. Of course, ultimately this is an empirical question. For example, I found (Tyler, 2010) that employees distinguished between shared moral values and judgments of the ethicality of management decision making, with the two found to be distinct but correlated concepts ($r = .22$, $p < .001$).

TABLE 8.2

The Influence of Managerial Ethicality on Values and Behaviors

	Moral Value Congruence	Obligation	VRFB	ERB
Management is ethical	.43***	.16***	.15***	.08***
Management is competent	.26***	.06***	.08***	.07***
Time one measure	.30***	.55***	.48***	.60***
Adjusted R.-sq.	64%	38%	31%	39%

Source: From Tyler, Does the morality of management matter? Unpublished manuscript, New York University. 2010.

To the degree that judgments about the ethical character of management practices are found to shape employee behavior, I suggest this argues that values are again influencing the business environment through employee's attention to and concern about the ethical character of management decision making. This echoes the previous argument that moral value congruence matters. There are two empirical issues that need to be addressed concerning ethics: Do judgments about the ethics of management decision making matter, and do they matter separately from instrumental judgments about management competence?

Tyler (2010) addresses this question in an analysis of the role of ethical judgments in shaping employee behavior. Using panel data collected on a random sample of American employees, he contrasts the role of employee evaluations of management competence and management ethicality in terms of their influence in shaping both perceived moral value congruence, obligation to management and voluntary employee behavior. The results of this analysis are shown in Table 8.2, which is drawn from Tyler (2010). His findings suggest that ethical evaluations of management decision making have an independent influence upon both perceived moral value congruence and on voluntary employee behavior. He finds that evaluations of the ethical character of management shape perceived moral value congruence, perceived obligation to defer to management, and voluntary workplace behavior.

The findings of that study (Tyler, 2010) are striking because they show that employee evaluations of management ethicality influence both perceived moral value congruence and legitimacy. It is clear based on these findings that those employees who evaluate management policies and practices as being ethical view management as sharing their moral values and as having the right to make decisions that employees feel an obligation to accept. Tyler also finds that employees are more cooperative in their workplace behavior.

These findings support the prior argument that ethical values are a viable basis for building organizational cultures. Both judgments about the morality of ends in the form of consistency of policies with employee values and judgments about the ethicality of the means management used to make decisions distinctly shape what employees do in the workplace.

The findings also reinforce the importance of moral value congruence in organizational settings. In contrast to the view that moral values are fixed and cannot change, these findings suggest that perceived moral value congruence is responsive to judgments about the ethicality of the practices of management. If employees judge that their managers are making decisions ethically, they view them as sharing their moral values, and they more willingly work on their behalf. Further, employees are found to work more willingly for managers they view as employing ethic means to make decisions. This is distinct from evaluations of their competence, which also motivates employee cooperation.

While perceived moral value congruence and perceived ethicality of decision making clearly shape employee' reactions to management, from a management perspective both are limited in one crucial way. They both depend on employee's preexisting views about what is right and wrong, ethical or unethical. Either because they view management actions as consistent with their own moral values or because they view management practices as ethical, employees are more cooperative with management. However, these employee judgments draw on preexisting employee views about what is appropriate.

If for some business-related reason management found itself in the difficult position of having to enact policies or engage in practices that employees think are wrong or unethical in that situation, employee's values would undermine management's need for cooperation. Employees would be less willing to cooperate with management and to voluntarily behave in accord with rules and policies, as well as being less willing to engage in extrarole behaviors that help the company. Hence, the potentially positive role of values for companies comes with strings attached: Employees have to believe that management shares their moral values and is making decisions ethically. The fact that both evaluations draw on employee values draws an exogenous force into management calculations.

This issue of value conflict was discussed by Kelman and Hamilton (1989) in their examination of the conflict between the state and religion.

While the state benefits from the support of religious authority in many situations, when the state and religious authorities were in conflict, people were torn between two values: the legitimacy of the state and morality as defined by religious institutions and authorities. Here, employees can potentially be torn between their own moral values and ethical standards, however derived, and actions taken by management. And, as in the conflicts discussed by Kelman and Hamilton (1989), neither the state nor religious authorities can count on the loyalty of their followers as people wrestle with difficult issues of right and wrong when trying to balance these different values.

On a more mundane level, a similar conflict was discussed by Robinson and Darley (1995) in the area of law. Robinson and Darley noted that one important reason that people obey laws is that those laws accord with their sense of right and wrong. Hence, the law benefits when not only legitimacy but also morality dictate that following the law is the right thing to do. For example, murder is not only illegal but also immoral. Consequently, Robinson and Darley suggested that the legal system is on weaker ground, motivationally speaking, when it seeks to make illegal behavior that people do not generally regard as immoral. So, they suggested that the legal system should do so sparingly lest it undermine its broader authority.

In the case of Robinson and Darley's (1995) argument, the discussion is about ends. The law is a set of principles that may or may not accord with people's moral values. However, this argument can be extended to the ethicality of means. Leventhal (1980) pointed out that there is also an ethicality of procedures. This distinction has recently been highlighted by discussions within America about the procedures used to interrogate terror suspects. Many people have expressed concern that procedures they consider to be "torture" are used in the process of trying to gain information about terror plots. This concern is a concern about the procedure. Even if torture were found to yield accurate and valuable information, people would still object to it because it violates ethical principles about how to act. This is a means-based judgment that is distinct from the ends that are achieved.

The argument here is similar for management. If management is relying on the values of its employees to motivate employee behavior, it consequently needs to be sensitive to what those values are and consider carefully when it engages in policies (ends) and practices (means) inconsistent with what employees view as ethical and moral.

QUESTION 3. DOES THE GENERAL JUSTICE CLIMATE SHAPE JUDGMENTS ABOUT THE ETHICALITY OF CONDUCT AND THE MORALITY OF POLICIES?

Ideally, employees can be motivated to cooperate using a general management strategy that is not linked to specific content issues of right and wrong. Procedural justice and the strategy of process-based management that flows from it is such a strategy in that it argues that people will be loyal to authorities because of how they make decisions, distinct from what those decisions are. Hence, to the degree that procedural justice judgments matter to employees, their influence on employee behavior provides a broader management approach to building and maintaining an ethical culture (Tyler, 2007; Tyler & Blader, 2000, 2005).

In other words, in contrast to an issues-based determination of the morality of management and of the ethicality of management decisions, management would benefit by motivating the view that managers are ethical and have congruent moral values through the general style of management that they display in the workplace. In particular, I argue that process-based management can be a key to general judgments that management is ethical and has congruent moral values. For this to be the case, it is necessary that people be influenced by a broader set of procedural concerns than just the ethicality of management.

What Is Procedural Justice?

When employees indicate that their workplace is or is not procedurally fair, what do they mean? Answering this question is fundamental to understanding how to design workplaces that engage employee values and encourage rule and policy adherence. And, in particular, it is important to identify procedural elements that are distinct from ethicality.

Prior studies of procedural justice in work settings identify two key dimensions of an employee's procedural fairness judgments: fairness of decision making and fairness of interpersonal treatment. These two types of fairness can be evaluated at the organizational and work group levels. This creates four procedural factors: decision-making fairness at the organizational level, interpersonal fairness at the organizational level, decision-making fairness at the work group level, and interpersonal fairness at the work group level.

Studies suggest that employees are influenced by all four of these aspects of procedural justice. At the organizational level, employees evaluate the procedural fairness of their overall organization, its policies and procedures, the actions of the CEO and board. Separately, they assess the fairness of the procedures used by their work group supervisor and coworkers. At each level, both aspects of procedure, decision making, and interpersonal treatment, independently and collectively, contribute to overall procedural justice evaluations.

The most obvious aspect of procedures is that they are mechanisms for making decisions. When thinking about those mechanisms, employees evaluate fairness along several dimensions. First, do they have opportunities for input before decisions are made? Second, are decisions made following understandable and transparent rules? Third, are decision-making bodies acting neutrally, basing their decisions on objective information and appropriate criteria rather than acting out of personal prejudices and biases? Fourth, are the rules applied consistently across people and over time?

Quality of interpersonal treatment is found to be equally important. It involves the manner in which people are treated during the decision-making process. First, are people's rights as employees respected? For example, do managers follow the rules specified in organizational manuals or employment contracts? Second, is their right as a person to be treated politely and with dignity acknowledged, and does such treatment occur? Third, do managers consider employee input when making decisions, and are the decision makers concerned about employee needs and concerns when they make decisions? Finally, do the decision makers account for their actions by giving honest explanations about what they have decided and why they made their decisions?

Research shows that each of these four aspects plays a distinct role in shaping employee judgments about whether their workplace is fair (Blader & Tyler, 2003). This argument was supported by an empirical analysis in which the influence of the four elements of procedural justice was considered in each of the two studies we have been examining. The results (shown in Table 8.3) indicate that each element is independently important, with employees considering organizational-level issues of decision making and interpersonal quality of treatment and work group-/supervisor-level judgments of the same two issues.

TABLE 8.3

The Impact of Procedural Elements on Employee's Values and Behaviors

	Ethicality of Judgments		Moral Value Congruence		Voluntary Behavior	
	Management Ethical	Management Competent	Moral Value Congruence	Obligation	Rule Following	Extra-Role Behavior
Quality of decision making	0.17***	0.03	0.05**	-.03	0.03	0.01
Quality of interpersonal treatment	0.69***	0.29***	0.38***	0.12***	0.11***	0.05**
Distributive justice	-.03	0.13***	0.02	0.12***	0.06***	0.09***
Outcome favorability	0.05**	0.19***	0.17***	0.06**	0.03	0.02
Time one	0.14***	0.45***	0.44***	0.55***	0.51***	0.61***
Adjusted R.-sq.	67%	49%	50%	36%	30%	40%

Source: From Tyler, Does the morality of management matter? Unpublished manuscript, New York University. 2010.

In other words, managers can improve the justice culture of their organizations by focusing on two levels: the work group and the organizational levels. On each level, they can target two issues: the quality of decision making and the quality of interpersonal treatment.

Efforts to improve the quality of decision making could potentially involve managers discussing issues of importance with employees before making a decision; making efforts to more clearly articulate the procedures being used for pay and promotion decisions, as well as the criteria involved; highlighting the consistency in decision making across people to minimize the belief that some people receive favorable treatment or that others are subject to prejudice or other biases.

The quality of interpersonal treatment is improved when the focus is on respecting employees and their rights, both as employees and as people. People in all organizations value their good standing in the group, and treatment with courtesy and dignity affirms that they are valued and respected.

A second aspect of quality of interpersonal treatment is trust. Employees want to trust management and to believe that those making decisions care about their needs, concerns, and well-being. While studies often find that employees are cynical about their managers, they consistently show that employees who are asked about what they want in a workplace indicate that they want to work for people who they trust. Managers can communicate that they are trustworthy by listening to their employees and, when implementing decisions, accounting for their actions by explaining how they have considered the employees, that is, by acting using fair procedures.

Getting employee input does not mean that managers must do what employees suggest; regardless of the ultimate outcome, employees tend to accept management decisions when they feel that their perspective has been considered during the decision-making process, even if their preferred course of action is not taken. Nor do employees need voice for all decisions and procedures. I am by no means advocating management's abdication of the responsibility to make decisions. I do, however, suggest that transparency in the process of decision making will result in higher levels of employee buy-in and satisfaction.

The Influence of Procedural Justice

At this point, there is an enormous procedural justice literature, so it is safe to argue based on that research that creating a procedurally fair organization enhances voluntary rule following among employees. However, that literature has generally been directed toward enhancing legitimacy as a consequence of procedural justice (Tyler, 2006). A key issue in this discussion is moral value congruence, not legitimacy of authority. So, one empirical issue central to behavioral business ethics is the distinction between these two values and why it might matter in management settings. In particular, should we consider moral value congruence or focus on issues of legitimacy, the traditional focus of much of the regulation literature?

There are several ways to compare legitimacy and moral value congruence. One is theoretical. On that level, legitimacy has clear advantages over morality. Legitimacy is a sense of obligation to do whatever an authority or institution dictates, within some range of appropriateness. Consequently, legitimacy is traditionally considered under the control of management, while moral values are traditionally viewed as shaped by factors outside the control of management, both because moral values develop early in life and because they are shaped by family, culture, and religion. Hence, while management might benefit from acting morally, it could just as easily be the case that management practices would be contrary to an employee's moral values, leading to declines in rule-following behavior.

Given that legitimacy has advantages, why be concerned about morality? There are several reasons. First, as already noted, morality is not as static as is often supposed. In fact, studies suggest that legitimacy is less responsive to judgments of management ethicality than is morality. So, ironically management might be more able to shape views about whether it shares employee values by managing fairly. Further, morality is consistently found to be a distinct force shaping employee behavior, and it is important to understand whether the same social dynamics that shape legitimacy can also shape moral value congruence. As with law, moral value congruence can add to the influence of legitimacy, or it can undermine it depending on the circumstances.

In an effort to examine the influence of the organizational culture resulting from procedural justice, I (Tyler, 2010) compared the influence of procedural justice on ethicality, perceived moral value congruence, and voluntary employee behavior to that of policy favorability. Evaluations of outcome favorability are instrumental and reflect the degree to which employees believe that they benefit or are harmed by the consequences of management policies.

I (Tyler, 2010) found that procedural justice has a strong influence on both judgments of the ethicality of management procedures and moral value congruence. In particular, the general quality of interpersonal treatment through which management manages shapes employee values of management ethicality and morality. If employees feel that their rights are acknowledged, they are treated with respect and dignity; if management actions reflect a sincere desire to do what is best for employees, then management is regarded as making decisions ethically and sharing employees' moral values. This influence is distinct from a smaller influence of fairness of decision making, but fair decision making also shapes judgments of ethicality and moral value congruence. Hence, it is within the ability of management to influence both ethical or moral judgments and views about the legitimacy of management.

The findings of this (Tyler, 2010) study of employees were replicated in the Tyler et al. (2007) study of police officers and members of the military. Moral value congruence was influenced by procedural justice in both groups. So, if police officers or military personnel felt that their superiors were making decisions using fair procedures, they felt that those authorities shared their moral values.

What is especially striking about the procedural justice results is that they suggest not only that evaluations of ethicality and moral value congruence are responsive to management policies and practices but also that general strategies of management that involve creating an ethical or justice-based culture can shape these ethical judgments. Hence, there is an approach that is above the content of any particular issue but that motivates based on employees' desire to cooperate with organizations that they evaluate as managing via fair procedures.

The findings are especially interesting because they help to clarify judgments about ethicality. What does it mean to evaluate whether management is ethical? I previously noted the centrality of inferences about the intentions of the decision makers. And, consistent with that argument, my results (Tyler, 2010) suggest that inferences about the motives of managers ("trust" in their motivations) are a factor shaping evaluations of whether management procedures are ethical. Since research suggests that trust flows from procedural justice, this leads to clear suggestions for management. First, allow employees opportunities for input into decisions. Second, provide evidence that employee concerns are considered by explaining how they are being taken into account. This is facilitated by transparent and open procedures, as well as by explanations after decisions are made.

CONCLUSION

Voluntary acceptance is a desirable form of employee behavior because it frees companies to use their resources for productive purposes rather than having to enact costly surveillance and oversight mechanisms. While some surveillance is important, and the threat of sanctions is an essential component of regulation, companies can minimize the need for this costly set of regulatory mechanisms by emphasizing value-based self-regulation. Similarly, companies benefit when employees engage in voluntary extra role behaviors motivated by the desire to help their organization be successful. Hence, a key issue is what motivates these behaviors.

This chapter argues that the question of how to motivate voluntary behavior by employees is central to the field of behavioral business ethics. And, the findings outlined suggest that pursuing moral ends, making decisions using ethical procedures, and management via procedural justice all shape employee cooperation. Hence, designing organizational cultures around values makes sense, both from a regulatory perspective (Tyler & Blader, 2005) and in terms of motivating productivity by stimulating commitment to the organization and voluntary efforts to help it succeed (Tyler & Blader, 2000).

Unfortunately, from this perspective the recent U.S. response to business scandals such as Enron and WorldCom has been a major step in the wrong direction. In passing the Sarbanes Oxley law in 2002, the U.S. Congress undermined many of the best practices in which the most progressive companies voluntarily engaged in efforts to build ethical cultures. Those companies and others were pushed by the law into the realm of mandated activity by creating incentive- and sanction-based mechanisms designed to shape the regulation of businesses (see Tyler, Dienhart, & Thomas, 2008). Thus, ironically, the legislative response to a handful of ethical failures—admittedly spectacular and devastating—was to impose on *all* companies a set of the very sorts of rigid command-and-control-based compliance requirements that are inconsistent with the goal outlined in this chapter and do not take advantage of the motivational possibilities linked to morality, ethicality, and justice.

Beyond the enormous social costs and financial burdens incurred by the heightened level of vigilance require by Sarbanes Oxley, I suggest that such an approach is actually harmful to the goal of creating value-based cultures in which rule following is voluntarily, even enthusiastically, embraced, and employees are motivated to work voluntarily on behalf of their companies.

Ironically, this era of sanctions undermined an earlier value-based approach to business regulation that I would argue had a greater likelihood of success. For example, in 1994, Lynne Sharp Paine of Harvard, in her now-famous *Harvard Business Review* article, "Managing for Organizational Integrity," contrasted command-and-control compliance programs with value-based programs. A compliance approach rests on rules enforced by external force, usually the company itself, but with threats of civil and criminal punishment lurking in the background.

The values approach rests on employees governing their own behavior by choosing such behavior voluntarily because it is consistent with employee values about what is appropriate. Paine (1994) argued that the goal is to have the employees engage with the values of the organization, considering those values in the light of their own values and principles of appropriate conduct. When those values are accepted because employees believe that management is moral, that it makes decisions ethically, and that it manages through fair procedures, employees are more likely to comply with rules even when they are not monitored. Such employees come to be good stewards of the values of the company, which they view as consistent with their own values. This is reflected in their everyday behavior, in which employees take the responsibility to act in accord with policies and practices on their own. Further, employees willingly engage in proactive behaviors designed to help the company by doing their jobs well, by helping to instill company values in new employees, and through actively discouraging those who seek to violate those values and disobey rules and policies.

A study by Treviño (1999) was the first large-scale attempt to measure and compare the effectiveness of compliance-based and value-based business conduct programs. This study supported Paine's (1994) contention that a values approach is more effective than a compliance approach. The researchers surveyed 10,000 employees in six industries. Compared to compliance-based programs, value-based programs had fewer reports of unethical conduct, higher levels of ethical awareness, more employees seeking advice about ethical issues, and a higher likelihood of employees reporting violations. Two factors in particular were found to be much higher in a values program than in a compliance program: employee commitment to the company and perceived permission to deliver bad news.

Treviño (1999) also looked at ethical culture as a factor separate from formal programs, and here the results were especially striking. Culture had more influence on employee behavior than did either ethics or compliance programs, regardless of their focus. The top five features of cultures in which employees most frequently followed the rules were, in order of strength: supervisory leadership, fair treatment, rewarding ethical behavior (tied with fair treatment), executive leadership, and punishing unethical behavior. In other words, if we ask what were the most important things supervisors and executives did to create an ethical culture, these data suggest the key factors were treating employees fairly, rewarding ethical behavior, and punishing unethical behavior.

Research by Tyler and Blader (2000) further supported the importance of culture. Their studies found that estimates of the likelihood of being caught and punished for wrongdoing had a less-powerful influence on rule-related behavior than did two key values. The first value was the belief authorities were legitimate and ought to be obeyed. The second value was the belief that company policies were consistent with their moral values.

The Treviño (1999) and the Tyler and Blader (2000) studies make two important points. First, they show that engaging the internal values of employees, (i.e., the values they come into the work organization already holding) strongly influenced compliance behavior in the workplace. External threats of punishment had a weaker influence. Second, they suggested that the organizational culture can engage employee values to promote ethical and compliance behavior. The literature reviews in this chapter make clear that one aspect of these values was the belief that management shares the moral values of employees and morally appropriate actions.

The findings outlined in this chapter point to two aspects of management policies and practices that underlie this value-based approach. First, employees viewed the policies management as consistent with their own ethical principles. Second, employees believed that management generally managed ethically. This includes making decisions ethically and generally acting in ways consistent with the principles of procedural justice. Both of these approaches promoted voluntary employee behavior.

Finally, I argue that our answer to the question of whether values shape behavior in work organizations has important consequences. For example, when we ask why there have been failures in the business world, we can focus on misaligned incentives and cognitive errors. But, we can also focus on ethical actors indifferent to issues of right and wrong. These differing diagnoses of the problem lead to varying prescriptions about the solution (see Tenbrunsel, 2008, 2009). In particular, a value-based approach suggests a way of managing behavior in work organizations that is different from the predominantly sanction-based model that dominates both government and management in America today. In contrast to seeking to respond to the current crisis of management and business by ratcheting up sanctions for wrongdoing, this approach argues that we need to build cultures within business organizations that emphasize issues of morality, ethicality, and justice and stress motivating employees to act based on their own commitment to behaving appropriately.

NOTE

1. Based on a presentation at the Conference on Behavioral Business Ethics: Ideas on an Emerging Field, Chicago, May 21–23.

REFERENCES

Appiah, K. A. (2008). *Experiments in ethics.* Oxford, UK: Oxford University Press.

Blader, S. L., & Tyler, T. R. (2003). What constitutes fairness in work settings? A four-component model of procedural justice. *Human Resource Management Review, 13*(1), 747–758.

Blader, S. L., & Tyler, T. R. (2009). Testing and expanding the group engagement model. *Journal of Applied Psychology, 94,* 445–464.

Darley, J., Messick, D., & Tyler, T. R. (Eds.) (2001). *Social influences on ethical behavior in organizations.* Mahwah, N. J: Erlbaum.

Haidt, J. (2007). The new synthesis in moral psychology. *Science, 316,* 998–1002.

Heider, F. (1958). *The psychology of interpersonal perception.* New York: John Wiley & Sons.

Kamm, F. M. (1989). Harming some to save others. *Philosophical Studies, 57,* 227–260.

Kelman, H. C. & Hamilton, V. L. (1989). *Crimes of Obedience.* New Haven: Yale University Press.

Kohlberg, L. (1981). *The philosophy of moral development: Moral states and the idea of justice.* San Francisco: Harper and Row.

Leventhal, G. S. (1980). What should be done with equity theory? In K. J. Gergen, M. S. Greenberg, R. H. Weiss (Eds.). *Social Exchange* (pp. 27–55). New York: Plenum.

Lind, E. A., & Tyler, T. R. (1988). *The social psychology of procedural justice*. New York: Plenum.

Muir, W. K. (1967). *Law and attitude change*. Chicago: University of Chicago Press.

Ones, D. S., & Viswesvaran, C. (1998). Integrity testing in organizations. In R. W. Griffin, A. O'Leary-Kelly, & J. M. Collins (Eds.), *Dysfunctional behavior in organizations: Violent and deviant behavior* (Monographs in organizational behavior and industrial relations, Vol. 23, Parts A & B, pp. 243–276). Stamford, CT: Elsevier Science/JAI Press.

Paine, L. S. (1994). Managing for organizational integrity. *Harvard Business Review, 72*, 106–117.

Rest, J., Narvaez, D., Bebeau, M. J., & Thoma, S. J. (1999). *Postconventional moral thinking*. Mahwah, NJ: Erlbaum.

Robinson, P., & Darley, J. (1995). *Justice, liability and blame*. Boulder, CO: Westview.

Sandel, M. J. (2009). *Justice: What's the right thing to do?* New York: Farrar, Straus & Giroux.

Tenbrunsel, A. E. (2008). Ethics in today's business world. *Journal of Business Ethics, 80*, 1–4.

Tenbrunsel, A. E. (2009). New ideas for ethics research. *Journal of Business Ethics, 89*, 1–2.

Thomson, J. J. (1985). The trolley problem. *Yale Law Journal, 94*, 1395–1415.

Treviño, L. K. (1999). Managing ethics and legal compliance: What works and what hurts. *California Management Review, 41*, 131–151.

Treviño, L. K., Weaver, G. R., & Reynolds, S. J. (2006). Behavioral ethics in organizations: A review. *Journal of Management, 32*, 951–990.

Tyler, T. R. (2005). Promoting employee policy adherence and rule following in work settings: The value of self-regulatory approaches. *Brooklyn Law Review, 70*, 1287–1312.

Tyler, T. R. (2006a). Legitimacy and legitimation. *Annual Review of Psychology, 57*, 375–400.

Tyler, T. R. (2006b). Restorative justice and procedural justice. *Journal of Social Issues, 62*, 305–323.

Tyler, T. R. (2006c). *Why people obey the law*. Princeton, NJ: Princeton University Press.

Tyler, T. R. (2007). *Psychology and the design of legal institutions*. Nijmegen, the Netherlands: Wolf Legal.

Tyler, T. R. (2008). Psychology and institutional design. *Review of Law and Economics* (symposium issue on Law and Social Norms), *4*(3), 801–887.

Tyler, T. R. (2009). Legitimacy and criminal justice: The benefits of self-regulation. *Ohio State Journal of Criminal Law, 7*, 307–359.

Tyler, T. R. (2010). *Does the morality of management matter?* Unpublished manuscript, New York University.

Tyler, T. R. (2011). *Why people cooperate*. Princeton, NJ: Princeton University Press.

Tyler, T. R., & Blader, S. (2000). *Cooperation in groups: Procedural justice, social identity, and behavioral engagement*. Philadelphia: Psychology Press.

Tyler, T. R., & Blader, S. (2003). Procedural justice, social identity, and cooperative behavior. *Personality and Social Psychology Review, 7*, 349–361.

Tyler, T. R., & Blader, S. L. (2005). Can businesses effectively regulate employee conduct?: The antecedents of rule following in work settings. *Academy of Management Journal, 48*, 1143–1158.

Tyler, T. R., Boeckmann, R., Smith, H. J., & Huo, Y. J. (1997). *Social justice in a diverse society*. Denver, CO: Westview.

Tyler, T. R., Callahan, P., & Frost, J. (2007). Armed, and dangerous(?): Can self-regulatory approaches shape rule adherence among agents of social control? *Law and Society Review, 41*(2), 457–492.

Tyler, T. R., & Degoey, P. (1996). Trust in organizational authorities: The influence of motive attributions on willingness to accept decisions. In R. Kramer & T. R. Tyler (Eds.), T*rust in organizations: Frontiers of theory and research.* Thousand Oaks, CA: Sage.

Tyler, T. R., Dienhart, J., & Thomas, T. (2008). The ethical commitment to compliance: Building value-based cultures that encourage ethical conduct and a commitment to compliance. *California Management Review, 50,* 31–51.

Tyler, T. R., & Fagan, J. (2008). Why do people cooperate with the police? *Ohio State Journal of Criminal Law, 6,* 231–275.

Section 5

Bounded Ethicality

9

Ethical Immunity: How People Violate Their Own Moral Standards Without Feeling They Are Doing So

Jason Dana
University of Pennsylvania

George Loewenstein
Carnegie Mellon University

and

Roberto Weber
Carnegie Mellon University

INTRODUCTION

Ethics can play an important role in modern economic and organizational contexts. With frequent opportunities to misappropriate others' wealth, mislead other parties such as investors and consumers, and manufacture harmful products, the extent to which economic actors behave unethically and the conditions that lead them to do so become worthy topics of investigation. Indeed, following large-scale examples of individual and corporate malfeasance (e.g., the Nestle baby milk scandal, the WorldCom and Enron financial collapses, and the frauds committed by Bernie Madoff and others), academics, the press, and the public at large seek to understand why such acts were committed and how they might be prevented in the future.

One important question for understanding these events is whether those who were ultimately responsible started on their path recognizing that they were behaving unethically. By now, a rather broad and thorough experimental literature has shown that the desire to appear ethical to oneself and others can exert a powerful influence on human behavior. Even when given strong incentives for behaving in a selfish fashion, with pains taken to verify subjects' understanding of the setup, experimental subjects regularly engage in other-regarding behavior, such as punishing unethical acts by others with no benefit to oneself (Fehr & Gächter, 2002), behaving honestly when dishonesty is profitable and undetectable (Gneezy, 2005), and implementing distributional outcomes that are egalitarian, again often at the expense of one's own egoistic payoff (Fehr & Schmidt, 1999; Loewenstein, Thompson, & Bazerman, 1989). Yet, if ethics is such a powerful motivation, what can account for the seemingly endless corporate scandals, defrauding of investors and employers, and embezzlement? Are the people who commit these acts simply corrupt, or are there specific situations that tend to give rise to unethical behavior, even on the part of people who would like to view themselves as honorable and honest?

In this chapter, we suggest that a study of *behavioral ethics* that takes its cue from the burgeoning field of behavioral economics can explain when and why ethically minded individuals behave unethically. Much of the focus of behavioral economics has been on ways in which people's behavior falls short of fulfilling their own goals. For example, evidence of procrastination and dynamic inconsistency reveals that people are not always capable of following through on their own intertemporal preferences. Similarly, evidence that different but consequentially equivalent frames of a decision lead to different choices reveals that people sometimes contradict themselves due to minor variations in a choice context. Just as people often fail to achieve their own goals or behave consistently, due to systematic errors and biases in judgment and decision making and to varying subtle features of the choice context, people can also systematically fail to live up to their own ethical standards (see, e.g., Chugh, Bazerman, & Banaji, 2005). That is, they may fail to behave as ethically as even they themselves would wish. The study of behavioral ethics—as apart from normative or legal approaches that specify how individuals should or must behave—aims to understand how even well-intentioned people can sometimes behave unethically. Such an understanding can lead us to a broader understanding of the range of ethical failures in business, taking us beyond the view that those guilty of malfeasance are just "a few bad apples" (see De Cremer, 2009).

Much of the instruction that occurs in the business ethics courses that have become increasingly popular in business schools teaches students how to use ethical principles to discriminate between behaviors that are and are not ethical. An implicit assumption of such approaches, as Tenbrunsel and Messick (2004) noted, is that "by highlighting and emphasizing the moral components of decisions, executives will be more likely to choose the moral path." The study of behavioral business ethics can provide incremental usefulness beyond the traditional approach by helping to explain when and why people who know the rules, and wish to follow them, end up breaking them. Such an understanding can potentially help people to recognize and avoid these types of "ethics traps"; more important, it can provide insights into the design of institutions that reduce the prevalence of such traps, making it easy and natural for people to behave in conformity with their own ethical principles.

Why do people violate their own ethical standards? One important reason, which is our central focus in this chapter, is that they are able to persuade themselves that they are not doing so: People have a remarkable ability to rationalize unethical behavior or to actively position themselves (e.g., through avoidance of compromising information or through delegation of unethical activities to others) to achieve "ethical immunity" by not facing up to the consequences and obvious interpretations of their actions. As a result, people who would like to be honest, generous, and fair, and to see themselves as such, end up behaving dishonestly, selfishly, and in a way that harms others.

In the following sections, we discuss experimental research examining three different "tactics" people use to avoid holding themselves ethically accountable. Each line of research demonstrates that people behave more ethically when they are morally accountable for their actions—that is, when their actions clearly and directly reflect on their ethical standards. When it is possible to avoid such ethical accountability, however, people often do so and end up behaving less ethically. That is, people often seek to avoid moral accountability, perhaps paradoxically, so that they will not feel compelled to behave in accord with their own standards of ethics.

In the section "Diffusing Responsibility," we show that people faced with ethically difficult decisions often prefer to diffuse responsibility for the choice. This diffusion can occur both vertically (e.g., when people hire intermediaries to do their "dirty work") and horizontally (e.g., when people fail to behave in an ethical fashion themselves, based on the justification that others can be counted on to do so). In the section "Exploiting Uncertainty," we show that people sometimes prefer to be uncertain about the impact of their actions on others so that they can be more self-interested. Finally, in the section "Seeking Justifications," we show that people, often unwittingly, select and weigh information about what is fair in a way that favors themselves.

The research we discuss contributes to a growing body of literature that views ethical failures as something of which even ethical people are capable (Loewenstein, 1996). Indeed, ethical immunity does not occur because people are not, in fact, really ethical. Rather, it is precisely because people are ethical, or at least truly want to be at some level, that they go through the costly contortions that they do to allow themselves to be selfish or dishonest when in fact no one would punish them for their selfishness or dishonesty but themselves.

A NOTE ON METHODOLOGY: THE VALUE OF ECONOMIC LABORATORY EXPERIMENTS FOR UNDERSTANDING WHEN AND WHY PEOPLE WILL BEHAVE ETHICALLY

By now, a large literature on experimental games incorporating monetary incentives has shown that people put a real value on principles such as fairness and honesty. As examples, people often give up nonnegligible amounts of money so that an anonymous other can benefit (see review in Camerer, 2003), and people often forgo opportunities to lie for money even though it is clear they cannot be caught (Shalvi, Handgraaf, & De Dreu, 2011). These types of laboratory studies are helpful for understanding ethical behavior because they enable researchers to create very simple environments in which individuals can choose between acts that are unambiguously "ethical" (telling the truth, sharing wealth equally with another who has an equal right to it) and "unethical" (telling a lie for monetary gain, taking wealth from others without any right to it). In such studies, confounding selfish motives can be carefully controlled and hence eliminated as potential causes of behavior.

Take the example of ethical behavior in distributions of wealth. In the simple laboratory dictator game (Forsythe, Horowitz, Savin, & Sefton, 1994), a player in the role of "dictator" can divide an endowment of money with an anonymous other in any way he or she sees fit, with both individuals having equal right to the wealth. The game can be played only once, the identities of the players are never revealed (even to the experimenter), and the recipient is given no chance to retaliate or otherwise respond. In this way, we can distinguish a player's inherent desire to act ethically, by dividing wealth equally, from desires for impression management, quid pro quo, or avoiding punishment. Despite removing all of these selfish motives for sharing, giving across a variety of dictator game experiments remains stubbornly positive (Camerer, 2003).

While laboratory experiments often show that individuals exhibit a high propensity toward some ethical behaviors, this does not mean that they necessarily provide evidence about the degree to which people are or are not ethical or generous in other closely related contexts. Indeed, *no* research can provide such evidence because all research, including field research, necessarily focuses on a limited set of specific situations, with a particular set of characteristics (Falk & Heckman, 2009). Therefore, to say that "people are not selfish" or "people do not lie" from the evidence presented in a single laboratory or nonlaboratory paradigm is of questionable validity (as much as it would be to say that "people always lie" because one finds one domain, poker playing, in which they do so). The merit of the experiments that we review is that they facilitate understanding of the precise factors that cause people to be more or less ethical, holding other factors constant.

THREE TACTICS FOR ACHIEVING ETHICAL IMMUNITY

Diffusing Responsibility

One situation in which people can avoid accountability for difficult ethical decisions is when responsibility for these decisions and for the resulting consequences is diffused (Darley & Latane, 1968). The actions of other people often diffuse responsibility in a fashion that enables individuals to take self-interested actions they would eschew if acting unilaterally.

Here, we define two different types of diffusion of responsibility. *Vertical* diffusion of responsibility occurs when an intermediary is placed between the decision maker and the stakeholders in the decision, making the decision maker feel less responsible for the outcome. For example, firms may use "firing consultants," who provide little other service than carrying out the act of firing their employees, or firms may outsource functions to a contractor that subsequently pays its employees wages that are below the usual standards of the firm. *Horizontal* diffusion of responsibility occurs when decision makers rely on others to act in a stakeholder's best interests rather than doing so themselves. The "bystander effect" (Darley & Latane, 1968) is a classic example, whereby people can fail to intervene and help a person in distress when others are present but almost never do so when alone.

Recent research suggests that vertical diffusion by way of intermediaries changes the perception of responsibility for unethical outcomes, both by external observers and by those directly involved. For example, players who are unfair through intermediaries are less likely to be punished than players who make unfair choices themselves (Bartling & Fischbacher, 2010; Coffman, 2010). Thus, the same acts, when carried out through intermediaries, are often perceived as less unethical than when the same acts are carried out directly.

As Hamman, Loewenstein, and Weber (2010) demonstrate, even the extent to which individuals hold *themselves* accountable for their unethical actions is mitigated when acting through intermediaries. In one set of studies, "principals" could decide which of several "agents" to hire to decide how much of a fixed sum of money given to the principal would be shared with a third party (the "recipient"). Principals tended to fire those who gave a lot and hire those who gave little, to the point at which those agents who were "employed" were those who gave almost none of the dictators' money to recipients. Motivated to be hired, the agents' choices became increasingly favorable to the dictator through time, leaving the other party almost nothing. The result was that, relative to conditions in which dictators made the sharing decision individually (i.e., not through agents), much less was shared. Moreover, despite the fact that they had systematically hired agents who acted selfishly on their behalf, dictators who made the sharing decision via agents ended up feeling less responsible for the low payoffs realized by recipients. Delegation, it seems, makes it easier to secure selfish outcomes because one does not feel as morally accountable when someone else—even a person one has hired to do the job—is doing one's dirty work.

A similar conclusion regarding the perils of vertical diffusion of responsibility comes from an experiment by Ellman and Pezanis-Christou (2010). They considered production by two subjects, who acted as members of a firm, which yielded costs for a passive third party. Both subjects were involved in choosing a level of production for the firm, which determined their own payoff and the payoff of the third party. Ellman and Pezanis-Christou considered alternative organizational structures in which the decision is made vertically (one subject set the level of production and the other carried it out) or horizontally (both subjects jointly determined the level of production, either by reaching consensus or by having their suggested choices averaged), and they also varied the presence of communication between the two subjects.

Without communication, ethical production levels that limit the harm to the third party occurred significantly more often under a horizontal structure in which both subjects' suggestions were averaged to determine what the firm did than under vertical structures in which the responsibility was diffused (Ellman & Pezanis-Christou, 2010). However, under an alternative horizontal structure, in which firm members had to reach consensus, ethical behavior was just as low as under vertical structures—mainly because when teams compromise, they tend to choose the less ethical of the two initial suggestions. When communication between the subjects was allowed, however, the vertical structure yielded the most ethical outcomes of any organizational structure. Communication apparently provided subordinates with voice and greater responsibility in the process of selecting production levels, erasing the effects of vertical diffusion.

Although vertical diffusion led to greater selfishness in the experiments just described (when no communication was present), other research provides evidence that horizontal diffusion of responsibility can have a similar effect. Considerable research in psychology demonstrates bystander effects in which an increase in the number of potential interveners in a situation reduced the likelihood that ethical action will be taken (Darley & Latane, 1968). However, one problem with interpreting bystander effects is that they potentially confound two different phenomena. On the one hand, and consistent with the argument we have been advancing, people may not actually care much about whether the ethical action is taken if they do not feel responsible for its occurrence. On the other hand, and consistent with a free-rider problem, people may truly care about whether the ethical action is taken but would prefer not to incur the costs of taking the action themselves if there is a good chance someone else will do so.

Dana, Weber, and Kuang (2007) isolated the first effect with an economic game. In the game, two decision makers chose between two actions that yielded a monetary payoff for them and for a passive bystander. Each decision maker could ensure a fair outcome that yielded the same payoff for everyone, while an inequitable outcome that benefitted the two decision makers and harmed the third party resulted only if both decision makers selected it. In this setup, any decision maker who was interested in the equitable outcome could guarantee its implementation, but each decision maker could evade accountability for choosing the selfish option because his or her decision only led to this outcome if the other player made the same choice. Further, because all players would receive the same amount if one chose the fair option, no free-rider problem was present; that is, there was no material advantage to letting someone else ensure equity. The fact that subjects chose the selfish option almost twice as often as players in a baseline condition who did not have the option to diffuse responsibility supports the idea that horizontal diffusion of responsibility can encourage unethical behavior by making people feel less accountable for their own behavior.

Exploiting Uncertainty

Another important factor that can influence the extent to which individuals feel accountable for unethical behaviors is the presence of uncertainty. The research we review presents several examples in which individuals rely on uncertainty, usually regarding the consequences of their actions, as a justification for behaving unethically while maintaining the perception that one is ethical. Some of the studies show that people use the veil of uncertainty to hide unethical behavior (including possibly from themselves); other studies go a step further and show that people sometimes choose to remain willfully ignorant to provide themselves with such a veil.

As mentioned, many economic experiments measuring fair or ethical behavior in distributional choices suggest that many people are motivated by a pure sense of doing what is "right" in that they give when there can be no possibility of personal gain from doing so. A commonly drawn conclusion from this research is that people (e.g., dictators in the dictator game) genuinely value being kind to others. However, several experiments suggest that fairness motives are not so simple. For example, in experiments using the dictator game, people who would share money often kept all of it when the other party did not know a game was being played, that is, that money could have been shared (Dana, Cain, & Dawes, 2006; see also Broberg, Ellingsen, & Johannesson, 2007; Lazear, Malmendier, & Weber, 2010). Thus, when others are uncertain about our actions, we are much less likely to behave fairly, even when there is no chance at retribution (see also Andreoni & Bernheim, 2009).

A related set of experiments explored how behavior changes when decision makers are allowed to remain uncertain about the consequences of their own actions. The findings of these studies indicate that, when individuals can remain uncertain about the degree of harm imposed on others by their actions, unethical conduct becomes much easier.

In a binary version of the dictator game, Dana et al. (2007) showed that a majority of dictators preferred an equal and welfare-maximizing option to a selfish option that gave them more but also lowered the total payout to both parties. Although one might interpret this finding as showing that people care about the other party, an additional treatment added a superficial, and seemingly irrelevant, level of payoff uncertainty by obscuring the relationship between payoffs and actions. In this treatment, the decision maker's own payoffs for the two options were known and were the same as in the baseline case, but the payoffs to the other party were left uncertain. These payoffs could either be the same as in the baseline game, or reversed, so that the action that benefitted the decision maker also benefitted the recipient and maximized total payoff. The actual payoffs were determined by a coin flip, and the outcome was not initially known to the decision maker. However, the decision maker could easily reveal the true payoffs by clicking on a "reveal game" button, in which case the true payoffs would be known.

If the ethical choice in the baseline game is to select the equality option, a comparable action is easily implemented in this "hidden information" treatment: A decision maker simply has to reveal the true payoffs and select whichever is the more generous option. However, dictators exploited uncertainty about the consequences so that they could be more selfish (Dana et al., 2007). Roughly half of dictators chose not to reveal the true payoffs, ultimately leading to a majority of choices being unfair. Thus, not knowing how another is impacted by one's action, even when one can easily resolve such uncertainty, provides the decision maker with ethical immunity to pursue self-interest while not feeling directly responsible for creating an inequitable outcome.

The finding by Dana et al. (2007) has been replicated in other experiments, which manipulated the exact payoffs and whether the default option was ignorance or information about the payoffs (Feiler, 2005; Grossman, 2010; Larson & Capra, 2009). In combination, all of these experiments suggest that people will sacrifice personal gain for the benefit of others when they know the exact consequence of their choices, but when there is even a little bit of uncertainty, which is irrelevant from a decision–theoretic point of view because it can be resolved at no cost, the same individuals will capitalize on this uncertainty about the consequences of their action—a form of ethical immunity—to pursue material gain.

Haisley and Weber (2010) provide an additional example of exploiting uncertainty to be more self-interested by showing that individuals manipulate their perceptions of ambiguity (i.e., lotteries in which there is uncertainty about the probabilities) to justify self-interested behavior. In their experiment, decision makers made a series of binary choices, with one choice option more equitable but the other (selfish) option yielded more money to the dictator and less to the recipient, on average. In case of the "self-interested" choice, the payoff to the recipient was also contingent on a lottery.

The experiment (Haisley & Weber, 2010) varied whether the lottery payment to the recipient was presented as "known" uncertainty (i.e., an explicit 0.5 chance to win) or "ambiguity" (the probability of winning could be anywhere between 0 and 1). When the probability of an adverse payout to the recipient was known, the dictator had very little room to manipulate subjective perceptions of likelihood. But, under ambiguity, the subject could plausibly convince him- or herself that the lottery faced by the recipient might be more favorable. That is, the authors hypothesized that dictators motivated to act selfishly, while wanting to believe they were not doing so, would rely on the ethical immunity provided by the ambiguous probabilities to convince themselves that what they were doing was "not that bad" for the recipient.

Consistent with the appeal of uncertainty as a means for obtaining ethical immunity, self-interested choices were more frequent under ambiguity than under known risk (Haisley & Weber, 2010). Moreover, subjects biased their subsequent (incentivized) estimates of the payoff to the recipient upward under ambiguity, but not under known risk, indicating that they had convinced themselves under ambiguity that these lotteries were indeed more attractive for the other party.

This research suggests that environments with greater uncertainty about the outcomes that result from one's choices are likely to yield less-ethical behavior. This is important, as many real-world situations in which individuals must make ethical choices are also frequently accompanied by uncertainty (e.g., about how much another will be harmed by actions that would benefit oneself).

Seeking Justifications

People avoid responsibility for behaving generously or ethically not only by avoiding information and situations that would hold them to account. Research on self-serving biases in judgments of fairness suggests that individuals also play "mind games" with themselves that serve a similar function. While supporting the general conclusion that people have a desire to be fair, this research shows that they gravitate toward the principles of fairness that most favor themselves. A classic example comes from a study by van Avermaet (reported in Messick, 1985) in which participants were instructed to fill out questionnaires until told to stop. When they finished, they were left with money to pay themselves and another participant who had already left. Participants were told one of four things: (a) The other subject put in half as much time and completed half as many surveys, (b) the other subject put in half as much time but completed twice as many surveys, (c) the other subject had put in twice as much time but completed half as many surveys, or (d) the other subject put in twice as much time and completed twice as many surveys.

Clearly, participants' sense of ethics served as a powerful constraint on behavior: Almost no one kept all of the money, which would be unjustifiably selfish and unfair because the other participant did similar work. How they shared the money, however, provides an interesting insight into human nature. Participants who worked twice as long and completed twice as many surveys kept twice as much money on average, a simple application of a merit principle to pay. Participants kept more than half of the money, however, both in the condition where they worked longer and completed less and the condition where they completed more and did not work as long. Again, behavior was consistent with a merit principle, but the principle chosen, on average, systematically favored the subject making the allocation. Finally, when participants completed only half as much and worked only half as long, they kept, on average, half of the money, consistent with a rule of equal division rather than merit (van Avermaet reported in Messick, 1985).

Similar results—suggesting that what constitutes a "fair" allocation is malleable toward judgments that favor the self—have obtained in numerous other experiments (Frohlich, Oppenheimer, & Kurki, 2004; Konow, 2000). What we can take away from this research is that most people are not unabashedly selfish; they have a desire to abide by some notion of what is fair or ethical. Yet, judgments of fairness can be systematically biased to favor the self. Much as people judge the actions they delegate to others or that they take under uncertainty as less diagnostic about their own ethical qualities, people judge fairness in a way that enables them to avoid the conclusion that they are seeking outcomes that are self-interested and unfair.

A series of experiments by behavioral economists (Loewenstein, Issacharoff, Camerer, & Babcock, 1992; Babcock, Loewenstein, Issacharoff, & Camerer, 1995) shows that this self-serving bias was caused by selective interpretation of information and also that it led, both in laboratory experiments and in a field study, to failures and impasse in negotiation. Simulating pretrial bargaining, Loewenstein et al. conducted bargaining experiments in which subjects were presented with case materials (depositions, police reports, etc.) from an actual lawsuit, randomly assigned to the role of either plaintiff or defendant, and asked to negotiate a settlement in the form of a payment from defendant to plaintiff. At the outset, the experimenters gave the defendants a monetary endowment to finance the settlement, and the division of the endowment the subjects agreed on through bargaining was what they took home as pay. The longer it took the parties to agree to a settlement, the more both were penalized by having the endowment of money they were dividing shrink. If they failed to settle, the defendant's payment to plaintiff, based on the smaller endowment size, was determined by a neutral judge who had reviewed all of the case materials. Before negotiating, both plaintiffs and defendants were asked to predict how the neutral judge would rule in the case and were also paid for the accuracy of this prediction.

Participants' estimates of a fair settlement were biased in a self-serving manner, leading to low settlement rates. Direct evidence that the self-serving bias played a role in this failure to settle came in the form of the predictions of the judge's ruling. Plaintiffs' predictions of the judge's award to them were, on average, substantially higher than those of defendants, despite the facts that the estimates were secret and had no bearing on the settlement and that both parties were paid to be accurate in their estimates. Further, the larger the discrepancy between a particular plaintiff's and defendant's estimates, the lower was their likelihood of settlement; hence, they both left the experiment worse off in terms of payment. This evidence suggests that self-serving biases are unintentional; people are often unable to avoid being biased, even when it is in their best interest to do so.

In subsequent experiments employing the same paradigm (Babcock et al., 1995), settlement rates were markedly improved by assigning participants their roles only after reading the transcripts. In this way, any motivation to interpret evidence as favorable to one side over another while reading and evaluating the materials was removed. Without a self-interested conclusion to reach, interpretations of fairness, as measured by predictions of the judge's ruling, looked more like those of a neutral third party than an interested party. More interestingly, diminishing the self-serving bias in this fashion dramatically increased settlement rates. This finding suggests that self-serving biases work by way of distorting the way that people seek out and weigh information when they perceive that they have a stake in the conclusion.

Using a similar approach, Haisley and Weber (2010), in the study of ambiguity and fairness discussed previously, used individuals' own initial, and naturally negative, perceptions of ambiguity to constrain the extent to which they could perceive ambiguity as favorable. Recall that the experiment found that dictators who were motivated to view ambiguity as favorable in that it justified self-interest did so and, as a result, behaved more selfishly. One treatment simply elicited preferences for ambiguity versus simple risk from dictators, prior to their finding out that they would have an incentive to view ambiguity favorably, This mild intervention, in which dictators simply had to express a preference (against ambiguity) prior to being motivated to view it favorably, was sufficient to constrain their subsequent actions and judgments—they no longer viewed ambiguity as favorable when it could help them, and as a result, they behaved significantly less selfishly. Thus, obtaining initial "unbiased" judgments of what is fair or ethical, or even about the likely consequences of uncertain events or processes, may be a powerful instrument for limiting the ability of individuals to deflect ethical accountability for their actions.

Sah and Loewenstein (2010) examined the rationalizations that physicians employ that enable them to accept gifts from pharmaceutical companies and medical device manufacturers, which most outsiders to the profession view as barely disguised bribes. Physicians in the early stages of their careers were asked in a survey about the acceptability of receiving various gifts from industry. Some of the physicians were first asked questions about the sacrifices they made in medical training. Others were also asked the sacrifice question and in addition were asked a question that implicitly suggested the idea that these hardships might justify acceptance of gifts. A control group was simply asked about the acceptability of receiving gifts with no prior priming questions. Reminding physicians of the sacrifices they had made in obtaining their education resulted in gifts being evaluated as more acceptable, and even though most residents disagreed with the hinted-at rationalization, exposure to it further increased the perceived acceptability of gifts. Reminders of hardships such as being overworked and having large amounts of debt apparently led physicians to conclude that they deserved gifts.

A research study using a die-under-cup paradigm further demonstrates the value decision makers place on having self-justifications for ethically questionable behavior (Shalvi, Dana, Handgraaf, & De Dreu, 2011; task adapted from Fischbacher & Heusi, 2008). Participants were asked to roll a die that was placed under a cup by shaking it. Then, through a small hole in the top of the cup, participants privately observed the result and were to be paid in dollars whatever number they said they rolled. They were further instructed to roll the die a few additional times to convince them that it was fair. This procedure made it transparent that even after the participants left, no one could observe what they rolled. The results revealed two interesting patterns. While the distribution of reports differed significantly from that of a fair die roll, the amount of apparent lying was modest, with about 37% of participants reporting that they rolled a six. Perhaps more interestingly, the distribution of reports very well fit the distribution that would be expected if one were reporting the best of three rolls, raising the possibility that people were willing to report the best roll that they had even though they were instructed that they were to report only the first roll.

To test this possibility directly, the procedure was changed in two ways (Shalvi et al., 2011). First, participants were allowed to inspect the die prior to rolling to ensure that it was legitimate. Then, they rolled the die under the cup once and observed the result. The experimenter then passed around a box, and each participant swept the cup (and thus the die) into the box, effectively hiding their result from ever being seen. Reports from this procedure were significantly lower on average, indicating less lying for material gain. Further, the distribution of reports differed significantly from the best-of-three distribution. It seems that participants needed justifications to be able to lie, even though they were the only ones privy to both the lie and the justifications. Having the opportunity to roll the die multiple times thus benefitted the participants, who could roll until they saw a better number and then feel that their report was less of a lie.

CONCLUSIONS

In this chapter, we show that, although most people are motivated to be ethical, self-interest often manages to trump ethics. But, the unethical conduct is not simply the result of people rationally deciding to forgo ethical considerations in pursuit of self-interest. Instead, the way in which people arrive at unethical conduct is more psychologically complex. Specifically, when the context surrounding an ethical choice provided individuals with the opportunity to not have their ethical selves held to account, people often exploited this lack of accountability to behave unethically without feeling they had done so. Put differently, while we may find it desirable to behave ethically, we may find it even more desirable to behave unethically without feeling like we have done so.

Ethical Immunity in Organizations

Although ethics traps exist in most, if not all, spheres of life, they are likely to be especially common and treacherous in business settings, where people often have limited responsibility for, as well as ability to monitor the consequences of, their individual actions. Indeed, common features of business environments are likely to facilitate the use of each of the three methods of achieving ethical immunity that we discussed in this chapter.

First, decision making in most businesses tends to be diffused, both vertically and horizontally, making it easy for people to avoid accountability for their own actions by "pointing the finger" at others. For example, the responsibility for ensuring accurate bookkeeping typically rests with unit accountants, internal auditors, the company chief financial officer (CFO), and external auditors. If all of these individuals perceive only limited involvement, or sometimes perhaps even passive involvement, then we might expect to see the kinds of unethical conduct demonstrated in experiments.

Second, decision making in business contexts is also typically characterized by high degrees of uncertainty. For example, in product safety decisions uncertainty about the degree of harm caused or the conditions under which harm may occur may provide decision makers with ethical cover. Moreover, the fact that businesses can often manipulate the kind of research conducted and disseminated regarding product safety—as the tobacco industry infamously did for decades—creates a striking parallel with those experiments in which people's ethical conduct is diminished when they have the ability to strategically fail to acquire relevant information.

Finally, business contexts may offer many of the kinds of justifications we discussed that facilitate unethical conduct. For instance, the obligation created by representing an organization or client may allow individuals to believe that the ethical act is equivalent to the one that best satisfies the firm's need for profit. Indeed, arguments by scholars—such as Milton Friedman's well-known claim that "the social responsibility of business is to increase its profits" (1970)—may present ethically conflicted managers with the necessary justification for rationalizing unethical conduct. Another important element of business contexts is competition, which may contribute to the often-used justification that people feel like they have no choice but to commit an unethical act.

Attacking Ethical Immunity Through Greater Self-Accountability

Beyond helping to predict and explain people's likelihood to behave unethically, the study of behavioral ethics can also suggest means of discouraging unethical behavior and encouraging ethical behavior. As noted in the introduction, we are skeptical of attempts to engender ethical behavior that rely on people to recognize when they face an ethical dilemma and to successfully navigate themselves around ethical traps. While normative and legal approaches may be useful in helping professionals to define ethical boundaries, they are unlikely to provide much traction when it comes to preventing those same people from crossing those boundaries.

Instead, we believe that, just as "choice architecture" (Thaler & Sunstein, 2008) can be used to design institutions that help boundedly rational people to make better decisions, institutions and information mechanisms can be designed to hold individuals accountable for their own behavior, even if only to themselves, encouraging ethical behavior by disarming mechanisms that enable ethical immunity. To enhance ethical behavior, all the research just reviewed suggests, we need to create decision-making settings that establish a kind of *self-accountability* that makes it more difficult for people to avoid being confronted with the fact that they are violating their own ethical standards.

In one of the experimental conditions of a study discussed, Haisley and Weber (2010) provided a demonstration of how greater self-accountability can enhance ethical behavior. In one condition, prior to making their choices, dictators were asked to decide whether they liked or did not like ambiguity for themselves. In this condition, the impact of ambiguity on selfish behavior disappeared. That is, by having subjects state, up front, their attitudes toward known risk versus ambiguity, they subsequently became "constrained" by these initial attitudes and were not able to self-servingly manipulate their perceptions of uncertainty.

Efforts to increase self-accountability can already be seen in a variety of professional and corporate settings, although they have generally not been interpreted in such terms. For example, new standardized conflict-of-interest disclosure forms for medical journals likewise require authors not only to list any conflicts they face but also to write affirmatively that they have no conflicts if none are listed. Increasing numbers of states are requiring unemployed persons to file frequently to renew unemployment benefits, probably because affirmatively stating that one is unemployed is more difficult for a person who has recently obtained employment than is failing to report such a change in employment status.

Closing Comments

The research reviewed in this chapter can be viewed as a glass half empty (as we have done), emphasizing that people are not as inherently ethical as prior research might suggest. However, it could also be viewed as a glass half full, in the sense of identifying a broad class of situations in which people do, in fact, behave ethically, honestly and generously. The key feature of these situations is the existence of moral accountability or, equivalently, the lack of what Dana et al. (2007) have called "moral wiggle-room." The good news is that when people are, in effect, held to account for their behavior, all of the research suggests that they are very likely to behave in an ethical fashion.

REFERENCES

Andreoni, J., & Bernheim, B. D. (2009). Social image and the 50–50 norm: A theoretical and experimental analysis of audience effects. *Econometrica, 77*(5), 1607–1636.
Babcock, L., Loewenstein, G., Issacharoff, S., & Camerer, C. (1995). Biased judgments of fairness in bargaining. *American Economic Review, 85*, 1337–1342.
Bartling, B., & Fischbacher, U. (2010). *Shifting the blame: On delegation and responsibility.* Working paper.
Broberg, T., Ellingsen, T., & Johannesson, M. (2007). Is generosity involuntary? *Economics Letters, 94*(1), 32–37.
Camerer, C. (2003). *Behavioral game theory: Experiments on strategic interaction.* Princeton, NJ: Princeton University Press.
Chugh, D., Bazerman, M., & Banaji, M. (2005). Bounded ethicality as a psychological barrier to recognizing conflicts of interest. In D. Moore, D. Cain, G. Loewenstein, & M. Bazerman (Eds.), *Conflicts of interest: Problems and solutions from law, medicine and organizational settings.* London: Cambridge University Press.
Coffman, L. (2010). *Intermediation reduces punishment (and reward).* Working paper.
Dana, J., Cain, D. M., & Dawes, R. (2006). What you don't know won't hurt me: Costly (but quiet) exit in a dictator game. *Organizational Behavior and Human Decision Processes, 100*, 193–201.
Dana, J., Weber, R., & Kuang, J. (2007). Exploiting moral wriggle room: Behavior inconsistent with a preference for fair outcomes. *Economic Theory, 1*, 67–80.
Darley, J., & Latane, B. (1968). Bystander intervention in emergencies: Diffusion of responsibility. *Journal of Personality and Social Psychology, 8*, 377–383.
De Cremer, D. (2009). Being unethical or becoming unethical: An introduction. In D. De Cremer (Ed.), *Psychological perspectives on ethical behavior and decision making* (pp. 3–13). Greenwich, CT: Information Age.
Ellman, M., & Pezanis-Christou, P. (2010). Organisational structure, communication and group ethics. *American Economic Review, 100*, 2478–2491.
Falk, A., & Heckman, J. (2009). Lab experiments are a major source of knowledge in the social sciences. *Science, 326*, 535–538.
Fehr, E., & Gächter, S. (2002). Altruistic punishment in humans. *Nature, 415*(6868), 137–140.
Fehr, E., & Schmidt, K. M. (1999). A theory of fairness, competition and cooperation. *Quarterly Journal of Economics, 114*, 817–868.
Feiler, L. (2005). *Patterns of information avoidance in binary choice dictator games.* Working paper.
Fischbacher, U., & Heusi, F. (2008). *Lies in disguise, an experimental study on cheating.* TWI Working Paper 40, Thurgau Institute of Economics, University of Konstanz, Germany.

Forsythe, R., Horowitz, J., Savin, N. E., & Sefton, M. (1994). Fairness in simple bargaining experiments. *Games and Economic Behavior, 6*, 347–69.

Friedman, M. (1970, September 13). The social responsibility of business is to increase its profits. *The New York Times Magazine.*

Frohlich, N., Oppenheimer, J., & Kurki, A. (2004). Modeling other-regarding preferences and an experiment. *Public Choice, 119*, 91–117.

Gneezy, U. (2005). Deception: The role of consequences. *American Economic Review, 95*, 384–394.

Grossman, Z. (2010). *Understanding strategic ignorance.* Working paper.

Haisley, E., & Weber, R. (2010). Self-serving interpretations of ambiguity and other-regarding behavior. *Games and Economic Behavior, 68*, 614–625.

Hamman, J. R., Loewenstein, G., & Weber, R. A. 2010. Self-interest through delegation: An additional rationale for the principal-agent relationship. *American Economic Review, 100*(4): 1826–46.

Konow, J. (2000). Fair shares: Accountability and cognitive dissonance in allocation decisions. *American Economic Review, 90*, 1072–1091.

Larson, T., & Capra, C. M. (2009). Exploiting moral wiggle room: Illusory preference for fairness? A comment. *Judgment and Decision Making, 4*(6), 467–474.

Lazear, E. P., Malmendier, U., & Weber, R. A. (2010). *Sorting, prices, and social preferences.* Working paper.

Loewenstein, G. (1996). Behavioral decision theory and business ethics: Skewed tradeoffs between self and other. In D. M. Messick & A. E. Tenbrunsel (Eds.), *Codes of conduct: Behavioral research into business ethics* (pp. 214–227). New York: Russell Sage Foundation.

Loewenstein, G., Issacharoff, S., Camerer, C., & Babcock, L. (1992). Self-serving assessments of fairness and pretrial bargaining. *Journal of Legal Studies, 12*, 135–159.

Loewenstein, G., Thompson, L., & Bazerman, M. (1989). Social utility and decision making in interpersonal contexts. *Journal of Personality and Social Psychology, 57*, 426–441.

Messick, D. (1985). Social interdependence and decisionmaking. In G. Wright (Ed.), *Behavioral decision making* (pp. 87–109). New York: Plenum.

Sah, S., & Loewenstein, G. (2010). Effect of reminders of personal sacrifice and suggested rationalizations on residents' self-reported willingness to accept gifts: A randomized trial. *Journal of the American Medical Association, 304*(11), 1204–1211.

Shalvi, S., Dana, J., Handgraaf, M. J. J., & De Dreu, C. K. W. (2011). Justified ethicality: Observing desired counterfactuals modifies ethical perceptions and behavior. *Organizational Behavior and Human Decision Processes, 115*, 181–190.

Shalvi, S., Handgraaf, M. J. J., & De Dreu, C. K. W. (in press). Ethical maneuvering: Why people avoid both major and minor lies. *British Journal of Management, 22*, 16–27.

Tenbrunsel, A. E., & Messick, D. M. (2004). Ethical fading: The role of self-deception in unethical behavior. *Social Justice Research, 17*, 223–236.

Thaler, R., & Sunstein, C. (2008). *Nudge: improving decisions about health, wealth, and happiness.* New Haven, CT: Yale University Press.

10

Ethical Discrepancy: Changing Our Attitudes to Resolve Moral Dissonance

Lisa L. Shu, Francesca Gino, and Max H. Bazerman
Harvard University

INTRODUCTION

People have ample opportunity to behave either immorally or unethically during the course of their daily lives. They may decide not to contribute to a donation box for their coffee, lie to a colleague regarding the quality of a report they wrote, overclaim credit for a successfully completed project, overcharge their clients for the work they have done, or bring home some office supplies at the end of the day. While this may sound like an unrealistic day, research suggests otherwise. Several studies have found that people lie and cheat on a daily basis and much more often than they dare to admit (DePaulo, Kashy, Kirkendol, Wyer, & Epstein, 1996; Fischbacher & Heusi, 2008; Gino, Ayal, & Ariely, 2009; Gino, Norton, & Ariely, 2010; Mazar, Amir, & Ariely, 2008; Schweitzer, Ordóñez, & Douma, 2004). For example, one study found that when newspapers are sold out of a box with on-your-honor payment into a cash box, people pay on average one third of the stated price (Pruckner & Sausgruber, 2006). Another study, in which payment was based entirely on self-reports of performance and individual cheating could not be identified, showed participants inflated their self-reported performance by 10% on average (Mazar et al., 2008). Taken together, these studies suggest that when given the opportunity to act dishonestly, a surprisingly large number of individuals do cross ethical boundaries (Ayal & Gino, 2011).

In contrast to this bleak state of ethics, the vast majority of us hold very positive images of ourselves as good and moral individuals (Aquino & Reed, 2002) who resist shining a critical moral light on our own behavior. Most of us care that we are considered to be ethical individuals by others and see ourselves as more ethical than others (Tenbrunsel, 1998; Zhong & Liljenquist, 2008). How then, do we explain these views given the routine and persistent acts of dishonesty that prevail in everyday life?

One set of explanations comes from an emerging literature on "bounded ethicality," which argues that humans are constrained in systematic ways that favor self-serving perceptions, which in turn can result in behaviors that contradict our own ethical standards (Banaji, Bazerman, & Chugh, 2003). Banaji and Bhaskar (2000) described bounded ethicality as a manifestation of Simon's bounded rationality in the domain of ethics. This research portrays the systematic and predictable psychological processes that lead people to engage in ethically questionable behaviors that are inconsistent with their own preferred ethics (Banaji & Bhaskar, 2000; Banaji et al., 2003; Bazerman & Tenbrunsel, 2011; Chugh, Banaji, & Bazerman, 2005). As a result, we engage in behaviors that we would actually condemn if we were more aware of our behavior. Examples of bounded ethicality include unintentionally overclaiming personal credit for group work, implicitly discriminating against out-group members while favoring in-group members, overdiscounting the future when others will pay the consequences, and falling prey to the influence of conflicts of interest.

While the bounded ethicality perspective emphasizes how unethical behavior results from our lack of awareness, another perspective emerges from volumes of literature on the surprising magnitude to which many of us will explicitly cheat with full awareness (Ayal & Gino, 2011; Gino et al., 2009, 2010). Our recent research, which we discuss in detail further in this chapter, examines how we explicitly violate ethical standards while maintaining a positive view of our own ethicality. Thus, we address the psychology that accounts for both bounded ethicality and explicit unethical actions, both of which lead to behavior inconsistent with beliefs.

We begin by discussing the well-documented tendency to overweigh the importance of the individual and to underweigh the importance of the situation. We then discuss asymmetries in how people judge their own moral and immoral actions versus those of others, as well as the discrepancies in evaluating the same good and bad deeds depending on whether they have already occurred or are about to happen. Next, we address the question of how people tend to reconcile their immoral actions with their ethical goals—through the process of "moral disengagement" (Bandura, 1986, 1990, 1991, 1999; Shu, Gino, & Bazerman, 2011). Then, we examine how our mind selectively "forgets" information that might threaten our moral self-image. We close with an attempt to identify strategies to close the gap between the unethical people we are and the ethical people that we strive to be.

THE POWER OF THE SITUATION

Several theories in moral psychology (e.g., Kohlberg, 1981; Rest, 1986) as well as in economics (e.g., Frank, 1987) discuss morality as a relatively stable character attribute—an individual is endowed with the trait or not or is settled in a particular stage of moral development. These trait-based views of morality predict moral behavior to be relatively consistent across time and situation. Because morality is a character trait that someone possesses (or does not possess), the trait-based view implies that individuals can be diagnosed and categorized in their morality, which is then conceptualized as static and predictable. For example, Kohlberg's moral development model (see Kohlberg, 1981) argues that moral behavior is determined by the stage of a person's moral reasoning. In particular, the model suggests that people at more developed stages make moral decisions superior to those at earlier stages (Gibbs, Basinger, & Fuller, 1992; Rest & Navarez, 1994). Importantly, Kohlberg (1981) argued that "the nature of our sequence is not significantly affected by widely varying social, cultural, or religious conditions. The only thing that is affected is the rate at which individuals progress through this sequence" (p. 25).

Extending Kohlberg's model, Rest (1986) identified four discrete steps involved in ethical decision making: awareness, judgment, intention, and behavior. Rest argued that people may go through these stages in different orders with different levels of success. Effectively completing one stage does not imply the success of subsequent stages. Thus, an individual may possess moral judgment but fail to establish moral intent and ultimately fail to behave ethically.

More recently, research in social psychology has proposed a different approach to the moral self (see, e.g., Monin & Jordan, 2009; Zhong,

Liljenquist, & Cain, 2009). In contrast to the static trait-based treatment of morality, the social psychology perspective emphasizes the power of the situation in helping or hindering moral judgment and behavior. This perspective acknowledges there are individual differences in moral development but emphasizes the factors outside the individual—factors in the environment—to be powerful predictors of ethical behavior. Several well-known experiments are commonly discussed in support of this account emphasizing the power of situational influences. For instance, in the famous Milgram experiments, an experimental assistant (an accomplice) asked each study participant to play the role of a teacher and administer "electric shocks" to another participant ("the learner") (who was really a confederate or experimental assistant) each time the learner made a mistake on a word-learning exercise. After each mistake, the participant was asked to administer a shock of higher voltage, which began to result in increasingly "apparent" and audible distress from the learner. Over 60% of the study participants shocked the other participant-accomplices through to the highest voltage, which was marked clearly with potential danger (Milgram, 1974). These results suggest that it is not individual character that causes one to inflict great pain on an innocent person, but rather the situation in which an authority demands obedience. Similarly, in another famous study, the Stanford prison experiment (see Zimbardo, 1969), Stanford undergraduates were randomly assigned to be either guards or prisoners in a mock prison setting for a 2-week experiment. After less than a week, the experiment was abruptly stopped because the guards were engaging in sadism and brutality, and the prisoners were suffering from depression and extreme stress. Normal Stanford students had been transformed by the mere situational conditions created for the experiment—with minimal instructions from the experimenter. These classic studies demonstrate the extent to which the situation affects our moral behavior. More recently, studies in the social psychology and organizational behavior literatures have identified other situational factors influencing individual dishonesty and ethical conduct, such as job context, incentive structures, and organizational culture (Ferrell, Gresham, & Fraedrich, 1989; Treviño, 1986), or surprisingly subtle influences such as ambient lighting (Zhong, Bohns, & Gino, 2010), use of fake products (Gino et al., 2010), and environmental wealth (Gino & Pierce, 2009).

With this abundance of evidence on the power of situation, Monin and Jordan (2009) suggested that our own conception of the moral self is not stable and trait based; rather, it is dynamic and influenced by situational factors that fluctuate from moment to moment. As a consequence, the inputs to ethical decision making are not only the character traits within the individual but also the tug of factors arising from the context of the decision.

In this chapter, we build on work from the social psychology perspective and present evidence from our own research as well as that of others suggesting morality is *situational,* *dynamic,* and *constantly redefined.* Through the situational lens backed by recent empirical evidence, we examine how people tend to change how ethical they are and how honestly they behave over time by redefining what being ethical means.

THE INFLUENCE OF UNETHICAL OTHERS

While moral beliefs may appear to be personal and unchanging, the environment exerts a surprising amount of influence. Specifically, in an organization and in any other social context, individuals have the opportunity to observe the consequences of the decisions and actions of others. Those observed behaviors in turn yield significant influence over our own personal morality.

Gino et al. (2009) disentangled three ways in which the unethical behavior of another influences our own behavior. First, when observing another person's dishonesty, one may update one's internal estimate of the consequences of the dishonest behavior by reducing the expected likelihood of getting caught, in accordance with rational crime theory as proposed by economists (Allingham & Sandmo 1972; Becker 1968). Observing another's unethical behavior changes the cost–benefit analysis of the behavior: While the gain may be fixed, the behavior seems less costly if someone else got away with it (see Hill & Kochendorfer, 1969; Leming, 1980).

But, as Gino et al.'s experiments (2009) suggest, we can also make the opposite prediction about the influence of another's dishonesty: Observing another's behavior makes morality more salient, and increasing the personal relevance of ethics will predict more moral behavior. Mazar et al. (2008) found that drawing people's attention to moral standards reduced dishonest behaviors. Participants who were given a moral reminder (the Ten Commandments) before exposure to an opportunity to cheat for financial gain cheated substantially less than those who were not given such a reminder. When ethics are made salient, people attend to their personal standards of ethics and become more morally stringent. Because moral relevance varies with situational cues, if we observe another's bad behavior, we may pay more attention to our own behavior and increase our engagement with ethical standards.

A third way the behavior of another affects our own morality is through affecting our understanding of the underlying social norms (Cialdini & Trost, 1998). The same behavior in different environments can imply different sets of norms according to norm-focus theory (Cialdini, Reno, & Kallgren, 1990; Reno, Cialdini, & Kallgren, 1993). Cialdini et al. (1990) demonstrated that participants who watched someone else litter subsequently reduced their littering behavior when the environment was clean, but the reverse occurred when the environment was dirty: The observer subsequently littered more. Hence, the interaction of another's behavior with the context in which it is observed adds another nuance to the story of the source of morality.

Social identity theory makes a distinction in how we learn about social norms (Tajfel, 1982; Tajfel & Turner, 1979, 1986): We are more motivated to model our behavior after that of an in-group member rather than that of an out-group member. In support of social identity theory, Gino et al. (2009) found that when people observed an in-group member behaving dishonestly, they were more likely to engage in dishonesty, but the effect disappeared when observing an out-group member. The spread of unethical behavior across individuals is like a billiard ball model in which the force of another rogue ball can negatively derail our own ethical direction—but only if the other wears the same stripe or solid that we do (i.e., the other is a member of our in-group).

How can individuals be so weak spined that they simply follow an in-group member's unethical behavior instead of challenging it? One possibility is that individuals in group contexts may not even necessarily recognize the behavior to be unethical. Gino and Bazerman (2009) described blindness to unethical behavior in an organization as perpetrated by the "boiling frog syndrome" (Senge, 1994). As folk legend goes, a live frog tossed into a pot of hot water will jump out before it cooks. To successfully boil a frog, one must let it sit in a pot of tepid water, place it over heat, and let the temperature rise a degree at a time. The frog will fall asleep bathing in comfortably warm water and will stay asleep as the water begins to boil, never having the chance to exert the strength to escape its environment. Similarly, a gradual deterioration in ethics—when the steps are so incremental that they are undetectable—can lead individuals and their organizations down a precipitous path toward ever-more-deviant behavior.

ASYMMETRIES IN ETHICAL JUDGMENTS

Research has established multiple divergences in how people think about their own ethicality versus that of others. Messick, Bloom, Boldizar, and Samuelson posited that, "We believe that we are fairer than others because we think that we do fair things more often and unfair things less often than others" (1985, p. 497). Related work has found that these beliefs extend to other contexts: We commonly think that we are more honest and trustworthy (Baumhart, 1968; Messick & Bazerman, 1996) and do more good deeds than others (Alicke, 1985; Baumeister & Newman, 1994).

We are predictably more critical of others' ethics than of our own ethics and are more suspicious of others' motives behind good deeds (Epley & Caruso, 2004; Epley & Dunning, 2000). We assume others are more self-interested and more motivated by money for the same behaviors in which we engage (Miller & Ratner, 1998; Ratner & Miller, 2001). We also more easily recognize others' conflicts of interests than we can recognize our own; because we view ourselves as moral, competent, and deserving, this view obstructs our ability to see and recognize conflicts of interests when they occur in our own behavior (Chugh, Banaji, & Bazerman, 2005).

The self-serving notions described create an asymmetry in our conceptions of personal morality: We are predisposed to favor ourselves over others as champions of ethical behavior. Yet, not all asymmetries in ethical judgment are intentionally self-serving. Chugh et al. (2005) argued that computational limitations, in addition to motivation toward self-worth, are involved in ethical decision making. Computational limitations include bounded awareness and depleted cognitive capacity—both of which are not driven by self-serving motivations.

Caruso, Gilbert, and Wilson (2008) identified one such computation limitation by demonstrating that when it comes to unethical actions, it is indeed better to seek forgiveness than permission. Their studies show that we judge the same behaviors as less permissible, more unethical, and more deserving of harsher punishment if it is going to happen in the future than if it happened in the past. The authors argued this "wrinkle in time" in ethicality judgments fits as part of the broader phenomenon wherein the future is more evocative than the past; the future feels psychologically closer than an equally distant past because we are always moving closer to the future and farther from the past. Thus, an event in the future is more able to elicit stronger affective responses compared to an equivalent event in the past.

Kahneman and Tversky (1979) established that people weigh losses more heavily than they do equivalent gains. Kern and Chugh (2009) showed that the asymmetry in how gains and losses are viewed also has an impact on ethical judgment: People judge the same behavior differently when facing a potential loss than when facing a potential gain, even when the two situations are identical. People are viewed as more unethical if a decision is presented in a loss frame than if the decision is presented in a gain frame. This asymmetry is exacerbated when participants are put under time pressure and can be eliminated when participants are instructed to "take their time." This provides yet another demonstration of how the demanding and intensive executive work life creates the conditions most ripe for lapses in ethical judgment (Chugh, 2004).

MORAL DISENGAGEMENT

Cognitive dissonance exists when there is a discrepancy between one's actual behavior and one's values or attitudes (Festinger & Carlsmith, 1959). Given that people care to perceive themselves as moral, decent, and ethical (Aquino & Reed, 2002), dishonest behavior should lead to self-censure (Bandura, 1990; Bandura, Barbaranelli, Caprara, & Pastorelli, 1996). If people aim to minimize the gap separating their moral standards from their real actions, they will generally refrain from behaving in ways that violate their standards. But, when actions and goals become unaligned, individuals feel the distress of cognitive dissonance—a form of psychological tension that arises when beliefs and behavior are at odds (Festinger, 1957). Elliot and Devine (1994) described dissonance as a form of psychological discomfort; when behavior typically labeled as negative is attributed to one's own choice rather than another's force, there is dissonance motivation, or discomfort that can be reduced by attitude change (Fazio & Cooper, 1983). In moral domains, people attenuate this distress either by modifying their behavior to bring it closer to their goals or by modifying their beliefs (Baumeister & Heatherton, 1996). These changes in beliefs can be alarmingly durable over time. Senemeaud and Somat (2009) showed that attitude change from a counterattitudinal essay-writing task persisted as long as 1 month after participants wrote their essays.

Bandura and others explained how individuals reduce cognitive dissonance in cases of dishonest behavior (Bandura, 1990; Bandura et al., 1996; Detert, Treviño, & Sweitzer, 2008). People whose actions are at odds with their moral standards will modify their beliefs about their bad actions through moral disengagement to alleviate cognitive dissonance. Moral disengagement repackages detrimental conduct in a way that is personally acceptable by relabeling the questionable behavior as morally permissible (Bandura et al., 1996). This may take any of the following forms: by portraying unethical behavior as serving a moral purpose, by attributing behavior to external cues, by distorting the consequences of behavior, or by dehumanizing victims of unethical behavior. Together, these ways to morally disengage explain how individuals recode their actions by shifting the boundary between ethical and unethical behaviors.

Even children possess from an early age the capacity to morally disengage. Mills studied how temptation changes children's attitudes toward punishment of dishonesty (Mills, 1958). Specifically, Mills varied the level of temptation to cheat on a competitive task for grade-school children and then measured the attitudes of these children toward cheating. His participants faced either high temptation (high rewards and low probability of being caught) or low temptation (low rewards and high probability of being caught). As expected, high temptation led to increased cheating, and the children who succumbed to temptation expressed increasingly lenient attitudes toward cheating, while those who resisted temptation became stricter toward cheating.

Paharia and Deshpande (2009) investigated situations in which consumers intended to purchase products that may have been produced through the use of unethical manufacturing practices (e.g., use of child labor). After declaring their intention to purchase such products, consumers will morally disengage to justify the decision to buy something that may have employed unethical manufacturing practices. They hold more lenient views toward questionable labor practices after they find out a product they would like to purchase might have been produced via unethical manufacturing.

In related research, Shu et al. (2011) found that when the opportunity to cheat for financial gain is present, individuals who cheated will morally disengage to repackage cheating behavior as permissible. In four studies, people justified their cheating through moral disengagement and exhibited motivated forgetting of moral rules that might otherwise limit their dishonesty, setting off on a slippery path toward ever-more-lax ethical standards. After succumbing to the temptation to cheat, people changed their beliefs toward cheating and redefined unethical behaviors to be more permissible. Yet, the studies also provide evidence that such a slide toward further ethical transgressions can be prevented by simple interventions, such as increasing people's awareness of ethical standards. For instance, in one of Shu et al.'s (2011) studies (Study 3), half of the participants were given the opportunity to cheat by overreporting performance on a problem-solving task they completed under time pressure, while the remaining half of the participants did not have such opportunity. The study also manipulated whether participants read an honor code at the beginning of the study versus not. The honor code was presented to participants as a separate task on comprehension and memory. After the problem-solving task, participants completed a questionnaire that included questions related to moral disengagement with items such as, "Sometimes getting ahead of the curve is more important than adhering to rules," and "If others engage in cheating behavior, then the behavior is morally permissible." Shu et al. (2011) had two main predictions: (a) that providing the opportunity to cheat would lead to increased moral disengagement, as compared to a control condition wherein cheating was not possible, and (b) that reading an honor code prior to the problem-solving task would reduce moral disengagement. The results of this study supported both predictions.

Thus, making morality salient not only reduces cheating in these studies but also keeps individuals' judgments scrupulous. Although dishonest behavior led to moral leniency and the forgetting of moral codes, honest behavior led to moral stringency and diligent recollection of moral codes.

MOTIVATED FORGETTING

Individuals are curators of their own collections of memories; they act as "revisionist historians" when recalling the past (Ross, McFarland,

Conway, & Zanna, 1983). People recall features selectively in ways that support their actions. They engage in "choice-supportive memory distortion" for past choices by selectively overattributing positive features to options chosen while simultaneously overattributing negative features to options overlooked (Mather & Johnson, 2000; Mather, Shafir, & Johnson, 2000). This effect disappeared for experimenter-assigned choices (Benney & Henkel, 2006; Mather, Shafir, & Johnson, 2003), yet reemerged when experimenters led participants to false beliefs about previous choices such that individuals continued to champion for the features of the option they thought they had chosen (Henkel & Mather, 2007).

Motivated memory errors are generally beneficial in reducing regret for options not taken and in sustaining general well-being. But, such systematic memory errors represent problems in accuracy, accountability, and learning (Mather et al., 2000). They have a particularly toxic effect in the domain of ethical decision making. Business executives are faced with increasingly complex rules—many of which were created explicitly to curtail questionable business practices that have emerged over the prior decade. If memory is selective, and if selection is arbitrated by motivation, then one convenient way to bolster one's self-image after behaving unethically is to revise one's memory. Individuals who only recall rules that favor their self-image could perpetuate their ignorance of rules created explicitly to change their behavior.

Shu and Gino (2010) found that individuals showed motivated forgetting of moral rules after deciding to behave unethically. Participants who were given opportunity to behave dishonestly to earn undeserved money by overreporting their performance on a problem-solving task were exposed to moral rules (e.g., an honor code or the Ten Commandments) prior to the task. Those who cheated were more likely to forget moral rules after behaving dishonestly, despite financial incentives to recall the rules accurately—even though they were equally likely to remember morally irrelevant information—when compared to those who did not cheat. For instance, in one of their studies, participants were asked to engage in a series of tasks that, in their eyes, were unrelated. For the comprehension and memory task, participants read both an honor code and the Ten Commandments. The study also included a problem-solving task participants were asked to engage in under time pressure. The task was designed such that participants could lie about their performance and thus earn money they actually did not deserve. The study varied the

232 • Lisa L. Shu, Francesca Gino, and Max H. Bazerman

order in which the two memory tasks (the one about the honor code and the one about the Ten Commandments) were presented to participants; participants completed one of the memory tasks before engaging in the problem-solving task in which they had the opportunity to cheat and the second one after the problem-solving task. The results of the study show that all participants remembered the same number of moral items in the task they completed before cheating but differed in the number of moral items they remembered in the task they completed after the problem-solving task. Participants who cheated by overreporting performance on the problem-solving task recalled fewer items of the moral code compared to participants who did not cheat and compared to participants in a control condition who did not have the opportunity to cheat on the problem-solving task. Thus, as the results of Shu and Gino's (2010) studies show, people appear to conveniently forget moral rules as a complementary strategy to moral disengagement after acting dishonestly.

CREATING MORE ETHICAL BEHAVIOR

Morality and memory are both malleable dimensions that reset to align with action. Given the goal to perceive oneself as moral and good, when a mismatch between action and goal occurs, people either change the action or change the goal. We close with an attempt to identify strategies that will help the moral self win this important match. If changes in beliefs and memory conspire to cover our trail of unethical deeds, what opportunities exist to position ourselves toward the ethical people that we aspire to be? We offer three suggestions.

One answer to reducing unethicality is that simply drawing people's attention to moral standards drastically reduces dishonest behaviors (Mazar et al., 2008). Making morality salient decreased people's tendency to engage in dishonest acts and preserved the rigidity of their ethical judgments. Shu et al. (2011) demonstrated that making morality salient decreased moral disengagement by changing the likelihood of engaging in unethical behavior. In these studies, a simple signature following an honor code dramatically lowered cheating behavior—even in a highly tempting environment. Many personal and organizational decisions require self-regulation of ethical behavior (e.g., punching time cards, filing taxes, submitting unbiased consolidated balance sheets to auditors), and it is important not to underestimate the role of situational cues in encouraging ethical behavior. Even simple interventions such as initialing a statement of firm values could nudge individuals toward more ethical decision making.

Fiske and Taylor (1991) summarized evidence that while decision makers try to perceive and encode all information, certain aspects of incoming information systematically receive more attention due to their saliency, vividness, and accessibility. The evidence presented in this chapter suggests that ethical decisions may be no different from other decisions in this respect as they are positively influenced by the salience of ethical standards. Future research uncovering other manipulations that can raise such ethical salience and vividness could prove particularly important in improving the current understanding of how discrepancies between ideal and actual moral selves can be reduced.

A second set of strategies for improving ethics comes from the well-documented literature on preference reversals between what people choose in separate versus joint decision making (Bazerman & Moore, 2009). This research documents that when people think about one option at a time ("between-subjects" experience), they are more likely to base their judgments on emotions than when they compare two or more options simultaneously ("within-subjects" experience). Moral dilemmas often invoke intuitive judgments of right and wrong that spring from immediate emotional responses to a given predicament. Emotions can sometimes lead to ethical failures that people later regret, failures that could be avoided by increased deliberation and analytical thought. Bazerman, Gino, Shu, and Tsay (2011) have documented multiple applications of joint evaluation as an effective tool that can help decision makers manage their emotional assessment of morality in favor of a more deliberate and analytical assessment of moral dilemmas.

For instance, Paharia, Kassam, Greene, and Bazerman (2009) explored the extent to which emotions influence judgments of price gouging. Paharia et al. used a real-world case to motivate their research: In 2005, the news reported that a well-known pharmaceutical company, Merck, had sold the rights to two of its relatively unprofitable cancer drugs to a smaller and lesser-known company, Ovation Pharmaceuticals. After the purchase, Ovation raised the price of the drug by 1,000%. However, Merck continued to manufacture the drugs. Probably due to Ovation's low public profile, this large increase in price for the drug did not trigger major outrage from the public. In examining this example, Paharia et al. (2009) suggested that observers would have responded differently and significantly more negatively if Merck was the company raising the price of the drugs directly. To test this hypothesis, Paharia et al. (2009) designed a study that compared the difference between raising prices directly versus indirectly. All study participants read that, "A major pharmaceutical company, X, had a cancer drug that was minimally profitable. The fixed costs were high, and the market was limited. But, the patients who used the drug really needed it. The pharmaceutical was making the drug for $2.50/pill (all costs included), and was only selling it for $3/pill." Then, some participants evaluated the ethicality of Action A, while others evaluated the ethicality of Action B:

A. The major pharmaceutical firm (X) raised the price of the drug from $3/pill to $9/pill.
B. The major pharmaceutical firm (X) sold the rights to a smaller pharmaceutical. In order to recoup costs, company Y increased the price of the drug to $15/pill.

The results of the study showed that participants who read Action A judged the behavior of Company X to be more unethical than those who read Action B, despite the smaller negative impact of Action A on patients. In addition, Paharia et al. (2009) asked a third group of participants to judge both possible actions simultaneously. In this case, preferences reversed. When participants could compare the two scenarios, their ratings were such that Action B was more unethical than Action A. These results indicate that a joint evaluation format reduced the influence of intuitive emotional judgment in favor of the influence of more deliberate analytical judgment. Thus, another viable strategy to avoid potentially costly ethical failures may be as a simple as changing the response mode used in making ethical decisions.

Finally, Stanovich and West (2000) distinguish between System 1 and System 2 cognitive functioning. System 1 refers to our intuitive decision processes, which are typically fast, automatic, effortless, implicit, and emotional; System 2 refers to reasoning that is slower, conscious, effortful, explicit, and logical. Moore and Loewenstein (2004) argue that our intuitive System 1 responses are more likely to be vulnerable to unethical temptations than our more reflective System 2 thoughts. This suggests that getting people to think more before acting, in more reflective and analytical ways, would be a useful way to nudge our actual selves closer toward the ethical selves we imagine.

These strategies all require that we cast our rose-tinted self-perceptions aside in favor of a truthful look at behavior—ethical vulnerabilities and all. Through understanding the differences between who we think we are, who we aspire to be, and how an outsider would perceive us, we can begin to uncover the biases that cloud our self-perceptions and identify our everyday ethical shortcomings relative to our espoused moral standards. Bringing this ethical discrepancy into resolution will be the first pivotal step toward seeing a positive shift in ethical behavior.

REFERENCES

Alicke, M. D. (1985). Global self-evaluation as determined by the desirability and controllability of trait adjectives. *Journal of Personality and Social Psychology, 49*(6), 1621–1630.

Allingham, M. G., & Sandmo, A. (1972). Income tax evasion: A theoretical analysis. *Journal of Public Economics, 1*, 323–338.

Aquino, K., & Reed, A. (2002). The self-importance of moral identity. *Journal of Personality and Social Psychology, 83*(6), 1423–1440.

Ayal, S., & Gino, F. (2011). Honest rationales for dishonest behavior. In M. Mikulincer & P. R. Shaver (Eds.), *The social psychology of morality: Exploring the causes of good and evil*. Washington, DC: American Psychological Association.

Banaji, M. R., Bazerman, M., & Chugh, D. (2003). How (un)ethical are you? *Harvard Business Review, 81*, 56–64.

Banaji, M. R., & Bhaskar, R. (2000). Implicit stereotypes and memory: The bounded rationality of social beliefs. In D. L. Schacter & E. Scarry (Eds.), *Memory, brain, and belief* (pp. 139–175). Cambridge, MA: Harvard University Press.

Bandura, A. (1986). *Social foundations of thought and action: A social cognitive theory*. Englewood Cliffs, NJ: Prentice Hall.

Bandura, A. (1990). Selective activation and disengagement of moral control. *Journal of Social Issues, 46*, 27–46.

Bandura, A. (1991). Social cognitive theory of moral thought and action. In W. M. Kurtines & L. Gewirtz (Eds.), *Handbook of moral behavior and development* (Vol. 1, pp. 45–103). Hillsdale, NJ: Erlbaum.

Bandura, A. (1999). Moral disengagement in the preparation of inhumanities. *Personal and Social Psychology Review, 3*, 193–209.

Bandura, A., Barbaranelli, C., Caprara, G., & Pastorelli, C. (1996). Mechanisms of moral disengagement in the exercise of moral agency. *Journal of Personality and Social Psychology, 71*, 364–374.

Baumeister, R. F., & Heatherton, T. F. (1996). Self-regulation failure: An overview. *Psychological Inquiry, 7*, 1–15.

Baumeister, R. F., & Newman, L. S. (1994). Self-regulation of cognitive inference and decision processes. *Personality and Social Psychology Bulletin, 20*, 3–19.

Baumhart, R. (1968). *An honest profit: What businessmen say about ethics in business.* New York: Holt, Rinehart and Winston.

Bazerman, M. H., Gino, F., Shu, L. L., & Tsay, C. (2011) Joint evaluation as a real world tool for managing emotional assessment of morality. *Emotion Review, 3*, 1–3.

Bazerman, M. H., & Moore, D. A. (2009). *Judgment in managerial decision making* (7th ed.). New York: Wiley.

Bazerman, M. H., & Tenbrunsel, A. E. (2011) *Blind spots: Why we fail to do what's right and what to do about it.* Princeton, NJ: Princeton University Press.

Becker, G. (1968). Crime and punishment: An economic approach. *The Journal of Political Economy, 76*, 169–217.

Benney, K. S., & Henkel, L. A. (2006). The role of free choice in memory for past decisions. *Memory, 14*(8), 1001–1011.

Caruso, E. M., Gilbert, D. T., & Wilson, T. D. (2008). A wrinkle in time: Asymmetric valuation of past and future events. *Psychological Science, 19*, 796–801.

Chugh, D. (2004). Societal and managerial implications of implicit social cognition: Why milliseconds matter. *Social Justice Research, 17*(2), 203–222.

Chugh, D., Banaji, M., & Bazerman, M. (2005). Bounded ethicality as a psychological barrier to recognizing conflicts of interest. In D. Moore, D. Cain, G. Loewenstein, & M. Bazerman (Eds.), *Conflicts of interest: Challenges and solutions in business, law, medicine, and public policy.* New York: Cambridge University Press.

Cialdini, R. B., Reno, R. R., & Kallgren, C. A. (1990). A focus theory of normative conduct: Recycling the concept of norms to reduce littering in public places. *Journal of Personality and Social Psychology, 58*, 1015–1026.

Cialdini, R. B., & Trost, M. R. (1998). Social influence: Social norm, conformity, and compliance. In D. T. Gilbert, S. T. Fiske, & G. Lindzey (Eds.), *Handbook of social psychology* (Vol. 2, pp. 151–192). New York: McGraw-Hill.

DePaulo, B. M., Kashy, D. A., Kirkendol, S. E., Wyer, M. M., & Epstein, J. A. (1996). Lying in everyday life. *Journal of Personality and Social Psychology, 70*(5), 979–995.

Detert, J. R., Treviño, L. K., & Sweitzer, V. L. (2008). Moral disengagement in ethical decision making: A study of antecedents and outcomes. *Journal of Applied Psychology, 93*(2), 374–391.

Elliot, A. J., & Devine, P. G. (1994). On the motivational nature of cognitive dissonance: Dissonance as psychological discomfort. *Journal of Personality and Social Psychology, 67*, 382–394.

Epley, N., & Caruso, E. M. (2004). Egocentric ethics. *Social Justice Research, 17*, 171–187.

Epley, N., & Dunning, D. (2000). Feeling "holier than thou": Are self-serving assessments produced by errors in self- or social prediction? *Journal of Personality and Social Psychology, 79*(6), 861–875.

Fazio, R. H., & Cooper, J. (1983). Arousal in the dissonance process. In J. T. Cacioppo & R. E. Petty (Eds.), *Social psychophysiology* (pp. 122–152). New York: Guilford Press.

Ferrell, O. C., Gresham, L. G., & Fraedrich, J. (1989). A synthesis of ethical decision models for marketing. *Journal of Macromarketing, 9*, 55–64.

Festinger, L. A. (1957). *A theory of cognitive dissonance.* Stanford, CA: Stanford University Press.

Festinger, L., & Carlsmith, J. M. (1959). Cognitive consequences of forced compliance. *Journal of Abnormal and Social Psychology, 58*, 203–211.

Fischbacher, U., & Heusi, F (2008). *Lies in disguise. An experimental study on cheating.* Thurgau Institute of Economics, Research Paper Series, 40.

Fiske, S. T., & Taylor, S. E. (1991). *Social cognition.* New York: Random House.

Frank, R. (1987). If homo economicus could choose his own utility function, would he want one with a conscience? *American Economic Review, 77,* 593–604.

Gibbs, J. C., Basinger, K. S., & Fuller, D. (1992). *Moral maturity: Measuring the development of sociomoral reflection.* Hillsdale, NJ: Erlbaum.

Gino, F., Ayal, S., & Ariely, D. (2009). Contagion and differentiation in unethical behavior: The effect of one bad apple on the barrel. *Psychological Science, 20*(3), 393–398.

Gino, F., & Bazerman, M. H. (2009). When misconduct goes unnoticed: The acceptability of gradual erosion in others' unethical behavior. *Journal of Experimental Social Psychology, 45*(4), 708–719.

Gino, F., Norton, M., & Ariely, D. (2010). The counterfeit self: The deceptive costs of faking it. *Psychological Science, 21*(5), 712–720.

Gino, F., & Pierce, L. (2009). The abundance effect: Unethical behavior in the presence of wealth. *Organizational Behavior and Human Decision Processes, 109*(2), 142–155.

Henkel, L. A., & Mather, M. (2007). Memory attributions for choices: How beliefs shape our memories. *Journal of Memory and Language, 57,* 163–176.

Hill, J., & Kochendorfer, R. A. (1969). Knowledge of peer success and risk of detection as determinants of cheating. *Developmental Psychology, 1,* 231–238.

Kahneman, D., & Tversky, A. (1979). Prospect theory: An analysis of decisions under risk. *Econometrica, 47*(2), 263–291.

Kern, M., & Chugh, D. (2009). Bounded ethicality: The perils of loss framing. *Psychological Science, 20*(3), 378–384.

Kohlberg, L. (1981). *Essays on moral development, vol. 1: The philosophy of moral development.* New York: Harper & Row.

Leming, J. S. (1980). Cheating behavior, subject variables, and components of the internal-external scale under high and low risk conditions. *Journal of Educational Research, 74,* 83–87.

Mather, M., & Johnson, M. K. (2000). Choice-supportive source monitoring: Do our decisions seem better to us as we age? *Psychology and Aging, 15,* 596–606.

Mather, M., Shafir, E., & Johnson, M. K. (2000). Misremembrance of options past: Source monitoring and choice. *Psychological Science, 11,* 132–138.

Mather, M., Shafir, E., & Johnson, M. K. (2003). Remembering chosen and assigned options. *Memory & Cognition, 31,* 422–433.

Mazar, N., Amir, O., & Ariely, D. (2008). The dishonesty of honest people: A theory of self-concept maintenance. *Journal of Marketing Research, 45*(6), 633–644.

Messick, D. M., & Bazerman, M. H. (1996). Ethical leadership and the psychology of decision making. *Sloan Management Review,* 9–22.

Messick, D. M., Bloom, S., Boldizar, J. P., & Samuelson, C. D. (1985). Why we are fairer than others. *Journal of Experimental Social Psychology, 21,* 480–500.

Milgram, S. (1974). *Obedience to authority: An experimental view.* New York: Harper and Row.

Miller, D. T., & Ratner, R. K. (1998). The disparity between the actual and assumed power of self-interest. *Journal of Personality and Social Psychology, 74*(1), 53–62.

Mills, J. (1958). Changes in moral attitudes following temptation. *Journal of Personality, 26*(4), 517.

Monin, B., & Jordan, A. H. (2009). Dynamic moral identity: A social psychological perspective. In D. Narvaez & D. Lapsley (Eds), *Personality, identity, and character: Explorations in moral psychology* (pp. 341–354). Cambridge, UK: Cambridge University Press.

Moore, D., & Loewenstein, G. (2004). Self-interest, automaticity, and the psychology of conflict of interest. *Social Justice Research, 17*(2), 189–202.

Paharia, N., & Deshpande, R. (2009). *Sweatshop labor is wrong ... unless the shoes are really cute! Strategies of moral disengagement in consumer behavior.* Unpublished working paper.

Paharia, N., Kassam, K. S., Greene, J. D., & Bazerman, M. H. (2009). Dirty work, clean hands: The moral psychology of indirect agency. *Organizational Behavior and Human Decision Processes, 109*, 134–141.

Pruckner, G., & Sausgruber, R. (2006). *Trust on the streets: A natural field experiment on newspaper purchasing.* University of Copenhagen. Department of Economics (formerly Institute of Economics).

Ratner, R. K., & Miller, D. T. (2001). The norm of self-interest and its effects on social action. *Journal of Personality and Social Psychology, 81*(1), 5–16.

Reno, R. R., Cialdini, R. B., & Kallgren, C. A. (1993). The trans-situational influence of social norms. *Journal of Personality and Social Psychology, 64*, 104–112.

Rest, J. R. (1986). *Moral development: Advances in research and theory.* New York: Praeger.

Rest, J. R., & Navarez, D. (1994). *Moral development in the professions: Psychology and applied ethics.* Hillsdale, NJ: Erlbaum.

Ross, M., McFarland, C., Conway, M., & Zanna, M. P. (1983). The reciprocal relation between attitudes and behaviour recall: Committing people to newly formed attitudes. *Journal of Personality and Social Psychology, 45*, 257–267.

Schweitzer, M. E., Ordóñez, L., & Douma, B. (2004). The role of goal setting in motivating unethical behavior. *Academy of Management Journal, 47*(3), 4220432.

Senemeaud, C., & Somat, A. (2009). Dissonance arousal and persistence in attitude change. *Swiss Journal of Psychology, 68*(1), 25–31.

Senge, P. M. (1994). *The fifth discipline: The art and practice of the learning organization.* New York: Currency Doubleday.

Shu, L. L., & Gino, F. (2010). *Sweeping dishonesty under the rug: How unethical actions lead to moral forgetting.* Unpublished working paper.

Shu, L. L., Gino, F., & Bazerman, M. H. (2011). Dishonest deed, clear conscience: Self-preservation through moral disengagement and motivated forgetting. *Personality and Social Psychology Bulletin, 37*(3), 330–349.

Stanovich, K. E., & West, R. F. (2000). Individual differences in reasoning: Implications for the rationality debate? *Behavioral and Brain Sciences, 23*, 645–665.

Tajfel, H. (1982). Social psychology of intergroup relations. *Annual Review of Psychology, 33*, 1–39.

Tajfel, H., & Turner, J. C. (1979). An integrative theory of intergroup conflict. In W. G. Austin & S. Worchel (Eds.), *The social psychology of intergroup relations.* Monterey, CA: Brooks-Cole.

Tajfel, H., & Turner, J. C. (1986). The social identity theory of inter-group behavior. In S. Worchel & L. W. Austin (Eds.), *Psychology of intergroup relations.* Chicago: Nelson-Hall.

Tenbrunsel, A. (1998). Misrepresentation and expectations of misrepresentation in an ethical dilemma: The role of incentives and temptation. *Academy of Management Journal, 41*, 330–339.

Treviño, L. K. (1986). Ethical decision making in organizations: A person-situation inter-actionist model. *Academy of Management Review, 11*, 601–617.

Zhong, C., Bohns, V. K., & Gino, F. (2010). Good lamps are the best police: Darkness increases dishonesty and self-interested behavior. *Psychological Science, 21*, 311–314.

Zhong, C. B., & Liljenquist, K. A. (2008). *Morality and hygiene.* Unpublished Manuscript.

Zhong, C. B., Liljenquist, K., & Cain, D. M., (2009). Moral self-regulation: Licensing & compensation, In D. De Cremer (Ed.), *Psychological perspectives on ethical behavior and decision making*. Greenwich, CT: Information Age.

Zimbardo, P. (1969). The psychology of evil: A situationist perspective on recruiting good people to engage in anti-social acts. *Research in Social Psychology, 11*, 125–133.

Author Index

A

Adams, J.S., 4
Agle, B., 91, 150, 151, 154, 166
Ahuja, G., 63
Alexander, L., 32
Alicke, M.D., 227
Allingham, M.O., 225
Allison, S.T., 109
Ambrose, M.L., 36, 52, 124
Amir, O., 221
Andreoli, N., 50, 55
Andreoni, J., 209
Anmmeter, A.P., 150
Appiah, K.A., 19, 174
Aquino, K., 24, 118, 155, 165, 166, 167, 222, 228
Argyris, C., 96
Ariely, D., 221
Arnaud, A., 48, 50
Ashford, S.J., 92
Ashforth, B.E., 149, 159
Ashkanasy, N.M., 91
Avolio, B.J., 83, 85, 91
Ayal, S., 221, 222
Ayer, A.J., 19

B

Babcock, L., 212, 213
Bachrach, D.G., 23
Bagozzi, R.P., 54
Ball, S.W., 108
Banaji, M.R., 5, 7, 11, 22, 123, 202, 222, 227
Bandura, A., 58, 64, 91, 154, 223, 228, 229
Barbaranelli, C., 228
Bardes, M., 58, 87
Bargh, J.A., 31, 94
Barndollar, K., 94
Barnett, T., 50, 57
Baron, J., 117, 134

Barsade, S.G., 35
Barsky, A., 25
Bartling, B., 206
Basinger, K.S., 223
Bass, B.M., 153
Bauman, C.W., 151
Baumeister, R.F., 23, 131, 227, 229
Baumhart, R., 227
Bazerman, M.H., 4, 5, 7, 11, 22, 25, 69, 124, 202, 222, 223, 226, 227, 233
Beams, J.D., 53
Beauchamp, T.L., 26
Bebeau, M., 98, 174
Becker, G., 225
Beer, J.S., 31, 32
Beersma, B., 112
Bell, M.P., 159, 161
Beller, S., 126, 127
Bender, A., 127
Bennett, R.J., 124
Benney, K.S., 231
Bergman, R., 95
Bernard, J., 27
Bernbeneck, A.F., 108
Bernheim, B.D., 209
Berridge, K.C., 35
Berry, C.M., 24
Berry, J.W., 136
Berscheid, E., 108
Bersoff, D.M., 5
Beu, D.S., 82
Bhaskar, R., 222
Bies, R.J., 20
Bilsky, W., 28
Bing, M.N., 150
Bingham, P.M., 124
Bjorklund, F., 28
Blader, S.L., 124, 176, 179, 181, 187, 188, 193, 195
Blair, I.V., 25

Subject Index